PUBLICATIONS OF THE DEPARTMENT OF ENGLISH
UNIVERSITY OF COPENHAGEN

VOLUME 7

Niels Davidsen-Nielsen

NEUTRALIZATION AND ARCHIPHONEME

Two Phonological Concepts and Their History

This book is for

Marianne

Mette

Hans

Marie

Niels Davidsen-Nielsen

NEUTRALIZATION AND ARCHIPHONEME

Two Phonological Concepts
and Their History

Universitetsforlaget i København
AKADEMISK FORLAG/Wilhelm Fink Verlag
COPENHAGEN 1978

Publications of the Department of English
University of Copenhagen

General Editors
Graham D. Caie, Michael Chesnutt,
Claus Færch

Published with the financial support of the
Faculty of Humanities, University of Copenhagen

Printed in Denmark by
J. J. Trykteknik a/s, Copenhagen

CONTENTS

6

2

7

PREFACE

The reception of the concept of neutralization, eager acceptance in some quarters, total rejection in others, affords a beautiful example of how people, scholars included, react, in language matters, in a largely ethnocentric fashion. If a new notion is helpful in accounting for some features of one's mother tongue, it is hailed as a basic implement of the linguist's kit. But if it is of no use there, it is cast aside as an intolerable burden.

The consonantal system of Russian, the way the French handle their vowels are best understood if we keep in mind that what is true at one point in the utterance is no longer true in another context. On the contrary, it is handier to take English consonants at their face value and to consider the reduced vowel of unstressed syllables as a vocalic unit in its own right. No wonder then if the concept of neutralization was first established and illustrated by Russian and French speaking linguists, while British and American scholars stood aloof.

Whenever those who operate with neutralization want to explain, to an English speaking audience, what it is all about, they automatically have recourse to the loss of aspiration in stops after /s/, as the only illustration available in their language. A very poor illustration at that, since voice remains distinctive in *asbestos* as opposed to *asperity*, and it would be worth while checking whether the average American around the White House pronounces the first name *Zbigniew* of a well-known political adviser as if it began like *spigot*.

But, of course, there is more to it than just linguistic ethnocentricism. Nothing is more characteristic of the Saussurean approach to language than the concept of neutralization. It is clear that if language units only exist, as stated by the Genevan master, by virtue of their being distinct from others of the same type, their identity cannot be determined on the sole basis of their perceptible shape, but by reference to the ones that belong to the same commutation class. Two physically identical segments in different surroundings may well stand for different units if their relations to the segments

appearing in the same contexts are different. Two physically different segments in different surroundings may well stand for the same
unit if their relations to the segments appearing in the same contexts
are the same.

In a similar vein, it has been said that understanding a language
is knowing that, at a certain point in the utterance, a segment has
been chosen by the speaker among a given number of other segments,
each one of which he might have chosen had his message been different. But if this is true, it cannot be immaterial if, in a definite context, the choice happens to be limited. Of course it could be, and has
been, argued that we should posit different systems in different contexts, and this is actually the only sensible presentation in some
cases: Russian stressed vowels /í é á ó ú/ as against unstressed
/i a u/. But if a certain unit, in positions of minimal differentiation,
stands in its relations to the other units in just the same way as two
units in positions of maximal differentiation, would it not be regret-
table if that peculiar situation were not mentioned?

Suppose a language where [t], in word final position, stands as
the only non-nasal apical, but where, word-initially, /t/ as a *voiceless* non-nasal apical is in opposition to /d/, a *voiced* non-nasal
apical. Word final [t] is exhaustively definable by means of the
features that are common to /t/ and /d/ where they compete.

Now, a practical problem arises: what graphic equivalents shall
we choose to visualize the relationships existing among the units?
This, which sounds perfectly marginal, has actually played a decisive
role in the history of the concept.

In our previous illustration, word final [t] is linguistically *both*
/t/ *and* /d/, and its most faithful graphic rendering is probably
/t/d/. In the case of vowels, the use of a letter without diacritic
for the archiphoneme (say /e/) and with two different diacritics
for the separate phonemes (/é/ and /è/) is also commendable and
certainly handier. But, unfortunately, what has generally prevailed
is the use of a capital, say /T/ for word final [t] as the archiphoneme.
Now let us posit, in our hypothetical language, a unit that sounds
[sat] in isolation, but [sad-] when followed by some flexion, say
/-a/ in /sada/. If [sat] is presented as /sad/t/, our public may accept
the view that, when passing from /sad/t/ to /sada/, the identity of
the base is not affected. If, however, the pair is presented as /saT/
and /sada/, all people concerned, linguistic specialists included, will
jump to the conclusion that we are faced here with a T/d alternation,
i.e., the replacement of a unit by another one.

If should be perfectly clear that a *phonetic* difference which is entirely conditioned by its *phonic* context, because the speakers of the language have never learned to produce there a distinction they make elsewhere, has nothing in common with the *morphologically* determined replacement of one *phoneme* by another in a context where the one is just as pronounceable as the other.

This writer does not know of any phonologist, including himself, who, at some point in his career, has not stumbled in this respect. Baudouin de Courtenay did, and Trubetzkoy should have known better than to suggest the misleading 'morphonology' for what was pure and simple morphology. The same could be said about Bloomfield and his followers' 'morphophonemics'. As late as 1949, Roman Jakobson was not aware of a difference between alternants and neutralization products.

For regular flounderers, the easiest way out is of course to deny the existence of phoneme systems and to camouflage their disregard for one of the basic steps in the description of language by applying the term phonology to the examination of morphological alternations. May I suggest that, in order to avoid a number of delicate problems, we should discard linguistics as an awkward and roundabout approach to a harmonious combination of psychology, logic, mathematics, and literature?

We must be thankful to Niels Davidsen–Nielsen for his painstaking survey of the various problems connected with neutralization and archiphoneme. He has centered his attention on the phonological uses of the concept of neutralization, which is exactly what we should expect, considering the conditions in which it originated. However, he does not bypass the various attempts to make use of the notion on the plane of significant units. It may be worth while mentioning in this connection that Hjelmslev's isomorphic approach prevented him from distinguishing between syncretism, as a formal confusion coinciding with the preservation of a difference in meaning suggested by context or situation, and the neutralization of meaningful oppositions, as the impossibility of distinguishing between two meanings, irrespective of whether formal differences are preserved or suppressed.

Some of us, in these days, have given up attempts to communicate with any group engaged in the study of language but the one that operates with a given basic set of notions. Not so Niels Davidsen–Nielsen. Not only has he been collecting information from all quarters, but his intention has obviously been to disseminate that information among scholars of all persuasions. He has not been deterred from his design by the current inexistence of a common terminological denominator, and there is little doubt that only thanks to such attemps as his may we hope one day to restore some measure of mutual understanding among the linguists of the world.

André Martinet

ACKNOWLEDGEMENTS

I would like to offer my sincere thanks to a number of persons and institutions that have helped me during the preparation of this book.

Eli Fischer-Jørgensen, who has for many years not only been a source of inspiration to me but also taken an active interest in my work, has given me many valuable critical comments on the manuscript. Hans Basbøll, who has read the entire manuscript as well, and Jørgen Rischel, who has read substantial sections of it, have also provided me with extremely helpful and perceptive criticism. Without the generous and liberal assistance of these three scholars the task of completing this book would have been harder and the result poorer.

I would like to thank John Dienhart for thoroughly checking the English of the text and, in so doing, giving me a good deal of constructive criticism as well. I am also grateful to André Martinet, who has suggested a number of changes and additions, particularly in the final chapter, and who has kindly undertaken to write the preface. The present work has greatly benefited from the help of these two linguists as well.

Among the many phonologists to whom I owe special thanks for assistance are Cathrine Høgsbro Holm, who has given me advice on aspects of French phonology, and Tsutomu Akamatsu, who works within the same area of phonology as myself and with whom I have had many rewarding discussions on the subject of neutralization.

I am indebted to the Faculty of Humanities, University of Copenhagen, for financially supporting the publication of this volume and for awarding me a three years' research fellowship, the latter part of which was devoted to studies on neutralization. My own department has backed me up in several ways, among others by releasing me from teaching and administrative duties for one term, thereby enabling me to finish this book, and by financially supporting visits to foreign universities which I have undertaken for purposes of research.

For assistance received in the final phases of the work I would like to thank the following: Anna Halager and Annette Götzsche

12

for typing the manuscript; Berit Rundqvist for compiling the index; the general editors of this series of publications — Graham Caie, Michael Chesnutt, Lis Christensen, Claus Færch — for accepting my manuscript and handling the problems of publication in collaboration with Akademisk Forlag.

Finally, my family deserve great thanks for their constant support during the writing of this book. In particular, my wife has for many years put up with my long working hours with tolerance and good spirits.

Copenhagen, May 1978   Niels Davidsen-Nielsen

Chapter 1
INTRODUCTION

In this book the concepts of 'neutralization' and 'archiphoneme' are
traced historically from their introduction in 1929 by members of
the Prague circle through various phonological schools to recent
theories of phonology. It is hoped that such a historical discussion
will help the reader to acquire a thorough and balanced understanding of these controversial and important phonological concepts.
In the description of the roles assigned to neutralization and archiphonemes in specific phonological theories I will attempt (as far as
possible) to take up the unbiased attitude of a neutral observer but
not to refrain from criticism when this is called for. There exists an
extensive literature on these two concepts, but it is scattered in a
large number of papers and books, and the present book, which
summarizes and discusses the most important contributions, may
therefore also serve as a reference work. In a final chapter my own
views on neutralization and archiphonemes are put forward. Yet
another contribution to the discussion of these concepts may perhaps seem uncalled-for, but as pointed out by Šaumjan (1968, p. 6)
the critical analysis of concepts can hardly be overstressed as it may
lead to the replacement of old concepts (explicanda) by new, more
precise and revealing concepts (explicata).

Although 'neutralization' and 'archiphoneme' have been with us
for nearly fifty years they cannot be characterized as well established
concepts. As a matter of fact they have given rise to a good deal of
confusion and miscomprehension, which has prevented them from
eventually gaining general acceptance. One reason for widespread
misunderstanding among linguists is no doubt that the phonologist
who developed the concept of neutralization, N.S. Trubetzkoy, has
himself vacillated considerably in his interpretation of the units
occurring in position of neutralization. In particular Trubetzkoy's
notion of 'archiphoneme representative' is a factor which has ob-
structed a clear understanding of the concepts under discussion (cf.
Akamatsu 1975). The most common misconception is that the concept of the archiphoneme is (historically) derived from, and thus

presupposes, that of neutralization, cf. Schane 1968, where the archiphoneme is described as "a special neutralized segment" (p.711),
and Hooper 1974, where it is stated that "Trubetzkoy 1971 [the
English translation of Trubetzkoy 1939, NDN] developed the notion
of archi–phoneme to account for contextual neutralization of
phonemic contrasts" (p. 18). In point of fact, the archiphoneme
does not, according to Roman Jakobson and Trubetzkoy, the originators of the two notions under discussion, presuppose the neutralization of a phonological opposition. Only if one has phonologists
such as Martinet in mind is it correct to say that one concept is
derived from the other. This particular misunderstanding, however,
is in no way surprising. If Jakobson's concept of archiphoneme had
not been available to Trubetzkoy when he elaborated his theory of
neutralization in the thirties, he could hardly have avoided introducing a similar concept himself. If it is assumed, for example, that
the opposition between the Russian phonemes /t/ and /d/, which
is operative initially in words, is neutralized in word–final position
where words like *rot* 'mouth' and *rod* 'race' are pronounced alike, it
is natural to inquire into the nature of the phonological unit that
appears in this position:

> the opposition between /t/ and /d/ is 'neutralized' in
> word–final position. This insight, which was fundamentally
> inspired by de Saussure, *necessarily leads to the postulation
> of a new unit, the 'archiphoneme'* (Kortlandt 1972, p. 22,
> my italics).

> Man darf aber nicht übersehen, dass als Folge der Neutra-
> lisierung *eine prinzipiell neue phonologische Einheit ent-
> steht*, die mit keinem der Glieder der neutralisierten Oppo-
> sition zusammenfällt (Šaumjan 1967, p. 134, my italics).

According to de Saussure the elementary linguistic components have
not an absolute but a purely relative, negative and oppositional
value. Influenced by this conception of language, post–Saussurean
phonologists have established the phonemes of a given language by
means of the commutation test. Even in theories such as those of
Daniel Jones and the post–Bloomfieldians, where the phoneme is
regarded as a class of phones, and where phones constitute the
point of departure in the phonemic analysis, the drawing up of
minimal pairs has been an important analytical tool ("minimal pairs
are the analyst's delight, and he seeks them whenever there is any

hope of finding them", Hockett 1955, p. 212). By application of
the commutation test a number of contrastive (commutable) units
are uncovered in a given position. The next natural step in the establishment of a phoneme inventory is to identify these units with units
uncovered in other positions. However, this operation is not simple
and straightforward, for in most languages the number of contrastive
units established in one position differs from the number established
in some other position. For this very reason some phonologists (the
Firthians, Twaddell, cf. chapter 3) refrain from identification in
such cases and set up separate phoneme inventories in each position.
The result of such a *polysystemic approach* is that the total inventory
of phonemes becomes large, complicated and unwieldy, and although
it can be argued that appropriateness is more important than simplicity the criticism can still be (and has indeed been) levelled at this
approach that it threatens to atomize phonology. By far the majority
of phonologists have therefore been prepared to identify units
established in one position with units established in other positions
even in those cases where the number of contrasts is not the same.
This operation, however, may be performed according to different
criteria, leading to different results, as will appear from the following
example.

In German there are six contrastive stop segments initially in
words and medially in uncompounded words between vowels —
[p b t d k g] — which are kept apart phonetically by means of
different places of articulation and by means of voicing (and/or
aspiration, tenseness). These contrasts can be exemplified with the
words *passe, Bass, Tasse, das, Kasse, Gasse* and *Raupen, rauben,
baten, baden, Haken, Hagen*. Finally in words there are only three
contrastive stop segments — [p t k] — which are kept apart by means
of differences in place of articulation only, cf. words like *rieb, riet,
Sieg* (these and the above examples are taken from Moulton 1962).
The problem confronting the phonologist is which of the contrastive
initial and medial stop segments the final labial, dental and velar stop
segments should be identified with. Should [-t], for example, be
identified with [t-, -t-], with [d-, -d-], or perhaps with both [t-,
-t-] and [d-, -d-]?[1] In such cases of multiple complementarity

---

1) Since [-t] shares the contrastive properties 'stop closure', 'orality' and
'dentality' with [t-, -t-] and [d-, -d-], I shall take it for granted that it is
either or both of these units it should be identified with, rather than with
[p-, -p-], [k-, -k-], [f-, -f-], [n-, -n-] or any other contrastive units established in initial and medial position.

three different solutions have been proposed (besides the polysystemic analysis): 1) a *phonetically based either-or analysis,* where the final [-t] in words like *Rat* and *Rad* is identified with the [t-, -t-] of words like *Tag, bitte* according to the criterion of phonetic similarity; 2) a *morphologically based either-or analysis,* in which the [-t] of *Rat* is identified with [t-, -t-] on the basis of alternants like *Rate* (dative case), whereas that of *Rad* is identified with [d-, -d-] on the basis of alternants like *Rade* (dative case);[2] 3) a *both-and analysis* (or 'both and neither', cf. Hockett 1955, p. 165), according to which [-t] is identified with [t-, -t-] as well as with [d-, -d-]. The reasoning underlying this third interpretation is that the oppositions between *t* and *d,* between *p* and *b,* and between *k* and *g,* which have been found to be operative initially and medially in German, are inoperative, suspended, or *neutralized* under certain conditions, viz. in word-final position, where only labial, dental and velar stops are distinguished. In words like *lieb, und* and *Tag* the final stops are thus supposed to represent what the corresponding voiced and voiceless stops occurring in initial and medial position have in common, i.e. the products, or intersections, of the classes *p* and *b, t* and *d, k* and *g* (labial stop, dental stop, velar stop). Now if *lieb, und* and *Tag* are in this manner interpreted as /li:$<$p/b$>$, un$<$t/d$>$, tɑ:$<$k/g$>$/, a new type of phonological unit, which is fundamentally different from the phoneme, has in fact been introduced. Such neutralization products of two (or more) phonological units occurring in other positions are indeed recognized in several phonological theories, where they go under names such as 'hyperphonemes', 'archiphonemes' and 'syncretism'. A graphical representation of the three methods of identification is given in the following table, where broken lines indicate that the final stops in German are identified with *p, t, k* in words like *stopp! Rat, Stock* and with *b, d, g* in words like *grob, Rad, Tag* on the basis of alternants like *stoppen, Rate, Stocke* and *grobe, Rade, Tage:*

---

2) I shall not here discuss the problems concerning the morphologically based identification of units that do not share features which set them apart from all other segments of the language in question (cf. the preceding footnote). In Danish, where the opposition between *p, t, k* and *b, d, g* is also inoperative word-finally, morphologically minded phonologists may wish to identify the [ʃ] of *citation* [sitʰaˈʃoʔn] 'citation, quotation' and the final stop of *citat* [siˈtʰaʔtʰ, siˈtaʔd] 'quotation' in spite of the fact that the common features of these segments are shared by [s] as well.

17

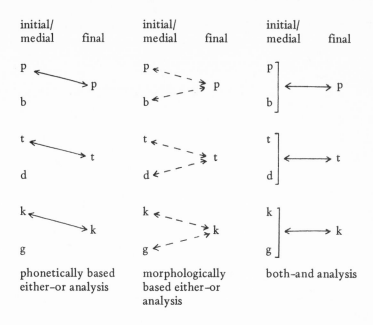

| | phonetically based either-or analysis | morphologically based either-or analysis | both-and analysis |

Of the approaches outlined above the either–or analyses seem preferable from the point of view of economy, as the inventory of phonemes established according to these methods will obviously be smaller than the inventory of phonemes established by a both-and analysis or by a polysystemic analysis. In its second version the either–or analysis also has the advantage of providing a smoother transition between phonology and grammar. It should be pointed out, however, that a non–arbitrary either–or analysis is often quite difficult (in some cases perhaps impossible) to carry through. If identification is based on phonetic similarity the analyst runs into serious difficulties 1) in the cases where a contrastive sound segment occurring in the position with fewer contrasts is phonetically intermediate between two contrastive sound segments occurring in the position with a larger number of contrasts, 2) when there is free variation in the position with fewer contrasts between two sound segments both of which occur as contrastive units in the position with a larger number of contrasts. In English, for example, there are six contrastive plain stops initially in words, but after initial *s* there are only three contrastive stop segments, which are distinguished by differences in articulatory place only, cf. *spill, still, skill*. These post-initial stops differ from the initial sounds of *pill, till, kill* by being unaspirated and from the initial sounds of *bill, dill, gill* by being

2

invariably voiceless, and it is therefore difficult non-arbitrarily to identify them with one rather than the other of the two initial stop series on the basis of phonetic similarity. In Danish, secondly, there are six contrastive stop consonants initially in words – [pʰ b̥ tʰ d̥ kʰ g̊] – but only three contrastive word-final stops, which are kept apart by differences in place of articulation only.[3] These final contrastive units oscillate between aspirated and unaspirated pronunciation, i.e. words like *lap* 'patch', *ladt* 'loaded' and *lak* 'lacquer' are sometimes pronounced [lapʰ, latʰ, lakʰ] and sometimes [lab̥, lad̥, lag̊]. In such cases it seems impossible to identify the final stops with one of the initial stop series rather than the other on the basis of phonetic similarity. Even if problems like these are disregarded, or could be solved, the analyst who adopts an either-or approach based on the criterion of phonetic similarity may be charged with 'phoneticism': it may be argued, for example, that the greater phonetic resemblance of final stops in German to the initial *p, t, k* series than to the initial *b, d, g* series is a non-functional criterion and therefore phonologically irrelevant (this resemblance can plausibly be attributed to a mechanical, physiologically determined devoicing in final position). If an either-or analysis is based on morphological alternations, on the other hand, difficulties may arise when a morpheme is realized in one way only. Whereas the final stops of German *bunt* and *Bund* can be identified with respectively [t-, -t-] and [d, -d-] on the basis of alternants like *bunte, Bunde,* the final stop of *und* can be identified with neither of these initial/medial stops since this morpheme is invariably realized as [unt]. Again, even if problems of this type are disregarded, the analyst who adopts an either-or approach based on the criterion of alternation may be charged with 'grammaticism' ("to sacrifice the results of the phonological analysis in order to simplify the presentation of the meaningful units", Martinet 1973 (1965), p. 94).

The both-and analysis is less simple than the either-or approach, but it is not as complicated as the polysystemic approach. In the both-and analysis archiphonemes (or hyperphonemes) are postulated in

---

3) I am referring to the most common type of Danish in which [ɣ] has been lost completely and assuming that [ð] should be interpreted as a separate phoneme. If [ð] is analysed as a syllable-final variant of /d/, i.e. if a word like *mad* [mað] 'food' is interpreted as /mad/, it is of course impossible to operate with final neutralization of /t/ : /d/, cf. a word like *mat* [matʰ, mad̥] 'weak'. After the loss of [ɣ], however, this analysis has lost most of its foundation.

addition to 'regular' phonemes, but they are not as heavy a load on the inventory as separate positional phonemes, since any neutralization product, for example <t/d>, can be referred to, and therefore regarded as derived from, two or more regular phonemes, for example /t/ and /d/. The analyst who employs this method might therefore claim that it strikes a happy medium between the either–or method and the polysystemic method by stating no more determinacy in the pattern than can actually be found and by avoiding an atomization of phonology. However, it can be objected that this particular way of avoiding the horns of a dilemma is a logically unsatisfactory artifice ('both and neither'). Even if this particular objection could be refuted the analyst who prefers the both–and method is faced with the problem of deciding to what extent it should be employed. Initially in English words only [s] can begin a triple consonant cluster (cf. *split, string, scream*), and this [s] might therefore be identified with all the contrastive consonantal segments established in other positions, i.e. it could be interpreted as an archiconsonant. However, phonologists who recognize neutralization do not normally in a case like this select an 'and' interpretation, but prefer to identify the non–constrastive *s*-sound with the contrastive *s*-sound occurring in other positions. This implies that they operate with *defective distribution* of all the other consonants which cannot occur in this position, just as the phonetically minded either–or analyst regards German /b d g/ as somewhat defective phonemes since they are assumed never to occur in word–final position. On closer inspection it turns out, then, that the both–and analyst in some cases accepts an either–or interpretation as well. Now, if defective distribution is recognized in addition to neutralization the question immediately arises of what criterion to use in distinguishing between these two notions. Unless a clear and principled answer to this question can be given the approach to identification based on the theory of neutralization is open to criticism.

We have seen that the identification of contrastive units established in different positions places the phonologist in a dilemma and that there are several possible ways of solving it. The particular way in which the analyst tackles this problem is indicative of the phonological school that he may or may not belong to. For example, an either–or analysis based on phonetic similarity is characteristic of the London school of Daniel Jones and of the Leningrad school. An either–or approach based on morphological alternations, on the other hand, is the typical approach adopted in generative phonology.

If the polysystemic approach is preferred by the phonologist he may be a member of the prosodic school of J.R. Firth, or he may be working within the framework of W. Freeman Twaddell's phonemic theory. Finally, the both-and approach is particularly characteristic of the Prague school, which introduced it.

The differences in approach to the problem of identification have so far been outlined in a rather heavy-handed manner. In order to present a fuller picture it should be pointed out that if the various linguistic theories are regarded in their totality, these differences fade out somewhat and manifest themselves largely in the choice of *level* on which a given approach is preferred and in the relative significance attributed to the various levels. In Hjelmslev's glossematic theory, for example, a both-and approach is adopted on the level of actualized representations, but on a more abstract level — that of idealized representations — the glossematist adopts a morphologically based either-or approach. Basically the same applies to the Prague and Moscow schools of phonology. In both these theories neutralization plays a prominent part on one level, but on a higher level a grammatically based either-or analysis is carried out, and in the Moscow school this abstract phonological level is regarded as extremely important. In the American structuralist school, furthermore, where a phonetically based either-or approach is adopted in the phonemic part of the description, an either-or analysis based on morphological alternations is introduced in the morphophonemic part of the description. Although the differences in approach are therefore not as clear-cut as it appears from the preceding paragraphs, it must be maintained that the question of identification clearly divides the waters. It is not the case that the three solutions to the problem of identification discussed above are all recognized, although on different levels, in any of the various phonological schools. In some theories the both-and analysis is not recognized on any level, in other theories the phonetically based either-or analysis plays no role (except, perhaps, in a very primitive phonetic sense), and in one or two theories, where alternations virtually pass unnoticed, there is no room for the morphologically based either-or analysis.

In the following chapters the arguments adduced in support of each of the different analyses will be dealt with in some detail. Before we proceed to this discussion, however, one particular approach which might shed new light on the problem of identification must briefly be mentioned. In the phonetically based either-or analysis the criterion of identification is objective realization, i.e.

the physiological–physical correlates of the functional units occurring in the position with fewer contrasts are taken into account. Now it might also be rewarding to examine the *psychological correlates* of these units. Evidence of this type could be obtained by investigating writing systems, children's spellings, the acquisition of speech, language change, slips of the tongue, the treatment of loanwords, etc. If, for example, units occurring in the position with fewer contrasts were symbolized in writing systems by special letters, or if there was here free variation between two letters consistently kept apart in the position with a larger number of contrasts, this would seem to be an argument against the either–or analyses and in support of the both–and analysis or, in the former case, the polysystemic analysis. Psychological evidence has not played an important part in phonological analyses, except in the early days of Prague phonology and in Sapir's work, but in recent studies the need for and relevance of psycho–linguistic investigations have been emphasized. According to Šaumjan (1967, p. 135f), for example, it is an important task to supplement the abstract investigation of phonological systems with investigations of the empirical correlates of the abstract units which are postulated. In addition to theoretical phonology and phonetics Šaumjan proposes to establish a separate discipline called *experimental phonology,* and in this discipline the examination of psychological data will naturally be of great importance. In the investigation of problems of identification such psychological data could be a useful check on the various analyses which are put forward. I shall return to this problem in the final chapter.

Chapter 2
PRAGUE PHONOLOGY

2.1. Roman Jakobson

The concept of the archiphoneme was introduced in 1929 by Roman Jakobson in a monograph on historical Russian phonology. In the introduction to this monograph, where fundamental notions are discussed, Jakobson establishes a number of phonological concepts. It is through these concepts, and by taking into account not only functional but also psychological properties, that he reaches the concept of archiphoneme. A *phonological opposition* is a phonetic difference which may serve to differentiate meanings. In English, for example, /teɪ/ : /lɪ/ of *take it, lick it* and /t/ : /f/ of *take it, fake it* both constitute phonological oppositions (my example). A term of a phonological opposition is called a *phoneme* if it cannot be decomposed into smaller phonological sub-oppositions. According to this definition the term /t/ of the opposition /t/ : /f/ is a phoneme, whereas /teɪ/ of the opposition /teɪ/ : /lɪ/ is not. An opposition may be composed of *correlative phonemes* or of *disjunctive phonemes*. By a *correlation* is understood a binary opposition which applies to more than one pair of phonemes. If the phonemes /p b t d k g f v θ ð s z/ occur in a given language, the correlation of voice will be abstracted by the linguistic consciousness, and the speaker-hearer will be able to think of it independently of the separate oppositional pairs. The psychological reality of this concept appears from traditional Slavonic assonances, where voiced and voiceless consonants "rhyme" with respectively voiced and voiceless ones, whereas "the pairing of voiced with voiceless consonants is inadmissible" (Jakobson 1962, p. 634). But in the same way that the speaker-hearer may abstract the differentiating property from a correlative opposition he may abstract the common core which unites the terms of such an opposition. This common core, which is called an *archiphoneme*, is also a psychologically real entity. In Czech and Serbian rhymes, for example, the phonemic difference between short and long vowels is ignored (Jakobson 1962, p. 635).

In his monograph on Russian, Jakobson expresses his theory of archiphoneme in the following way (p. 8f):

> En prenant pour de départ la délimitation des notions établie ci-dessus, nous pouvons dégager une entité nouvelle, essentielle pour la phonologie, à savoir l'*archiphonème*. L'archiphonème, d'une part, n'est pas susceptible d'être subdivisé en oppositions de phonèmes disjoints plus menues, et d'autre part ne saurait posséder avec un autre archiphonème un substrat commun isolable par la conscience linguistique, c'est-à-dire que l'archiphonème ne saurait être corrélatif d'un autre archiphonème. L'archiphonème est une idée générique, c'est une unité abstraite, qui peut unir un ou plusieurs couples de variantes *corrélatives* (de phonèmes corrélatifs).

In order to illustrate this theory Jakobson sets up the inventory of archiphonemes in modern Russian. For example, the correlative vowel phonemes /í/ (accented) and /i/ (unaccented) are united into one archiphoneme, and the same goes for consonantal phonemes such as /r/, /r'/ (palatalization), /z/, /s/ (voice) and /d/, /d'/, /t/, /t'/ (palatalization and voice). But also /é/, /ó/ and /j/, which stand outside the correlations, and which may therefore be regarded as 'phonèmes hors couple', meet the conditions placed by Jakobson on archiphonemes. It holds good of Russian archiphonemes like <á/a> and /j/, then, that they cannot be broken down into oppositions formed by two disjunctive phonemes (the former archiphoneme, on the other hand, can be broken down into an opposition consisting of two correlative phonemes) and that they do not share any common substrate which may be isolated by the linguistic consciousness with any other archiphoneme. Jakobson's archiphonemes are thus constituted partly by the correlation pairs (<á/a>, <r/r'>, <s/z>, etc.), partly by phonemes without corresponding correlative phonemes (/j/, /é/, etc.). In the monograph nothing is said about neutralization.

In *Projet de terminologie phonologique standardisée* (1931) we find practically the same definition of the archiphoneme as in Jakobson's monograph: "Unité phonologique qui, d'une part, ne saurait être corrélative d'une autre unité phonologique et qui, d'autre part, n'est pas susceptible d'être subdivisée en disjonctions plus petites" (p. 316). But units of this type, which emerge if the correlation marks are removed from the language, and which therefore also include the unpaired phonemes, are now called *archiphonèmes fondamentaux*. In addition to this entity, however, another related entity is recognized, which is termed *archiphonème*, and which is defined in the following way (p. 315): "Élément commun de deux ou plusieurs phonèmes corrélatifs, qu'on peut concevoir abstraction faite des propriétés de corrélation." According to the *Projet*-definitions /s z/, /á a/, /r r'/ and /t t' d d'/ in Russian are thus both archiphonemes and fundamental archiphonemes. On the other hand Russian /j/, /é/ and /ó/ are no longer archiphonemes, but only fundamental archiphonemes. That Jakobson himself must have accepted this revision appears from the fact that he later defined the archiphoneme as "the common core of two phonemes within a correlated pair" (1962, p. 634f).

2.2. N. S. Trubetzkoy

According to Roman Jakobson (1962, p. 314) *N. Durnovo* was the first linguist who broached the important problem of *neutralization* of phonological oppositions (already in 1927). However, it was above all N. S. Trubetzkoy who, in a large number of papers and books, developed this concept (1929, 1931, 1933a, 1933b, 1934, 1936a, 1936b, 1939). In his monograph on Polabian dating from 1929 it is pointed out that the correlative properties of phonemes may in certain positions lose their phonological value. In Polabian the opposition between voiced and voiceless obstruents was inoperative before obstruents (except /v/ and /j/), since the voicing of an obstruent was regulated by that of the following obstruent, cf. examples like [röezgă, daiskă]. In this position the obstruent phonemes therefore appeared in the linguistic consciousness in their "von der 'Stimmbeteiligungsvorstellung' abstrahierten Gestalt" (p. 122), and they may accordingly be transcribed with special (Greek) letters: /Röσgă, dαισkă/ (see below as regards the capital letter in the first word). Similarly, the palatalization correlation was only operative before the vowels [o α u ă š], not before other vowels, nor before consonants, nor in final position, and both the unpalatalized *p*-sounds in a word like [püp] 'priest' were consequently perceived by the speaker-hearer as " 'weder harte noch weiche' *P*-Laute" (p. 123). In those cases where the palatalization opposition was inoperative it would also be reasonable to use special symbols (capital letters), and, for example, to transcribe [ṕαs, röezgă] as /ṕɑS, Rӧσgǎ/. The neutrality of sound images such as /σ/, /P/ etc. could, however, be somewhat disturbed by phonetic and morphological associations. In [daịskǎ] and [rӧezgǎ], for example, [s] and [z] would thus be associated by the speaker of Polabian with the phonetically identical entities occuring in words like [posmǫ̌] and [sǫzmǎ], where voicing was phonetically valid. The transcriptions /daiσˢkǎ/ and /rӧσᶻgǎ/ are therefore psychologically more appropriate than the ones cited above with /σ/ alone. According to Trubetzkoy, the sibilants were here associated with a certain, although very weak, feeling of voice/voicelessness. In an example like [laiskǎ] 'fox' the sibilant was associated with /s/ by the speaker-hearer not only phonetically but also morphologically, since the derived form [laisɑickǎ] 'vixen' contained an s-sound which was distinctively voiceless. In this case, therefore, the transcription /Laị̌σˢkǎ/ would be psychologically the most appropriate. In spite of these phonetic and morphological associations Trubetzkoy is of the opinion that the correlative property of a phoneme may in some positions be virtually lost: "Es gibt Stellungen, in denen alle Eigenschaften eines Phonems im Sprachbewusstsein deutlich hervortreten; in anderen Stellungen aber verblassen einige Eigenschaften desselben Phonems und werden nur ganz undeutlich perzipiert" (p. 125f).

In his monograph Trubetzkoy also touches on the phenomenon which has later been termed 'segment redundancy' (i.e. the case where some feature values may be predicted on the basis of others within the same segment): in Polabian, /j/ may in all positions be regarded as a consonantal phoneme which is neutral with respect to voice as well as to palatalization. According to Trubetzkoy, however, there is an important psychological difference between this and the contextually determined invalidation of a correlative opposition.

In an article on phonological systems dating from 1931, Trubetzkoy points out that, with a few exceptions, the opposition between palatalized and corresponding plain consonants in Russian loses its phonological value before palatalized and plain dentals, since in these two positions only palatalized and plain sounds respectively occur. As examples [śt́inã̄, śĺėt] and [stọ̀ł, słȍn, snȍp] are mentioned (Trubetzkoy's transcription). The presentation of phonological phenomena is still psychologically oriented, and Trubetzkoy now entertains the idea that the consonants appearing in this environment are spontaneously perceived by the native speaker of Russian as plain because a plain consonant, such as /s/, constitutes the naturally *unmarked* member in the palatalization correlation (the idea of phonetic and morphological associations, on the other hand, is not followed up). It is added, though, that through careful self-observation the Russian speaker will rid himself of this impression and regard, for example, the [s'] in [št′inằ, śl′èt] as a cross between a palatalized and an unpalatalized consonant ("nicht ganz hart, nicht ganz weich", p. 99). It is also pointed out that the feeling of non-palatalization is in the case of the [s] of [stǫł, słȯn, snȯp] considerably weaker than in the case of prevocalic and final [s], whose plainness is phonologically valid. In the position of irrelevance the phoneme is according to Trubetzkoy transformed into the corresponding *archiphoneme*. The archiphoneme is defined in virtually the same way as in *Projet:* "*Als Symbol des Archiphonems* (d.h. des einer Korrelation zugrunde liegenden, von den betreffenden korrelativen Eigenschaften abstrahierten allgemeinen Lautbegriffs) *dient* . . ." (p. 98). Nothing is said about fundamental archiphonemes, i.e. about Jakobson's original archiphonemes.

The term 'neutralization' (Aufhebung, Neutralisierung) is used for the first time in the two articles published in 1933. According to Trubetzkoy the fact that neutralized phonemes are in many national orthographies symbolized by special written characters points towards their special status in the linguistic consciousness. In the Old Indic Devanagari alphabet, for example, a special symbol ('anusvara') is used for a nasal whose point of articulation is mechanically regulated by that of the following sound, and which has therefore no phonological value. Though it is especially correlative properties which are neutralizable, disjunctive properties may also be neutralized. For example, the opposition between nasals with different places of articulation is in many languages neutralized in preconsonantal position. In the article Trubetzkoy emphasizes that a neutralized phoneme should not be confused with the unmarked member of an opposition, "denn zwischen dem einfachen Fehlen und dem aktiven Verneinen einer Eigenschaft besteht ein grundsätzlicher Unterschied" (1933a, p. 112). We may therefore assume that Trubetzkoy is now (i.e. in 1933) of the opinion that the initial consonant of Russian [št′inằ] should be interpreted as the archiphoneme <s/s'> and not as /s/, in spite of what is said about linguistic consciousness and markedness in the 1931-article.

In a paper on phonological oppositions (1936a) and in *Grundzüge der Phonologie* (1939) Trubetzkoy abandons the division of oppositions into two classes only — correlations and disjunctions — and establishes a far more complex classification, which must be briefly mentioned.[1] According to their relations to the entire system oppositions are classified, first, into *bilateral* and *multilateral* ones. An opposition is bilateral if the totality of features shared by the two members does not recur in other members of the same system; as an example /t/ : /d/ in French, which are the only non-nasal apical stops in the system, may be adduced. If the shared features are found in other members as well, the opposition is multi-dimensional, cf. /p/ : /t/ in French, whose common properties (voicelessness and stop closure) recur in /k/. According to the same principle oppositions are classified into *proportional* and *isolated* ones. An opposition is proportional if the relation between its members is identical with that which exists between the members of other oppositions within the same system. As examples may be mentioned /t/ : /d/ and /p/ : /t/ in French, where the relations between the members recur in /p/ : /b/ and /b/ : /d/ respectively. On the other hand /r/ : /l/ in French is an isolated opposition. According to the mutual relation between the members of an opposition a distinction is drawn between *privative, gradual* and *equipollent* oppositions. An opposition is privative if one of its members possesses a property which the other lacks, cf. /ã/ : /a/ in French (as in *banc* — *bas*), the former member of which is characterized by the presence of nasality. An opposition is gradual if its members are characterized by different degrees of the same quality, cf. /i/ : /e/ in French, which represent two different degrees of mouth opening (as in *irriter* — *hériter*). An opposition which is neither privative nor gradual is termed equipollent and may be exemplified with /s/ : /ʃ/ in French (as in *sang* — *champ*). What was formerly a correlation is in Trubetzkoy's new classification system a bilateral, proportional, privative opposition. According to the scope of their distinctive validity, oppositions are lastly classified into *constant* and *suspendable* (supprimables, neutralisables) oppositions. However, this division only applies to bilateral oppositions. Psychologically there is a great difference between these two oppositional types, which may be explained in the following way: in the position of neutralization the members of a suspendable opposition are only combinatory variants of the same archiphoneme, i.e. of a

---

1) Cf. also Fischer-Jørgensen 1975, p. 28.

"phonème dont le contenu phonologique se réduit aux traits communs aux deux termes de l'opposition donnée" (1936a, p. 13), and even in those positions where such an opposition is operative its members break down into archiphoneme + a specific quality. It is much more difficult for the speaker–hearer to extract the archiphoneme from a constant opposition, which is not characterized by any "double existence."

Examples of constant and suspendable oppositions can be drawn from his article, 'Die Aufhebung der phonologischen Gegensätze' (1936b), where Trubetzkoy deals exclusively with the concepts of neutralization and archiphoneme. As an example illustrating a constant opposition he gives /e/ : /ɛ/ in Danish, the members of which are in all positions constrastive. As an example illustrating a suspendable opposition /e/ : /ɛ/ in French is adduced, the members of which are only kept apart in word-final position, cf. *les* : *laids* (otherwise only [ɛ] occurs in closed syllables and only [e] in open syllables, as in *perdre* ['pɛrdr] and *descendre* [de'sã:dr] respectively). The positions in which an opposition is neutralized are called *positions of suspension* ('Aufhebungsstellungen'), and those in which an opposition is phonologically valid are termed *positions of relevance* ('Relevanzstellungen'). The archiphoneme is characterized as "die Gesamtheit der Züge . . . die zwei Phonemen gemein sind" (p. 32), i.e. it does not presuppose neutralization and it can be abstracted from two phonemes only. Once again it is pointed out that only bilateral oppositions may be neutralized. In a German word like *Blatt* the initial consonant cannot be interpreted as the archiphoneme <b/d>, in spite of the fact that [dl] is an impossible initial sequence in German, for the phonological content of such an archiphoneme would be "stop closure", "orality" and "voice", and these features also characterize /g/ (*glatt*). Therefore one cannot speak of a suspension of the multilateral opposition /b/ : /d/.[2] As far as the psychological importance of the difference between constant and suspendable oppositions is concerned, the following is stated by Trubetzkoy (p. 30f):

---

2) The reader may well ask how it is then possible for Trubetzkoy to recognize neutralization in the case of /e/ : /ɛ/ in French. As the phonological content of <e/ɛ> must be "unrounded front vowel", which also characterizes /i/ and /a/, the opposition /e/ : /ɛ/ can hardly be anything but multilateral. It would appear that Trubetzkoy is guilty of an inconsistency here.

die konstanten phonologischen Gegensätze [werden] selbst
von phonetisch ungeschulten Mitgliedern der Sprachgemein-
schaft deutlich wahrgenommen, und die Glieder eines
solchen Gegensatzes werden als zwei verschiedene "Laut-
individuen" betrachtet. Bei den aufhebbaren phonologischen Gegensätzen ist die Wahrnehmung schwankend: in
den Relevanzstellungen werden beide Oppositionsglieder
deutlich auseinandergehalten, in den Aufhebungsstellungen
ist man dagegen oft nicht imstande anzugeben, welches von
beiden man eben gehört oder gesprochen hat. Aber selbst in
der Relevanzstellung empfindet man die Glieder eines aufhebbaren Gegensatzes nur als zwei bedeutungsdifferenzie-
rende Nuancen, als zwei zwar verschiedene, aber dennoch
eng miteinander verwandte Lauteinheiten, und dieses Ge-
fühl der intimen Verwandschaft ist für solche Oppositionsglieder besonders kennzeichend.

To a Frenchman the difference between the members of the suspendable opposition /e/ : /ɛ/ is thus felt to be much smaller than the
phonetically equivalent difference between the members of the constant opposition /i/ : /e/. But from a purely functional point of view
the difference between constant and suspendable oppositions must
also be regarded as extremely important, particularly for the following reason: on the basis those neutralizations where it is one of the
two members, and not an intermediate sound, which (phonetically)
appears in the position of suspension, one can determine that this
member is functionally *unmarked* (archiphoneme + zero), whereas
the non-occurring member is *marked* (archiphoneme + a specific
mark). In German, for example, /t/ thus constitutes the unmarked
member of the opposition /t/ : /d/, cf. examples like [bunt] (*bunt,
Bund*) and [rɑːt] (*Rat, Rad*).

In an attempt, apparently, at reconciling the conflicting views
advanced by himself that the unit occurring in the position of neutralization should be interpreted a) as the unmarked member of an
opposition (1931) and b) as the archiphoneme (1933), Trubetzkoy
introduces the notion of *archiphoneme representative*. The entity
appearing in the position of neutralization is now regarded as the
'Stellvertreter' of an archiphoneme:

In den Stellungen, wo ein aufhebbarer Gegensatz tatsäch-
lich aufgehoben ist, verlieren die spezifischen Merkmale

eines Oppositionsgliedes ihre phonologische Geltung, und relevant bleiben nur jene Züge, die beiden Gliedern gemein sind. In der Aufhebungsstellung wird somit ein Oppositionsglied zum Stellvertreter des *"Archiphonems"* des betreffenden Gegensatzes (1936b, p. 31f).

It should be pointed out that the archiphoneme representative is not to be understood simply as the manifestation of an archiphoneme, for in *Grundzüge der Phonologie*, where the ideas advanced in Trubetzkoy 1936b are repeated in slightly abbreviated form, it is stated explicitly that the archiphoneme representative is *realized* as a sound (p. 71). This implies that in addition to a phonetic level, Trubetzkoy operates with two phonological levels which differ in abstractness. For example, a German word like *und* will now be interpreted at the most abstract level as /un<t/d>/. At a less abstract but still phonological level the unmarked member of the opposition /t/ : /d/ is assumed to represent the archiphoneme <t/d>, i.e. *und* is here interpreted as /unt/ and its final segment regarded as a /t/ whose voicelessness has lost its relevance. At the phonetic level this archiphoneme representative is realized as [t]. This attempt to claim that the unit occurring in the position of neutralization is simultaneously an archiphoneme and the unmarked member of a neutralizable opposition (which represents the archiphoneme) is neither clear nor convincing. It has been criticized by Akamatsu (1975), who considers it a crucial contradiction, and who points out that the intervention of archiphoneme representatives considerably and unnecessarily reduces the importance of archiphonemes, which are now mere logical entities.

In conclusion it may be said about Trubetzkoy that besides being the pioneer of the theory of neutralization he is the Prague phonologist who along with Martinet has contributed most significantly to the discussion of this concept. In most of the publications mentioned above he attaches great importance to the intuitions of the native speaker, and we have seen that he has vacillated considerably in his interpretation of the segment occurring in the position of suspension. Should this segment be analyzed as an archiphoneme, as the unmarked member of the neutralized opposition, or as one of the oppositional members (marked or unmarked) on the basis of phonetic and/or morphological associations? After having been critized for taking the intuitions of the native speaker into account in the phonological analysis, Trubetzkoy himself repudiated "psychologism" in his later works. For example, it is stated in the section of *Grundzüge der Phonologie* dealing with phoneme definitions that one should avoid invoking the linguistic consciousness, for "das 'Sprachbewusstsein' ist entweder eine metaphorische Bezeichnung des Sprachgebildes ('langue') oder ein ganz vager Begriff, der selbst noch definiert werden muss und vielleicht gar nicht definiert werden kann" (p. 38). His attitude is now purely functional; but from such a viewpoint the concept of neutralization is still of great importance, and it should therefore, according to Trubetzkoy, be regarded as one of the cornerstones of phonology (p. 70).

2.3. V. Mathesius

We have seen above that in 1929 Jakobson introduced the notion of the archiphoneme and that in 1929, also, Trubetzkoy used the notion of neutralization (suggested first by N. Durnovo)[3] in his description of Polabian. It should not be overlooked, however, that in the same year both these concepts were in fact recognized by V. Mathesius. In an article on the phonological structure of Czech as compared with some non-Slavonic languages, particularly German, Mathesius makes a distinction between phonemes (sounds with a functional value) and modifying elements (sound properties with a functional value). Vowel quantity, for example, is considered a modifying element in Czech, and if a word like *rada* 'advice' is replaced by *ráda* 'eager' (fem.) this does not in the linguistic consciousness of the native Czech speaker constitute a change from one phoneme to another but a change in the 'aspect' of one and the same *a*-phoneme. Now whereas vowel quantity is regarded as a genuine modifying element in Czech, palatalization belongs among the 'eléments modificateurs non proprement dits'. If a word like *dýky* ['di:ki] 'dagger' (gen.sg.) is replaced by *díky* ['d'i:ki] 'thanks', this does not constitute a change in the aspect of one *d*-phoneme, but rather a change from one phoneme to another (very closely related) phoneme. Palatalized and unpalatalized consonants in Czech — such as /d'/ and /d/, /t'/ and /t/ — are linked together in the linguistic consciousness, and this is

---

3) In *Grundzüge der Phonologie* (p. 70) Trubetzkoy acknowledges his debt to Durnovo as regards the concept of neutralization: "der Unterschied zwischen aufhebbaren und konstanten phonologischen Gegensätzen . . . ist für das Funktionieren der phonologischen Systeme, wie es als erster N. Durnovo betont hat, ausserordentlich wichtig."

also the case with the bright and corresponding dark sibilants s/š, z/ž, c/č ('sifflantes et chuintantes'), as well as with voiced and corresponding voiceless consonants. Mathesius thus expresses virtually the same view as Jakobson, who abstracts the common core of two phonemes within a correlative pair, regards it as psychologically 'real', and terms it 'archiphoneme'.

Whereas the notion of archiphoneme is thus only implicit in Mathesius' paper, that of neutralization is recognized explicitly. For example, it is stated that in Czech and German the functional difference between voiced and voiceless consonants is eliminated in word–final position:

> Les deux langues concordent en ce que la différence dans la sonorité des consonnes n'a pas dans ces langues de valeur phonologique à la fin des mots. Ceci signifie qu'à la fin du mot, dans l'une et l'autre langues, on trouve confondus en un phonème unique les couples de consonnes b/p, d/t, v/f, z/s, h/x, et outre, en tchèque, d'/t', ž/š, en allemand g/k (Mathesius 1929, p. 81).

It appears, then, that in the year when Trubetzkoy pointed out that the correlative properties of phonemes may in certain environments lose their phonological value, virtually the same view was put forward by Mathesius. Like both Jakobson and Trubetzkoy, furthermore, Mathesius emphasizes the importance not only of functional but also of psychological properties in phonology.

2.4. A. Martinet

The linguist who, apart from Trubetzkoy, has studied the concepts of neutralization and the archiphoneme most thoroughly is André Martinet. In his article 'Neutralisation et archiphonème' dating from 1936, these two concepts are for the first time connected in such a way that 'archiphoneme' presupposes 'neutralization'. The archiphoneme is here defined in the following way (p. 54): "la notion d'élément commun de deux ou plusieurs phonèmes neutralisables, ou, mieux encore, ... celle d'*unité phonologique simple susceptible, en certaines positions, de se dissocier en deux ou plusieurs éléments phonologiquement distincts.*" In comparison with the previous definitions (Jakobson, *Projet*, Trubetzkoy), this represents a narrowing of the concept in the sense that archiphonemes can be extracted from neutralizable oppositions exclusively. Martinet argues for this view by saying that the archiphoneme, which without neutralization is a pure abstraction, only has a concrete manifestation value in the position of suspension. In this connection it should be mentioned that even to Trubetzkoy archiphonemes without neutralization are somewhat dubious entities, cf. *Grundzüge der Phonologie* (p. 76), where it is stated that the affiliation of two phonemes to one archiphoneme is far less evident if the opposition which they form is constant than if it is suspendable. To the present writer there is little doubt that the psychological reality of Martinet's archiphonemes is indeed greater than that of the archiphonemes discussed previously. For example, it seems highly probable that the common core of the opposition /e/ : /ɛ/ in French, which is neutralizable, is more 'real' to the speaker–hearer than that of /i/ : /e/, which is non-suspendable: "Un Français n'acceptera jamais de mettre sur la même plan l'opposition æ/e d'une part, les oppositions e/i et æ/a d'autre part, parce que les deux phonèmes e et æ sont sentis comme formant une unité supérieure E qui s'oppose comme telle à d'autres unités A (= a et α) et I (= i)" (p. 53). If one wishes to take the intuitions of the speaker–hearer into consideration in the linguistic analysis, the intimate connection between the members of a suspendable opposition must be indicated in the phonological description. Now whereas it can be said that Martinet narrows the concept of the archiphoneme in the sense that it is extractable from neutralizable oppositions only, it can at the same time be claimed that Martinet's archiphoneme is broader than Trubetzkoy's and that of the *Projet* in two ways: it may cover more than two phonemes, and it may cover phonemes which do not form a correlative opposition. In Russian, for example, /t t' d d'/ may thus be united within one archiphoneme, and the same applies to /e ɛ/ in French in spite of the fact that these two phonemes form a disjunctive opposition.

In an article published in 1946 Martinet comes to the conclusion that it is distinctive features ('les traits pertinents'), not phonemes, which are the basic units of phonology. This implies that neutralization may now be regarded as the loss of the relevance of a feature in certain positions, rather than as the suspension of an opposition formed by phonemes. Instead of saying that oppositions such as /d/ : /t/, /z/ : /s/, /b'/ : /p'/ in Russian are suspended in word-final position, we can say that the feature 'voice' loses its value in this environment. If neutralization is understood in this way it is possible, according to Martinet, to dispense with the concept of archiphoneme. (But if phonemes are still recognized it is natural to ask what kind of phoneme it is that appears in the position of neutralization.) Furthermore, Trubetzkoy's distinction between bilateral and multilateral oppositions, whose main function is to make it possible to distinguish between neutralization (only bilateral oppositions are neutralizable) and the absence of a phoneme in a given position can now be dispensed with. However, Martinet does not conclude decisively that such a conception of neutralization is superior to the traditional one. In the same article (p. 42) he dissociates himself from a psychologically oriented description of language:

> Or, le recours au sentiment linguistique ne saurait être considéré comme scientifiquement recommandable. Si nous voulons donner en peu de rigueur à notre discipline, il ne peut être question pour nous de nous livrer a l'analyse d'un sentiment, et ceci d'autant moins que ce sentiment ne peut être autre chose qu'un reflet laissé dans le subconscient par les expériences linguistiques du sujet. C'est sur les manifestations linguistiques elles-mêmes que nous devons faire porter notre observation.

Despite what has just been said about the consequences of regarding neutralization as loss of feature values, Martinet still operates with archiphonemes in *Phonology as Functional Phonetics* (1949), and the psychological and functional properties of these entities are discussed. For example, a Frenchman will accept the archiphoneme E as a justification of his own linguistic feelings. It is emphasized, however, that the psychological point of view is of secondary importance (1949, p. 6):

> linguistic feeling is a result of the functioning of the system. It is an effect and not a cause, and it is obvious that if we want to proceed scientifically, we should, as far as possible, examine causes rather than effects. The more so as it is much safer to study strictly linguistic data than the psychological reflexes of them.

In the description of the sound system of a language the list of phonemes should include archiphonemes, or it should at least be followed by indications showing to what extent phonetic differences retain their functional value. The linguist is warned against postulating neutralization (and archiphonemes) unless two or more phonemes stand in *exclusive relation,* i.e. are alone in sharing the sum total of their distinctive features except for one (this definition comes quite close to Trubetzkoy's definition of bilateral oppositions). For example, the opposition between /t/ and /p/ in English is not neutralized initially before /l/ — where only [p] occurs, never [t], cf. *play*, **tlay* — for these phonemes do not stand in exclusive relation, and we therefore cannot know for certain whether it is the opposition /p/ : /t/ which is suspended: it might just as well be /k/ : /t/, cf. *clay*. What we find here is a case of *defective distribution*, and none of /p/'s features lose their value in this position. In Martinet 1956 two phonemes are said to be in 'rapport exclusif' (exclusive relation) if they are distinguished by one feature only and if they are the only ones in the system displaying all the features which they have in common. It is added, however, that more than two phonemes may also stand in exclusive relation. In English, for example, /m/, /n/ and /ŋ/ fulfil the above conditions since they are the only phonemes in the language characterized by the feature 'nasality' and since they are distinguished from each other by one feature only (point of articulation). Unlike Trubetzkoy, then, Martinet does not insist that neutralization should be restricted to bilateral oppositions. In the same book the archiphoneme is defined as the set of distinctive features held in common by phonemes which are in exclusive relation (p. 42). This implies that it is no longer regarded as presupposing neutralization. If the archiphoneme is not accompanied by neutralization, however, it must be considered a pure abstraction. In Martinet 1968, it is pointed out that one should only recognize neutralization if the members of an opposition have in common a set of distinctive features which no other phoneme shares with them, i.e. if they are in an exclusive relation.

Defective distribution is not, however, the only pitfall awaiting the linguist. In the article 'De la morphonologie' (1965) Martinet points out the danger of confusing neutralization with morphologically conditioned phoneme *alternations*. A sharp distinction must be drawn between phonology and morphophonology. In particular one should be on one's guard against describing as morphological alternation what is in fact neutralization. What one finds in Russian examples such as *ryba* [rɨba] 'fish' ~ *rybka* [rɨpka] 'little fish', *pod oknom* [pǎd...] 'under the window' ~ *pod komom* [pǎt...] 'under the lump', and *ot okna* [ǎt...] 'from the window' ~ *ot goroda* [ǎd...] 'from the town' is *not* morphologically conditioned alternations between the phonemes /b/ and /p/, /d/ and /t/, but neutralization of the oppositions /b/ : /p/, /d/ : /t/ in the last–mentioned members

of the pairs. In Russian the opposition between voiced and corresponding voiceless phonemes is suspended before obstruents (except
/v/), and a Muscovite is simply unable to pronounce sequences of
obstruents which are not either voiced or voiceless throughout.
Therefore *rybka, pod komom* and *ot goroda* should be analysed as
/riPkă, păT-kómăm, ăT-górădă/, i.e. the leftmost obstruents in the
clusters should be interpreted as archiphonemes. To postulate the
phonological forms /rib-, pod-, ot-/ in these three examples would
be to sacrifice the results of the phonological analysis in order to
simplify the presentation of morphemes. By the same principle
English plural forms such as *sins* [sinz], *ells* [elz] and *eggs* [egz],
dogs [dɔgz] must be analysed as /sinz, elz/ and /egS, dɔgS/. For
whereas the English speaker is capable of producing sequences of a
nasal or lateral followed by a voiceless obstruent, cf. *since* [sins] and
else [els], he is unable to pronounce obstruent sequences which are
not either voiced or voiceless throughout. According to Martinet, a
phonological analysis consists in accounting for what phonic features
the native speaker–hearer is capable of producing, distinguishing, and
combining to form the words of the language. Whereas the three
Russian morpheme sequences mentioned above as well as *eggs, dogs*
in English thus exemplify neutralization, a genuine case of alternation is found in an Italian example like *amico* [amíko] 'friend' ~
amici [amíči] 'friends', for here the opposition /k/ : /č/ is not
suspended in the latter word, cf. an example like *stomaco* [stómako]
'stomach' ~ *stomachi* [stómaki] 'stomachs'. An Italian is perfectly
capable of pronouncing a [k] before [i].

Before moving on to other Prague phonologists we must briefly
mention how neutralizations are divided into different types and
how the phonetic realization of neutralized oppositions (archiphonemes) is described. According to the conditions under which
a suspension takes place, Trubetzkoy distinguishes between *contextually determined* and *structurally determined* neutralizations
(1936a, p. 37ff). Neutralizations of the former type are due to the
presence of certain adjacent phonemes; as an example the suspension
in Russian of the opposition between voiced and voiceless consonants
before obstruents (except /v/) may be mentioned. Neutralizations
of the latter type are dependent on the structure of the word (or

morpheme); as examples may be mentioned the suspensions in Russian of the opposition between voiced and voiceless consonants in word-final position and of the opposition /a/ : /o/ in unaccented syllables. As far as the phonetic realization of archiphonemes is concerned, it is stated by Martinet (1936, p. 55) that when two phonemes α and α′ are neutralized they may be realized phonetically as follows:

    (i) as [α] in some positions and as [α′] in others.
    (ii) exclusively as [α] or exclusively as [α′].
    (iii) indifferently as [α] or as [α′].
    (iv) as a third sound [α″].

An example illustrating the first type of manifestation is <e/ε> in French, which in open syllables is realized as [e] and in closed syllables as [ε]. The second type is represented by German <t/d>, which is realized exclusively as [t]. The third type may be exemplified with Danish <p/b>, which in one of the positions of neutralization (utterance-finally) is manifested indifferently as [p] or as [b], cf. a word like *lap* 'patch', which is sometimes pronounced [lap] and sometimes [lab] finally in utterances. As an example of the last realization type we may mention Russian <a/o>, which in unaccented non-pretonic syllables is realized as [ə]. A similar account of the phonetic realization of archiphonemes is given by Trubetzkoy (1936b, pp. 32-36; 1939, pp. 71-75).

2.5. A.W. de Groot

The Dutchman A.W. de Groot has dealt with the concept of neutralization in an important paper dating from 1939. De Groot differs from other phonologists working within the framework of Prague phonology by recognizing neither the concept of the archiphoneme nor of neutralization (although the article is entitled 'Neutralisation d'opposition'). Where Trubetzkoy, Martinet, and others would postulate neutralization, he operates with defective distribution instead. This appears from his description, for example, of the non-occurrence of the sound [e] in final closed syllables in French compared with the occurrence in this environment of [ε] as the 'phenomenon that in some positions a certain phoneme cannot be used, whereas that to which it is directly opposed can.' It is also apparent from the fact that the word "neutralization" is put in inverted commas. De Groot's rejection of neutralization and archiphonemes is a consequence of his conception of the phoneme. Unlike Trubetz-koy, for example, he does not regard the phoneme as primarily a distinctive unit but as a "signe linguistique avec une fonction *identi-fiante*, mais sans fonction symbolique" (p. 132, my italics). By virtue of this identifying function the phoneme is an independent positive entity, and in contradistinction to word accent, for example, it is recognizable without linguistic and/or situational context.[4] The distinctive function of the phoneme is a result of its identifying function and is not obligatory. In English, for example, /t/ is opposed to /d/ at the beginning of morphemes, but in the interior of morphemes after /s/ only the former of the two occurs, and these two phonemes are therefore only potentially distinctive ('virtuelle-ment distinctifs'). If the phoneme is regarded as a positive entity whose primary function is to identify word forms, it is not possible to operate with any phoneme which in one respect or another is "neutral", i.e. archiphonemes are ruled out:

> Un pareil phonème extra-oppositionnel à côté d'une opposition directe et corrélative de deux phonèmes non seulement ne se présente pas, il ne peut même pas se présenter à priori. C'est une contradictio in terminis, puisqu'un phonème, en vertu de sa nature, est virtuelle-ment distinctif à l'égard de tous les autres phonèmes du même système; un pareil troisième phonème (par exemple en russe un *t* à côté d'un *t̪* non-palatal et d'un *t'* palatal) ne pourrait dans aucune position avoir une fonction vir-tuellement ou actuellement distinctive à l'égard du membre sans marque de l'opposition (en russe dans ce cas à l'égard du *t̪*) (p. 137).

De Groot also operates with defective distribution in those cases where in a certain position two phonemes are not distinctively opposed to each other and where the manifestation is intermediary between the members of the opposition. In his opinion the inter-mediate manifestation is easy to explain as "économie de parole". If /b d g/ are absent after /s/ in English, /p t k/ are naturally given greater possibilities of phonetic variation and may therefore be realized without their normal fortis-character. De Groot does not

---

4) This argument has subsequently been disproved; cf. Ladefoged and Broad-bent 1957, where it is demonstrated that the linguistic context decisively influences the identification of vowels.

mention oscillating manifestation, found, for example, in a Danish word like *hat* 'hat', which is pronounced sometimes with [t] and sometimes with [d]. We may assume, however, that he would interpret such cases in the same way, i.e. by saying that in Danish the realization of /t/ is less constrained in final position as a result of the absence of /d/ in this position (or, alternatively, that /d/ has a larger domain of manifestation due to the lack of /t/). De Groot regards the linguistic consciousness as a factor which should be taken into account in linguistic analysis. In his 1936-article, Martinet points out that the disjunctive oppositions /e/ : /ɛ/, /ø/ : /œ/, and /o/ : /ɔ/ in French are perceived by the native speaker as more intimately connected than the remaining vowel oppositions except /a/ : /ɑ/, which is correlative, and he puts forward the hypothesis that this is due to the fact that they are neutralizable. De Groot accepts Martinet's observation but not his explanation. According to him the reason for the intimate connection between the members of these oppositions is the fact that these four pairs constitute the only *direct* oppositions in the French vowel system, i.e. they are the only ones whose members are kept apart exclusively by a peripheral element.[5] In order to make this interpretation intelligible it is necessary briefly to describe de Groot's analysis of the French vowels. He operates with the hierarchically ordered features ("marques") 'sonority' (which corresponds to 'height'), 'place of articulation', 'lip rounding', and "assourdissement", which presumably corresponds to 'laxness' ('tenseness') in Jakobson's system. (We shall disregard de Groot's treatment of the vowel [ə] as well as his feature 'vowel length', which is said to have practically no distinctive function in French, and which is consequently placed at the bottom of the hierarchy.) By means of these features de Groot arranges the French vowel phonemes in a table, which is here reproduced in the form of a tree diagram and with somewhat simplified terminology. Note that he operates with three degrees of sonority:

---

5) Une opposition est directe quand l'élément central ou la collection d'éléments centrale des membres de cette opposition est identique et que seulement un élément peripherique est different. Nous appelons une marque *a* plus centrale qu'une marque *b*, si dans le système en question un signe avec la marque *a* peut s'employer sans la marque *b*, mais non pas un signe avec la marque *b* sans la marque *a* (p. 131).

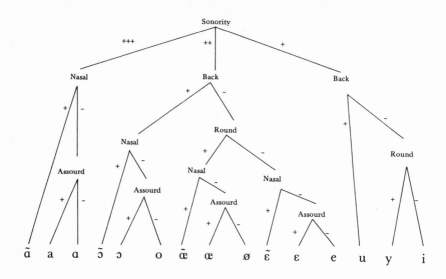

It appears from the diagram that /a/ : /ɑ/, /ɔ/ : /o/, /œ/ : /ø/, and
/ɛ/ : /e/ are the only "direct" oppositions in the French vowel
system, since the members of each of these oppositions are kept
apart by means of the peripheral element "assourdissement". (On the
other hand /i/ and /e/, for example, are distinguished from each
other by means of the non–peripheral feature 'sonority'.) This explains the intimate connection between the members of precisely
these oppositions: "Le rapport intime entre a et ɑ, entre ae et e etc.
ne résulte pas du fait que les oppositions a/ɑ, ae/e etc. sont 'neutralisables', mais du fait que ce sont des oppositions directes entre
des voyelles isolées et en effet les seules qui existent en français" (p.
145).

De Groot also rejects the orthographic arguments adduced by
Trubetzkoy (1933a) in order to demonstrate the psychological reality of neutralization. Trubetzkoy mentions that in Old Greek the
opposition between voiced and voiceless stops as well as that between aspirated and unaspirated stops was suspended before s. These
neutralized stop phonemes, whose phonetic manifestation he
refrains from discussing, were felt to occupy a place apart, and they
therefore had to be represented by special letters. Since they only
occurred before s, special letters were devised which represented the
whole sequence of neutralized stop + s, namely ξ (ksi) and ψ (psi).
Now according to de Groot, the creation of these letters was not due

to special stop phonemes, which were neither "tenues" nor "mediae" nor "aspiratae", but may be explained — just like the above-mentioned phonetic example dealing with English stops — as a tendency towards economy. It is comparable to the use in English of the grapheme & for Latin *et*.

According to de Groot "neutralization" is simply a kind of defective distribution. The same sound cannot be the manifestation of two different phonemes, and in fact the native speaker never finds it difficult to identify a particular sound: "en néerlandais je ne saurais mentioner à peine un seul cas òu l'on doute de quel phonème on se sert dans un cas déterminé" (p. 136). The notion of neutralization is psychologically unmotivated, for the feeling of an intimate connection between two phonemes which are unopposed to each other in certain positions does not arise if the opposition which they form is indirect. Conversely, such a feeling does present itself in the case of any direct opposition, whether "neutralizable" or not. De Groot argues that Trubetzkoy has been forced to introduce the concepts of neutralization and archiphoneme because he claims that in order for two sounds to be referable to different phonemes they must be *actually* distinctive. By laying down this condition he runs into serious difficulties with [h] and [ŋ] in English, Dutch, and German. These consonants are in complementary distribution, but as they do not share any features which set them apart from other sounds occurring in any of the three languages they cannot be interpreted as variants of the same phoneme. On the other hand they do not meet the condition of being actually distinctive. In order to get out of this dilemma Trubetzkoy resorts to the notion of 'indirect opposition': in German, [h] and [ŋ] are not directly contrastive, but both of them contrast with [p], cf. *hacken, packen, Ringe, Rippe*, and therefore they are indirectly opposed to each other. On closer inspection, however, this turns out to be an impossible solution (a rejection of Trubetzkoy's argument can be found in Fischer-Jørgensen 1975, p. 84*n*). De Groot points out that if phonemes are regarded as identifying entities, which are only potentially distinctive, there is no problem with these sounds at all: we recognize [h] and [ŋ] as different units when we meet them.[6]

---

6) De Groot's ideas about the identifying function of phonemes are reflected in Cohen 1952. In this book neutralization and archiphonemes are not recognized either, and after initial *s* in English the author assumes that there is defective distribution of /b d g/.

42

2.6. J. Vachek

A survey of the theory and practice of the Prague school has been given by Josef Vachek in *The Linguistic School of Prague* (1966). In this book Vachek emphasizes the importance of the concept of neutralization. On the other hand the archiphoneme is regarded as a largely unfruitful concept, which may perhaps be useful in structuring phonemic systems, but which has no justification in phonological representations of spoken utterances. In a Russian example like [s'v'eckə] 'candle', where Trubetzkoy because of the suspension of the palatalization opposition before palatalized /v'/ would operate with /Sv'-/ or perhaps /sv'-/ (i.e. where he would interpret the sibilant as an archiphoneme or as the unmarked member of the opposition /s/ : /s'/) most Prague phonologists would, according to Vachek, operate with /s'v'-/ instead. The unit in initial position is thus considered to be a palatalized sibilant, but at the same time these Pragueans recognize that the opposition between this phoneme and its correlative partner is here neutralized. In other words, the initial segment is regarded as a palatalized phoneme on the basis of its phonetic realization in spite of the fact that the palatalization opposition is neutralized. In support of this solution it is mentioned that the members of the given language community evaluate the archiphoneme as one of the phonemes subsumed under it and that in a phonemic representation of a spoken utterance there should not be units belonging to a level other than that of the phoneme. According to Vachek the archiphoneme is a subphonemic unit (recall that correlative phonemes can be broken down into common core + differential property).

This rejection of the archiphoneme does not, however, carry much conviction. In the first place, Vachek does not substantiate his claim that the segment in the position of suspension is evaluated as one of the phonemes appearing in the position of relevance. He simply states the following: "Even Trubetzkoy himself admits that the members of the given language community evaluate the archiphoneme, in the neutralized position, as this or that phoneme" (p. 62). But as mentioned above Trubetzkoy is in several of his works inclined to the opposite view (recall that he characterizes Russian [s'] in those positions where the palatalization opposition is suspended as "nicht ganz hart, nicht ganz weich"). Secondly, it seems self-contradictory to maintain, for example, that the final stop of German [rɑ:t] (*Rat, Rad*) is at one and the same time a

/t/ — which is kept apart from /d/ by being voiceless — and a unit whose voicing is neutralized. If the segment occurring in this position is a dental stop which is neutral with regard to voice, how is it then possible to interpret it as /t/ rather than as <t/d>? If the concept of neutralization is recognized it necessarily follows that 'neutralization products' must also be recognized, whether they are termed 'archiphonemes', 'hyperphonemes' or 'syncretisms'.

2.7. B. Trnka

The concepts of neutralization and archiphoneme are discussed by Trnka in his revised edition of *A Phonological Analysis of Present-Day Standard English* (1966).[7] In this book a somewhat different classification of phonological oppositions from the one proposed by Trubetzkoy (1936a, 1939) is carried out. Whereas oppositions are divided according to their relation to other members of the system into 'proportional' and 'isolated' the same way they are in *Grundzüge*, Trnka further classifies oppositions according to the relation between their members into *disjunct* oppositions, whose terms are distinguished from each other by two, or more, relevant features (e.g. /p/ : /v/), and *conjunct* oppositions, whose terms differ from each other by only one relevant feature. Oppositions of the latter type are subdivided into *privative* oppositions, where one term is differentiated from the other by an additional relevant feature (cf. /t/ : /d/, addition of 'voice') and *equipollent* oppositions, where both terms have the same relevant features with the exception of one which is different (cf. /p/ : /f/, 'plosive' vs. 'friction'). The sum of the relevant features common to both terms of equipollent oppositions is termed an *archiphoneme*. That archiphonemes can be extracted from equipollent oppositions only, and not from privative oppositions as well, is quite surprising considering Jakobson's conception of archiphoneme as the common core of two phonemes within a correlative pair.

Trnka allegedly recognizes *neutralization*, which is defined provisionally as "the suppression of conjunct oppositions in some of their positions in the word" (p. 29). This implies that localization

7) In an article dating from 1958 Trnka puts forward largely the same views as in the revised edition of *A Phonological Analysis of Present-Day Standard English*. In another paper (1939) he draws attention to a number of similarities between combinatory variants and neutralization of phonemes.

(place of articulation) oppositions, such as /m/ : /n/ in English, may also be neutralized, and his interpretation of neutralization is thus more comprehensive than that of Trubetzkoy (who only regarded bilateral oppositions as neutralizable). On the other hand Trnka rejects Trubetzkoy's theory that the sound occurring in the position of neutralization manifests an archiphoneme. In Czech the voice opposition is neutralized before the paired consonants /p b t d s z ʃ ʒ /, and in a word like *svatba* [svadba] 'wedding' the opposition between /t/ and /d/ is thus neutralized. However, the [d] of *svatba* cannot according to Trnka be interpreted as an archiphoneme <t/d> since /d/ occurs in the derived adjective *svatební* [svadebɲiː]. "If /d/ in /db/ had not the same bundle of relevant features as /d/ in *sady*, it would be a different phonemic unit, and the analogical transference ... could not have taken place. This and other cases of morphological analogy are apt to show that /d/ in both kinds of position [those of 'neutralization' and 'relevance'; NDN] is the same phoneme, and the same holds for /t/" (p. 30). By interpreting [d] in *svatba* as /d/ — the marked member of the opposition and the phonetically realistic choice — Trnka thus takes up the same position as Vachek. In those cases where the sound occurring in the position of neutralization is not — as in the example just quoted — identical with the phonetic implementation of one term of the oppositional pair, an archiphonemic interpretation, which would here be phonetically plausible, is also rejected by Trnka. What we find here is a 'neutralization variant' of one of the two phonemes entering into the opposition. In English, for example, the opposition betweeen nasal consonants is neutralized before /f/, but in a word like *comfort* the [ɱ], which is phonetically intermediate between [m] and [n], does not represent the archiphoneme <N> but is a neutralization variant of the phoneme /m/.

Trnka's argument against the archiphoneme is not really convincing. If it is theorized that the apical stop in *svatba* represents an archiphoneme <t/d>, then this archiphoneme if moved to the position of relevance in derived forms would obviously have to be disambiguated as either of the phonemes subsumed under it, i.e. it would cease to be an archiphoneme. In *svatební*, where the apical stop is moved to intervocalic position, it is hardly surprising that the archiphoneme of *svatba* is disambiguated as /d/. It is difficult to see why an analogical transference of a unit like <t/d> to the position of relevance in the shape of /d/ (or /t/) should be ruled out.

By interpreting the apical stop of [svadba] as /d/ rather than as

<t/d> Trnka rejects not only the archiphonemic analysis but also, in point of fact, the concept of neutralization itself. Neutralization is now understood in the following way: "The process of neutralization must be regarded ... as consisting in the exclusion of one of the terms of opposition from its specific phonemic contexts" (p. 30). Now if the analyst regards /d/ in Czech, for example, as 'excluded' in word-final position, i.e. if [t] in words like *let* 'flight' and *led* 'ice' are interpreted as /t/, he has *de facto* rejected the concept of neutralization and opted for 'defective distribution' instead. This, as we know, is the position taken up by the post–Bloomfieldians, but they would not speak of neutralization and (taking their basic approach into consideration) rightly so. If it is assumed that the opposition between /t/ and /d/ is neutralized word-finally in Czech, the apical stop occurring in this position must necessarily be 'neutral' with respect to the distinction /t/ : /d/, and in that case it cannot be interpreted as /t/. Trnka mentions that neutralization is a Prague concept which is rejected by most American descriptivists, but except for the word 'neutralization' the analysis proposed by himself would be endorsed by practically any American descriptivist. As pointed out in the *Introduction* as well as in the above discussion of Vachek's views, the recognition of neutralization entails the recognition of 'neutralization products' (archiphonemes). This causal relationship has been overlooked by both Vachek and Trnka, and consequently their views fall somewhere between 'neutralization' and 'defective distribution'.

2.8. E. Buyssens

In an article of 1972 Eric Buyssens has put forward some views on neutralization and archiphonemes which are similar to those held by de Groot and, in particular, by Trnka and Vachek. Like de Groot, Buyssens is of the opinion that phonemes have an *identifying* function, but whereas for de Groot this function is the primary one, the *distinctive* function is regarded as equally important by Buyssens. Like Vachek and Trnka, he argues that the notion of the archiphoneme has to be rejected since (in his view) it is not based on concrete facts as the phoneme is. Among his arguments the following are the most important: [8]

(1) Trubetzkoy's attempt to strengthen his archiphonemic theory

---

8) Some of these arguments are repeated in abbreviated form in Buyssens 1974.

by means of psychological phenomena, i.e. by adducing as empirical evidence a particularly intimate connection in linguistic consciousness between neutralizable phonemes, is a failure. In Dutch, for example, the opposition between voiced and voiceless consonants is neutralized word–finally, but the sounds occurring in this position are readily identified by the native speaker with the voiceless phonemes, as demonstrated by the fact that spelling reformers have proposed to write words like *heb, veld, lig* as *hep, velt, lich* instead. Unlike de Groot, however, Buyssens does not attempt to offer any alternative explanation in a case like /e/ : /ɛ/ in French, where a psychologically intimate relationship has often been postulated. Apparently he questions the validity of this example, for he states that the vowel of a word like *belle* is identified clearly by the native speaker with the /ɛ/ of *raie*.

(2) The archiphoneme is a unit of a different order from the phoneme, and since only units of the same order may be allowed to form oppositions, it is not permissible to operate with oppositions between archiphonemes and phonemes. This implies (my example) that the final segment of German *Rad* cannot be interpreted as an archiphoneme, for in that case *Rad* would be kept apart from a word like *Rahm* by means of the opposition $<t/d>$: /m/. In this connection it will be recalled that Vachek bans archiphonemes in a phonemic representation since they belong to a different level.

(3) Archiphonemes complicate the phonological description and are of no use. It is always simpler to assume that any sound manifests one phoneme only. Even in the case of intermediary realization Buyssens finds it simpler to say that one of the members of the opposition and the segment occurring in the position of neutralization are allophones of the same phoneme. He would thus regard the [pʰ] of *pin* and [p] of *spin* in English as allophones of the phoneme /p/ (or perhaps the [b] of *bin* and the [p] of *spin* as allophones of /b/).

(4) Recognition of archiphonemes leads to arbitrary decisions. In word-final closed syllables in French the vowels [u], [o] and [ɔ] represent three different phonemes, cf. *soûle* ≠ *saule* ≠ *sol*, but before final /r/ we only find [u] and [ɔ], as in *pour* ≠ *port*, never [o]. This implies that both the opposition between /u/ and /o/ and the one between /ɔ/ and /o/ may be considered neutralized in

this position, but if archiphonemes are recognized there is no knowing whether the words *pour*, *port* should be analysed as /p<u/o>r, pɔr/ or as /pur, p<o/ɔ>r/. In order to clear up dubious cases of this type Martinet (1960, p. 72) has proposed the criterion of *partial complementarity*: in French the front vowels [i], [e], [ɛ] and [a] represent different phonemes, cf. *riz ≠ ré ≠ raie ≠ rat*, but in closed syllables only [i], [ɛ] and [a] are found, as in *bile ≠ belle ≠ bal*. Here it can be decided that it is the opposition /e/ : /ɛ/ which is neutralized, for only these two sounds are partially complementary, the former occurring in open syllables and the latter in closed syllables. In the case of /o/ : /u/ vs. /o/ : /ɔ/ this criterion is also useful, [o] and [ɔ] being partially complementary in the sense that only the former sound occurs in final open syllables and only the latter before homosyllabic /r/. However, a decision that it is /o/ : /ɔ/ which is neutralized is less obviously reached here than in the case of /e/ : /ɛ/, for in nonfinal open syllables [ɔ] frequently occurs besides [o], and in nonfinal closed syllables [o] sometimes occurs besides [ɔ].

Buyssens concludes his attack on the archiphoneme in the following way (p. 55):

> En résumé, l'hypothèse de l'archiphonème n'a pas de fondement et ne joue aucun rôle dans la théorie de Troubetzkoy; en outre, elle se heurte à certains faits. Rappelons enfin que pour pouvoir dire qu'une opposition peut être pertinente dans telle position et neutralisée dans telle autre, il faut nécessairement admettre que le segment en position de neutralisation s'identifie avec l'un des phonèmes en position de pertinence; Troubetzkoy le dit explicitement: "un des termes de l'opposition devient le représentant de l'archiphonème" (p. 81) [quoted from the French translation of *Grundzüge*; NDN]. Les Américains ont donc raison de dire "Once a phoneme, always a phoneme".

It should be borne in mind, though, that Trubetzkoy's late proposal that the unit occurring in the position of neutralization is the archiphoneme representative, not the archiphoneme itself, is not really compatible with his own theory of neutralization. Secondly, it is incomprehensible to the present writer why the notion of neutralization should necessitate the identification of the sound occurring in the position of neutralization with one of the two phonemes appearing in the position of relevance. On the contrary, and as pointed out several times above, it is the opposite conclusion which forces itself upon the analyst who recognizes neutralization, namely, identification with both these phonemes.

The fact that Buyssens seconds the American slogan "Once a phoneme, always a phoneme" makes it natural for the reader to infer that he wishes to reject not only the archiphoneme, but also neutralization itself, and that he prefers to operate with defective distribution instead. This, however, is not the case. In a short paper of 1975, in which he replies to criticism levelled against him by R. Vion (see below), Buyssens states that such a conclusion should not be drawn (p. 36):

> C'est la conclusion inverse qui s'impose: puisque je n'ai pas mis en doute la validité de la notion de neutralisation, c'est que je l'accepte. Vion semble incapable de distinguer entre hypothèse et réalité: la neutralisation est un fait objectif, indiscutable; on ne peut nier que tel phonème est impossible dans telle position.

Buyssens' position is thus the same as that taken up by Trnka (according to whom neutralization is the exclusion in certain contexts of one of the terms of a conjunct opposition) and Vachek. As we have seen, however, this position is not tenable since it only makes sense to speak of neutralization if a unit is indeed 'neutral' with regard to the opposition between two (or more) phonemes. It is also difficult to see how neutralization — say, of /t/ and /d/ in word-final position in German — can be regarded as an objective fact rather than as a phonological interpretation. The facts would seem to be that the sounds [t] and [d] are found initially and medially in German words and that the former but not the latter of these sounds is found at the end of words. Whether these facts should be interpreted as neutralization is a matter that must be decided by the analyst.

In a recent paper (1977), in which he replies to criticism levelled at his approach by Akamatsu (cf. 2.10), Buyssens maintains the view that the notion of the archiphoneme is fallacious and should be rejected.

2.9. R. Vion

In a paper of 1974 dealing exclusively with the notions of neutralization and the archiphoneme Robert Vion takes the article by

Buyssens discussed above as his starting-point. In reply to Buyssens' contention that archiphonemes cannot be substantiated psychologically Vion argues that the members of an opposition like /e/ : /ɛ/ in French are indisputably linked in the mind of the native speaker and that this points towards the existence of an archiphoneme. Furthermore, even if the Dutch example adduced by Buyssens is correct it does not necessitate a rejection of the archiphoneme, for the feelings of the speaker-hearer do not constitute the objective of a phonological description: "A la limite, l'absence complète de conscience immédiate de l'archiphonème n'est pas un obstacle à sa validité linguistique" (p. 35).

As regards the phonological interpretation of French words like *pour, port,* Vion argues that it is only the opposition /o/ : /ɔ/ which is neutralized and that the correct analysis is consequently /pur, p<o/ɔ>r/. For one thing these two vowels are partially complementary: normally [o] occurs to the exclusion of [ɔ] in final and non-final open syllables, as in *chapeau, mollusque,* whereas [ɔ] occurs to the exclusion of [o] in non-final closed syllables and before final /r/, as in *poster, port.* On the other hand [u] and [o], both of which occur in final and non-final open syllables, as in *époux, chapeau* and *rouler, mollusque,* cannot as easily be considered partially complementary (it is only before final /r/ and in non-final closed syllables that [u] occurs to the exclusion of [o], cf. *pour, moustache).* Vion admits, however, that this is not a wholly satisfactory argument, for [ɔ] and [o] are not, in the positions of neutralization, in completely complementary distribution: in non-final open syllables [ɔ] is sometimes found as well as [o] (cf. *voleur* [vɔlœr, volœr]), and in non-final closed syllables [o] is sometimes found as well as [ɔ] (cf. *fausseté* [foste, fɔste]). According to Buyssens (1975, p. 37) this concession is not expressed with sufficient clarity by Vion, for in fact [ɔ] is extremely common in non-final open syllables, and there are even minimal pairs like *beauté* ≠ *botté* and *côté* ≠ *coté.* Buyssens therefore concludes that Vion manipulates the facts in order to make them conform to a preconceived theory.

Since the criterion of partial complementarity is not quite satisfactory in the case of *pour/port,* Vion resorts to another criterion, namely that of *indecision* on the part of the speakers in the choice of sound quality in the position of neutralization. Whereas speakers of French will never hesitate in their choice of [u] versus [o], they demonstrate a good deal of indecision as far as the vowels [o] and [ɔ] are concerned (for example, a word like *rococo* may be pronounced [rɔkɔko], [rɔkoko], and [rokoko]). Such indecision is not a constant property of neutralization, but when it does occur it provides an answer to the question of which of two (or more) oppositions should be considered neutralized. In this particular case it enables the phonologist to interpret *pour* and *port* unambiguosly — as /pur, p<o/ɔ>r/ — and at the same time to recognize the concept of the archiphoneme. To this Buyssens replies (1975, p. 37) that there is no true indecision in the case of French /o/ : /ɔ/. Some speakers will pronounce [o] where others pronounce [ɔ], and *vice versa*, but this is because their phonological systems differ. The individual speaker will never hesitate in his choice between these vowels, i.e. within one and the same phonological system no indecision can be found.

Vion also discusses the important question of the nature of neutralizable oppositions. As we know, Trubetzkoy restricts the concept of neutralization by permitting it to apply to bilateral oppositions only, and Martinet requires, only a little less restrictively, that the members of a neutralizable opposition should be in "rapport exclusif". According to Vion both these proposals are too restrictive (and he quotes a paper by Cantineau (1955), where a similar view is expressed). Nor does he consider the restrictions sufficiently weakened if the domain of neutralization is expanded to any but isolated oppositions, i.e. to proportional oppositions, for in French the opposition /i/ : /j/, which is isolated, must be regarded as neutralized in all positions except finally. Vion's own solution to the problem of delimitation is to say that only *phonemes which are adjacent in the system* ('phonèmes voisins') may be neutralized. This is a somewhat vague statement, but since the phonemes of a language are apparently arranged by Vion into a system on the basis of their distinctive features, it can probably be concluded that he regards any *minimal* opposition as neutralizable. In a given language the oppositions between /p/ and minimally different (neighbouring) phonemes like /b/, /f/ and /t/ can therefore be regarded as neutralizable. It should not be overlooked, however, that an opposition such as /r/ : /l/ in British English, which is by most phonologists considered minimal, must according to this proposal be regarded as neutralized in the post-vocalic part of syllables, where only [l] occurs; i.e. words like *ball* and *old* will have to be analyzed as /bɔ:<l/r>, əu<l/r>d/. From a psychological point of view this is not very plausible, except perhaps to speakers of Japanese.

In his paper Vion introduces the notion of *degree of relevance* ('degré de pertinence') of phonological oppositions. Oppositions which are constantly distinctive, such as /p/ : /b/ in French, are assigned the value '1', and oppositions which are never distinctive, such as [r] : [ʁ] in French, are given the value '0'. Neutralizable oppositions, which are distinctive but not constantly so, are characterized by a degree of relevance which is intermediate between 0 and 1. For example, the opposition /e/ : /ɛ/ in French may be assigned the value 0.25 as it is distinctive in only one out of four positions. On the other hand /p/ : /b/ in Russian, which is neutralized before obstruents and word-finally but remains distinctive elsewhere, has a degree of relevance which is considerably higher. The more closely the degree of relevance of a neutralizable opposition approaches 0, the more likely it is for the archiphoneme to be reflected in the mind of the speaker. This theory might help solve the problem mentioned by Buyssens: the phonemes /p/ and /b/ in Dutch are not felt to be intimately connected by the native speaker, for <p/b> in Dutch is a much 'weaker' archiphoneme than <e/ɛ> in French, i.e. its degree of relevance is considerably higher than 0.25.

Vion's conception of archiphoneme is summarized in the following way (p. 52):

> L'archiphonème est une unité distinctive libérée par une opposition entre phonèmes voisins dans le système, lorsque cette opposition voit son degré de pertinence évoluer entre 0 et 1. Cet archiphonème se définit comme *au moins* l'ensemble des traits pertinents communs aux phonèmes dont l'opposition se neutralise.

In the definition the italicized words make it possible to recognize archiphonemes not only in the case of bilateral oppositions but also in the case of multilateral oppositions. In French, for example, the phonemes /e/ and /ɛ/ (in the subsystem permitting differentiation) are distinguished from each other and from /i/ by means of the features 'second degree of vowel height' and 'third degree of vowel height'; their shared features — 'front' and 'unrounded' — are shared also by /i/, i.e. /e/ : /ɛ/ is a multilateral opposition. In the subsystem which permits neutralization, however, the archiphoneme <e/ɛ> is defined by the features 'front', 'unrounded' and 'open', i.e. it contains a feature in addition to those shared by /i/, /e/, /ɛ/, namely 'open', through which it is kept apart from /i/, which in this subsystem is characterized by the feature 'close', not by 'first degree of vowel height'. Notice also that in the definition the concept of archiphoneme presupposes that of neutralization. It should be pointed out, finally, that according to Vion there is complete solidarity between these two concepts: a rejection of archiphonemes is not conceivable unless it is accompanied by a rejection of neutralization.

2.10. T. Akamatsu

Tsutomu Akamatsu has contributed significantly to the clarification of the concepts of neutralization and archiphoneme in two recent articles. The first of these, dating from 1975, deals with Trubetzkoy's notion of *archiphoneme representative* (cf. 2.2 above). Akamatsu points out that if this notion is accepted the archiphoneme cannot *de facto* be recognized as an independent phonological unit which appears in the position of neutralization to the exclusion of either of two terms of a neutralizable opposition. In other words, the notion of archiphoneme representative vitiates that of archiphoneme. It can be shown, furthermore, that the archiphoneme representative — in contradistinction to the archiphoneme — is a totally unjustified concept. According to Akamatsu the only formulaic specification of a neutralizable opposition which is compatible with both these concepts is $abcd : abc$, where the letters refer to distinctive features. In German, for example, where according to Trubetzkoy the un-marked member /t/ of the opposition /d/ : /t/ represents the archi-phoneme $<d/t>$ in word-final position, both the archiphoneme and the unmarked member may be identified as abc; the marked member /d/, on the other hand, contains the features $abcd$, where d sym-bolizes the *feature* 'voiced'. This formula has to be rejected, how-ever, for a feature (e.g. 'voiced') can only be posited if another anti-podal feature ('voiceless') can be concomitantly posited to which it is opposable, i.e. features should be regarded as non-null units in opposition. Since an opposition like $d : \emptyset$ is inadmissible, the above formula will have to be replaced by $abcd : abce$, where in the German example e symbolizes 'voiceless'. But this (correct) formula is incompatible with the notion of archiphoneme representative, since it implies that the phonological content of an archiphoneme such as $<d/t>$ in German (abc) is no longer identical to that of either /t/ ($abce$) or /d/ ($abcd$). According to Akamatsu, Trubetzkoy's mistaken insertion of an archiphoneme representative between the archiphoneme and the phonetic realization is tied up with the tradi-tional and questionable Prague theory of marking, according to which the marked term of an opposition is considered equivalent to the unmarked member of that same opposition plus the "mark", which is described as a distinctive feature — a theory which corroborates the formula $abcd : abc$.

> Le concept traditionnel de "marque" présenté de cette façon est potentiellement dangereux parce qu'il laisse en doute en ce qui concerne la présence inéluctable dans le terme non marqué d'un trait pertinent dont la valeur est polaire et coordonnée à celle du trait pertinent (dit la "marque") dans le terme marqué et qui existe en face de celui-ci (1975, p. 98).

If the notion of archiphoneme representative is recognized, it becomes natural to re-interpret the 'neutralization' of a given opposition as *defective distribution* of the marked member of this opposition. Such a solution, Akamatsu points out, is not in the spirit of Trubetzkoy, who distinguishes clearly between neutralization (suspension of phonological opposition) and defective distribution. But Trubetzkoy's own mistaken theory of archiphoneme representative has paved the way for such an approach. Within the framework of functional phonology, however, it is inadmissible to say that /A/ and /B/ are opposed to each other in position X, but that the opposition between these two phonemes is neutralized in position Y, *where only A occurs* (cf. the criticism levelled at Vachek, Trnka and Buyssens in 2.6, 2.7 and 2.8). If /B/ is assumed not to occur in position Y, only the concept of defective distribution is called for, and there is no need to speak of neutralization at all. Akamatsu's conclusion, which I find convincing, is that the notion of archiphoneme representative is "un accessoire pernicieux", and should be abandoned completely. When that has been done the concept of archiphoneme will recover the full functional status as an independent phonological unit appearing in the position of neutralization to which it is entitled.

In the second of his papers on neutralization (1976) Akamatsu sets out to arbitrate the dispute between Buyssens and Vion discussed above. He finds Vion justified in criticizing Buyssens for attempting to retain a doctored concept of neutralization while at the same time rejecting the archiphoneme. These two concepts cannot be dissociated: "En effet, je dirai qu'en phonologie fonctionelle ces deux concepts sont complémentaires et qu'on n'a pas le droit de parler de l'un sans parler de l'autre" (Akamatsu 1976, p. 29). On the other hand, Akamatsu agrees with Buyssens that Vion in his discussion of the criterion of partial complementarity and French back vowels minimizes the fact that [ɔ] occurs frequently in non-final open syllables and that [o] is not rare in non-final closed syllables.

Akamatsu's views on neutralization and archiphoneme differ widely from those of Buyssens, and in most of the questions under debate he sides with Vion. On one important point, however, he takes a critical view of Vion's theory, namely as regards the criterion of 'indecision'. Although this criterion is interesting it is not, according to Akamatsu, theoretically quite satisfactory, and another and better criterion is available. The problem of establishing the identity of any neutralizable opposition, Akamatsu claims, can be solved by means of Martinet's criterion of *common base*. In this way it can be shown, for example, that it is the opposition /o/ : /ɔ/ which is neutralized in a French word like *port*, and that it is not the opposition /u/ : /o/ which is neutralized in *pour* instead (cf. 2.8 and 2.9). Akamatsu simply refers to Martinet (1968, p. 5f), but since the argument put forward in Martinet's article does not seem irrefutable, it is necessary to discuss it in some detail.

Martinet points out that in the case of French words like *pou* [pu], *pot* [po], *pas* [pɑ] and *poule* [pul], *pôle* [pol], *Paul* [pɔl], *pâle* [pɑl] there are apparently no grounds for deciding whether it is /o/ : /ɔ/ or /ɔ/ : /ɑ/ which is neutralized in final open syllable position; i.e. there are two possible identifications as shown in the following diagrams:

Final open syll.	Final closed syll.		Final open syll.	Final closed syll.
[u] ———— [u]			[u] ———— [u]	
[o] ⟨———— [o]			[o] ———— [o]	
⟍ [ɔ]			╱ [ɔ]	
[ɑ] ———— [ɑ]			[ɑ] ⟨———— [ɑ]	

According to the leftmost diagram *pou*, *pot* and *pas* are analyzed as /pu, p<o/ɔ>, pɑ/, and the common base of the members of the neutralized opposition is 'mid back vowel'. In the rightmost diagram the words are interpreted phonologically as /pu, po, p<ɔ/ɑ>/ and the common base is 'low back vowel' (Martinet does not, it should be noticed, consider the analysis /p<u/o>, pɔ, pɑ/, with 'high back vowel' as the common base). A non-arbitrary solution can be reached, however, if words like *bourre* [bur], *bord* [bɔr] and *barre* [bɑr] are taken into account. If these are compared with *poule, pôle, Paul, pâle* there are once again two possible identifications:

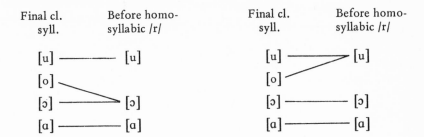

In the leftmost diagram *bourre, bord, barre* are analysed as /bur, b<o/ɔ>r, bar/, and the common base of the members of the neutralized opposition is 'mid back vowel'. In the diagram on the right the words are analyzed as /b<u/o>r, bɔr, bar/ and the common base is 'high back vowel' (we assume that only these two possibilities will be considered by Martinet and that the analysis /bur, bor, b<ɔ/a>r/, where the common base is 'low back vowel', is ruled out). Now if all three series of words are compared, there is only one of the analyses proposed which satisfies the demands of simplicity and generality, namely the following:

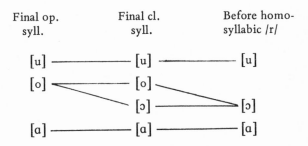

This identification implies that *pou, pot, pas, bourre, bord, barre* are interpreted as /pu, p<o/ɔ>, pa, bur, b<o/ɔ>r, bar/, i.e., the common base is 'mid back vowel'.

The preceding account is a — hopefully correct — reading of a short and condensed passage in Martinet's article. Now it seems to me that the proposed solution does not force itself upon the functionally minded analyst and that it presupposes the classification of [o] in *pot* as 'high mid' like [o] in *pôle* and of [ɔ] in *bord* as 'low mid' like [ɔ] in *Paul* (as shown in the above diagrams). However, if

56

one looks at features in a relativistic way, the only conclusions which can be drawn from the French data under discussion are that whereas there are four distinctive degrees of opening in the series *poule, pôle, Paul, pâle*, there are only three distinctive degrees of opening in both *pou, pot, pas* and *bourre, bord, barre*, and that 'mid' is represented by respectively [o] and [ɔ] in the last two series. Such an approach is expressed in the following diagram:

Final op. syll.	Final cl. syll.	Before homo-syll. /r/
high	1st degree	high
	2nd degree	
mid		mid
	3rd degree	
low	4th degree	low

If the data are arranged in this way there are three possible and equally simple identifications:

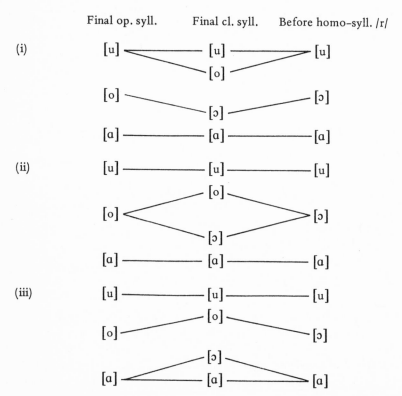

In (i) the feature 'high' in the systems with reduced contrast is identified with the first and second degrees of opening in the full system,
whereas 'mid' and 'low' are identified with respectively the third
and fourth degrees of opening, i.e. the words *pou, pot, pas, bourre,
bord, barre* are analysed as /p<u/o>, pɔ, pɑ, b<u/o>r, bɔr, bɑr/. In
(ii) 'high' is identified with the first degree of opening, 'mid' with
the second and third, and 'low' with the fourth, i.e. the above words
are interpreted as /pu, p<o/ɔ>, pɑ, bur, b<o/ɔ>r, bɑr/. In (iii) 'high'
and 'mid' are identified with respectively the first and second
degrees of opening, whereas 'low' is identified with the third and
fourth, i.e. /pu, po, p<ɔ/ɑ>, bur, bor, b<ɔ/ɑ>r/. Although the first
and third solutions are phonetically less realistic than the second
(cf. the forms /pɔ/ *pot* and /bor/ *bord*), they are just as acceptable
as (ii) from a functional point of view. Since [o] represents the phoneme /ɔ/ as well as the phoneme /o/ in (i) (cf. /pɔ/ *pot*, /pol/ *pôle*),
and since [ɔ] represents both /o/ and /ɔ/ in (iii) (cf. /bor/ *bord*,
/pɔl/ *Paul*), these two solutions presuppose the recognition of overlapping in different contexts. However, this particular type of overlapping is accepted by practically all phonologists.

Thus we see that Martinet's criterion of 'common base' does not
enable the phonologist to establish the identity of a neutralizable
opposition in any straightforward and unquestionable way. For this
reason Vion's attempt to solve the problem by means of the criterion
of 'indecision' should not be overlooked.

2.11. Concluding Overview

The notions of neutralization and the archiphoneme were introduced
independently of each other by respectively N.S. Trubetzkoy and
Roman Jakobson. However, they were soon linked together, either
wholly or partially. To Trubetzkoy himself, archiphonemes without
neutralization were somewhat dubious entities. Although Martinet
has considered the possibility of dispensing with the archiphoneme
by interpreting neutralization as loss of feature relevance (1946),
his basic view is that there is solidarity between the two concepts
and that the concept of the archiphoneme is derived from that of
neutralization. According to Vion, similarly, the two notions are
bound up with each other, and Akamatsu states explicitly that
neutralization and the archiphoneme are complementary and that
we have no right to speak about one concept without speaking about
the other as well.

The notions of the archiphoneme and neutralization have not only been introduced by the Prague school, but they also occupy the most prominent position in this particular theory. However, this does not mean that they are recognized by all Prague phonologists. For example, they are rejected by de Groot because he sees phonemes as positive entities whose primary function is to identify word forms. Other Prague phonologists — Vachek, Trnka, Buyssens — accept the notion of neutralization while rejecting that of the archiphoneme. In my opinion this position is untenable and involves a confusion of neutralization and defective distribution. If the analyst claims, for instance, that the opposition between voiced and voiceless obstruents in German, Russian, Turkish is 'neutralized' at the end of words since only voiceless phonemes occur in this position, he has in fact rejected the concept of neutralization and opted for defective distribution instead.

The question of what types of phonological oppositions may be neutralized has never been settled completely in the Prague school. It is generally agreed that only minimal oppositions are neutralizable, but beyond that opinions vary. According to Trubetzkoy only bilateral oppositions may be suspended (but in his practice he sometimes operates with neutralization of multilateral oppositions as well, e.g. of /e/ : /ɛ/ in French). Similarly, Martinet requires that for two or more phonemes to be neutralizable they should stand in exclusive relation. Vion, on the other hand, finds this solution too restrictive and only requires that neutralized phonemes should be adjacent in the phonological system ('phonèmes voisins').

In the early days of the Prague school psychological aspects of phonology were considered very important. In 1929 Jakobson stressed the psychological reality of the archiphoneme. In his monograph on Polabian dating from the same year, as well as in several later publications, Trubetzkoy attached great importance to the psychological reality of neutralization. Martinet, likewise, takes the linguistic intuitions of the speaker–hearer into consideration in his early work. Subsequently, however, both Martinet and Trubetzkoy have dissociated themselves from a psychologically oriented linguistic description and adopted a purely functional view, arguing that linguistic feeling is a result of linguistic function and cannot be investigated scientifically.

As mentioned in chapter 1 the concepts of neutralization and the archiphoneme have given rise to a good deal of confusion and miscomprehension. If particularly the latter notion is by some linguists regarded as almost occult this may partly be due to the somewhat infelicitous term 'archiphoneme' (which is easily associated with e.g. 'archetype') and to the use of capital letters. Had the Prague phonologists spoken of 'neutralization products' instead and used a type of transcription in which the neutralized phonemes themselves appear, it seems likely that the two concepts would have been accepted, or at least understood, by a larger number of phonologists.

Chapter 3

BRITISH AND AMERICAN PHONOLOGICAL THEORIES

3.1. W. Freeman Twaddell

With his monograph *On defining the phoneme* dating from 1935 W. Freeman Twaddell has contributed significantly not only to the understanding of the phoneme but also to the understanding of the concept of neutralization. Twaddell differs from most American structuralists in attaching great importance to paradigmatic contrasts; he is in fact much closer to the Praguians than to the Bloomfieldians. Of this he is well aware, for he points out that his descriptive procedure is very much like the 'phonology' of the Prague circle. On some points, however, Twaddell has reservations (p. 77):[1]

> If the valuable and suggestive work of many members of the Cercle Linguistique de Prague has not been wholly convincing to many students of language, it is (aside from its newness) because of the subjective mentalistic definition of units and a somewhat truculent denial of the relevance of phonetic analysis.

Even on these two points, however, the difference between Twaddell and the Prague phonologists cannot be considered marked. Twaddell rejects a physical as well as a mentalistic phoneme definition and regards the phoneme as an abstract fictitious unit. He looks upon the functional phoneme definition as a variety of the mentalistic definition (p. 60), since it explicitly or implicitly relates to the intention of the speaker. But in this connection it is worth remembering that the Praguians already in the early thirties took a critical view of the original psychological definition and that in their endeavours to remove the last traces of mentalism they were in complete harmony with Twaddell. To this it must be added that Twaddell may reasonably be considered a functionalist himself. Of the thirteen points of the procedure which he proposes for defining the phoneme the first

---

1) Page references are to *Readings in Linguistics* I, where most of chapter VII (which for our purposes is unimportant) has been omitted.

runs as follows: "In a given community there are like utterances and different utterances" (p. 69). The basis for deciding what is the same and what is different is "observable responses of members of the community as hearers",[2] but it is clearly implied that informants can only perceive differences of sound which serve to distinguish meanings, whereas they are unable to perceive differences between free phonetic variants.[3] Twaddell's attitude is thus the same as that taken up later by Hockett (1955, p. 144), who, instead of asking his informants whether two utterances mean the same, asks them whether they *sound* the same. As regards Twaddell's second objection — that the phonetic analysis is neglected — it should be remembered that on this point there is a great difference between theory and practice in the Prague school. It is true that the Prague phonologists proposed to draw a sharp line of demarcation between phonology and phonetics and that phonetics occupied a humble and quite unsatisfactory position in their theory, but in actual practice they freely made use of phonetic criteria in their phonological analysis.

The following comments are necessary in order to explain Twaddell's procedure: English forms like *pill, till, kill, bill* are minimally phonologically different since the corresponding phonetic events differ from each other in one phonetic fraction (roughly = 'segment'). As the last two fractions of the corresponding phonetic events are similar they furthermore constitute a class. On the basis of the articulatory differences in the initial segments (labiality, alveolarity, palato-velarity, voicing, etc.) this class may be considered ordered. The terms of such minimum differences, in this particular case *p, t, k, b,* are called micro-phonemes. If the above forms are now compared with *pen, ten, ken, Ben,* with *tapper, tatter, tacker, tabber* and with *nap, gnat, knack, nab,* it appears that the four classes are similarly ordered, since the corresponding phonetic events are similar and in a one-to-one relation. For example, *pill* differs from *till* in the same way that *pen* differs from *ten, tapper* from *tatter* and *nap* from *gnat,* and given the order *pill, till, kill, bill* there is only one ordering of the remaining three classes, namely the one cited above, which satisfies the requirements of a one-to-one relation. The micro-phonemes from the four classes may therefore be joined together in *macro-phonemes* (or simply 'phonemes'), a macropho-

---

2) A behaviouristic bias is clearly felt here.
3) As language users are normally attentive to socially important phonetic variation, this (implicit) assumption is undoubtedly incorrect.

neme being defined as the "sum of all similarly ordered terms (micro-phonemes) of similar minimum phonological differences among forms" (p. 69).

In a form like English *spill* the micro-phoneme corresponding to the post-initial fraction of the corresponding phonetic event cannot be identified with the initial micro-phoneme of *pill*, for the two units are not similarly ordered (for example, *bill* occurrs but not *sbill*). In other words, within the category of stop consonants we do not find exactly the same contrasts in the frame [s___ɪɫ] as in the frame [___ɪɫ], and therefore the micro-phoneme in *spill* cannot be identified with the initial micro-phoneme in *bill* either. To interpret *spill* as either /spɪl/ or /sbɪl/ would be to conceal rather than to reveal the phonological facts: "It appears arbitrary ... to assign the stop of *spill* to [p] *or to* [b]" (p. 67). In taking up this attitude Twaddell is in agreement with the Prague phonologists, but whereas the latter are of the opinion that the unit after *s* in *spill* represents both /p/ and /b/ in the sense that it may be regarded as the common denominator of these two phonemes (an archiphoneme), Twaddell concludes that it is a third phoneme, i.e. it is a case of neither /p/ nor /b/: "There appears to be no alternative to considering the stops of 'spill, spare, spin', etc. as corresponding to a *different phoneme* from the stops of 'pill, pair, nap, lip, tapper', etc." (p. 74, my italics).

According to Twaddell's method it is necessary to set up separate phonemes not only in cases of neutralization but also in those instances where practically all other phonologists would operate with defective distribution. In a form like English *plan* it would not be possible for Twaddell to identify the initial micro-phoneme with the *p* of *pan*, for the two units are not similarly ordered: within the articulatory range of stop consonants we do not find the same contrasts in the frame [___læn] as in the frame [___æn] (thus the form *tan* is possible and realized as a word in English, whereas the form *tlan* is impossible). The Prague phonologists would here equate the two units and operate with the phoneme /p/ in *plan* rather than with the archiphoneme <p/t>, for as *clan* is possible and realized as a word we cannot know for certain whether it is the opposition /p/ : /t/ or the opposition /k/ : /t/ which is suspended (cf. 2.2 and 2.4 above).

It should be added that Twaddell is aware of the difference between systematic and fortuitous absence of a phonological unit in a certain environment (as exemplified by the absence in English of respectively *t*lan and h*e*t). Thus although it is illegitimate to identify the initial micro-phoneme of *plan* with the initial micro-phoneme of *pan*, it is permissible to identify the micro-phonemes corresponding to the medial fractions of phonetic events like *beet, bit, bait, bat* in English with the micro-phonemes of *heat, hit, hate, hat,* in spite of the fact that *bet* occurs but not *het*. To be sure we do not within the articulatory range of front vowels find exactly the same contrasts in the frame [h__t] as in the frame [b__t], but this is accidental and therefore does not preclude identification.

Twaddell's refusal to equate dissimilarly ordered micro-phonemes implies that in the analysis of languages with neutralizations and defective distributions he has to set up a very large number of phonemes, and in this way his phonological description becomes quite elaborate, as he himself admits: "There is no denying that this definition is complicated and forbidding" (p. 74). But the price which must be paid for a more limited phoneme inventory is, according to Twaddell, a concealment of important phonological relations, and this particular type of economy often emanates from a wish to work out a simple system of transcription (cf. Daniel Jones and, later on, K.L. Pike). Now it is difficult to deny that the identification of a given micro-phoneme with another differently ordered micro-phoneme involves the disadvantages mentioned by Twaddell. If German *Tod*, for example, is interpreted as /to:t/ — as it normally is in early Anglo-American phonemics — the fact that there is no opposition between /t/ and /d/ in word-final position in this language is glossed over (it seems insufficient to state that German /d/ is a somewhat defective phoneme). As we have seen in the preceding chapters, however, it is possible to operate with fewer phonemes than Twaddell does without covering up neutralizations. And it should be added that for most linguists the endeavours to reduce the number of phonemes do not primarily stem from a desire to reach a simple system of transcription. The reason why practically all structuralist phonologists are prepared to identify micro-phonemes also in those cases where they are dissimilarly ordered (e.g. the *p*'s of English *plan* and *pan*) is that they wish to set up a relatively limited inventory of functional entities and in this way arrive at the simplest possible description. Notice also that examples like *plan-pan* and *spill-pill* receive the same treatment in Twaddell's theory: in both *plan* and *spill* it is a case of micro-phonemes which cannot be identified with certain other micro-phonemes, namely those occurring initially in *pan* and *pill* respectively, because the ordering is different.

Twaddell does not, in other words, distinguish between defective distribution and neutralization (see chapter 5 for a criterion according to which such a distinction may be made). In spite of these questionable points his monograph is of great value, as it explicitly formulates the foundation underlying the type of phonology that takes paradigmatic contrasts as its starting-point. What Twaddell sets out to do is to account for all phonological contrasts, and in this respect his description is perfectly consistent.

3.2. J.R. Firth and the Prosodic School

On several important points there exists a close relationship between the theories of Twaddell and J.R. Firth (and his adherents): (1) the polysystemic approach adopted by Firth is very similar to Twaddell's theory of micro-phonemes. Twaddell regards the macro-phoneme as nothing more than the sum of similarly ordered micro-phonemes, and in Firth 1935b (1957, p. 48) it is stated that the sound system of a language is "little more than a sum of all the possible alternances of sounds in all contexts." (2) Twaddell and Firth may both be characterized as nominalists (or, in Householder's terminology, hocuspocus linguists). As mentioned above Twaddell considers the phoneme an abstract fictitious unit, and Firth writes the following about phonological and other linguistic units: "Such constructs have no ontological status and we do not project them as having being or existence" (1950, p. 42 (1957, p. 181)). (3) Both of them are far more interested in appropriateness than in simplicity, and consequently their phonological descriptions are very complicated. In Firth 1948 (1957, p. 137) it is stated that the "suggested approach will not make phonological problems appear easier or oversimplify them" and in Palmer 1970 (p. xvi) the following: "If the full importance of prosodic analysis has not been recognized it may be because some of the solutions proposed seemed unnecessarily complex or even perverse." (4) Both phonologists have a bias towards behaviourism. For example, Firth writes about continental European phonology that "this systemic or phonological analysis of the sounds of a language is not inconsistent with *my own behavioristic method of contextualization*" (1935a (1957, p. 35), my italics). (5) Twaddell and Firth agree in rejecting totally the view that the purpose in performing a phonological analysis is to devise an adequate system of transcription, and both of them are of the opinion that most other phonologists fall into this trap. According to Twaddell most linguists' 'phonemes' ought really to be termed 'transcribemes', and Firth notes regretfully that "the Roman alphabet ... has determined a good deal of our phonetic thinking" (1948 (1957, p. 126)). It is a manifestation of this congeniality between the two linguists that in several of the prosodists' works reference is made to Twaddell and his "all too neglected monograph" (Robins 1957 (1970, p. 189)).

The *polysystemic* approach is one of the most important characteristics of Firth's phonological theory.[4] Firth operates not with one system of *phonematic units* (approximately = phonemes, cf. below) but, like Twaddell, with different systems in different positions. Furthermore different systems are established for grammatically different structures: "we may speak ... of the phonematic system of the concord prefixes of a Bantu language" (Firth 1948 (1957, p. 122)). He does not wish to identify functionally the terms of one phonematic system with the terms of others. To do so would be to disregard important phonological relations, since the phonematic units enter into widely different oppositions in different positions. This attitude originates in the importance he attaches to the principle of "contextualization", according to which the different phonetic contexts as well as the different grammatical, lexical and situational contexts that phonematic units occur in are taken into account:

> From the foregoing summary of a technique of contextualization it will be clear that no attempt is made to establish psychological or phonological relations between terms of different series. The contexts can be systematically analysed and various alternances constituted, but it does not follow that all these alternances or systems should be forced into a single theoretical architectonic scheme (Firth 1936 (1957, p. 73f)).

By way of example Firth (1935) mentions the nasal consonants in Marathi. In this language there are two nasal phonematic units in initial position (/m n/), and three in final position (/m n ŋ /); and in preconsonantal position, where the articulatory place of a nasal is automatically regulated by that of the following sound segment, there is only one, which in transcriptions may be symbolized as /n/. Now since the relations between the nasal consonants occurring in these three positions are completely different — a three–way alternation finally, a two–way alternation initially, and no alternation

---

4) The polysystemic view was put forward by Firth already in 1935, the year of publication of Twaddell's monograph.

preconsonantally — it would be inadmissible to identify, for example, the *n*-sounds occurring in the three positions. "Though writing them with the same symbol on practical phonetic grounds, I should not identify them in any way. That they are the same 'phoneme' is the very last thing I should say" (Firth 1935b (1957, p. 51)).

If the analyst rejects identification of units in one position with units occurring in another and operates with different systems in different positions instead, there is obviously no need for, or room for, the concept of neutralization (and 'defective distribution' disappears as well, since it is now impossible to speak of a 'higher' unit which is absent in certain positions). Like Twaddell, Firth refuses to equate the stops occurring after initial *s* in English with either /p t k/, or /b d g/, or with both these series at once. Provided that a bisegmental interpretation of these obstruent clusters is preferable to a monosegmental interpretation, it is three separate phonematic units which appear after *s*; "take the English word *stick*, which may be transcribed *stik* or *sdik*, according to the nature of the contextual conventions laid down. Discussions have taken place on the further and *quite gratuitous question* of whether 'the sound' after the *s* is to be identified with *t*'s or *d*'s in other contexts" (Firth 1936 (1957, p. 72), my italics).[5] The same example is mentioned by Robins in his book on general linguistics (1964), and Robins draws the same conclusion as Firth: "The concept of neutralization need not ... be invoked to deal with the non–comparability of some different systems that operate in different structural places" (1964, p. 168).

The reason why most phonologists differ from Firth and Twaddell in equating phonological units occurring in different positions, even if these are dissimilarly ordered, is obviously that they wish to restrict the inventory of functional units and thereby to arrive at a simple description (perhaps also at a psychologically plausible description). But as mentioned before, Twaddell and Firth attach far greater importance to appropriateness than to simplicity, and this attitude is not compatible with the identification of dissimilarly ordered phonematic units. As both Twaddell and Firth are antimentalists, a psychologically based identification is also ruled out. Since the concept of neutralization rests on the equating of one phonological element (itself psychologically indeterminate) with two or more other phonological elements, it follows that neutral-

---

5) In the same article Firth proposes a monosegmental interpretation of English *sp, st, sk.*

ization is a conceit which cannot be accepted by Twaddell and Firth.

In conclusion it should be pointed out that Firth's phonological theory differs from that of Twaddell in one important respect. The most characteristic feature of Firth's theory is that a very large part of the phonic material is assigned to *prosodies*, i.e. to elements which extend over, or are relevant to, units which are larger than a single segment. Prosodies are characterized by not being "placed", and they are therefore described as non-successive. The Firthians operate with syllable prosodies, such as length and stress; syllable-group prosodies, such as length- and stress-relations between syllables; and sentence prosodies, such as intonation. Since grammatical criteria are also included in the phonological analysis, they also operate with word prosodies, for example vowel harmony in Turkish and Hungarian. Furthermore, features with delimiting function, such as plosion, aspiration and affrication in languages where these occur only in certain positions (syllable-initially, for example) are regarded as prosodic (syllable-part prosodies). One of the advantages offered by such a syntagmatic method is claimed to be that one in this way avoids assigning (erroneously) a phonetic feature of a certain length to one of two neighbouring segments. In paradigmatically inclined phonemic descriptions of Russian, in which language palatalization extends over a consonant and an adjacent homosyllabic vowel, palatalization is thus allotted to the consonant, in spite of the fact that it is often the difference in the quality of the neighbouring vowel which stands out most clearly (cf. also that the Cyrillic orthography marks the difference between palatalization and non-palatalization by means of different vowel letters). But according to the Firthians this solution distorts the actual phonetic facts, and palatalization should be regarded as a syllable prosody instead (Robins 1957 (1970, p. 193f); 1964, p. 163f).[6] Although psychological evidence is not taken into account in prosodic analysis, Firth claims in support of his theory that prosodies are both spoken and heard. Practically any phonetic feature may by analysed, in one language or another, as a prosody. The features which are not treated as prosodies, but which are more reasonably regarded as segmental and successive, are assigned to phonematic units. These phonematic units cannot be considered identical with the phonemes of other

---

6) The prosodic interpretation cannot, however, be accepted without reservation, for syllable-initial consonants may be palatalized independently of syllable-final consonants, and *vice versa*.

68

phonological theories, since a number of their phonetic features
have been extracted and allotted to prosodies. They are thus ab-
stractions composed of fewer features than the phonemes of other
theories.

3.3. Daniel Jones

Daniel Jones and the American structuralists have in common that
they start out from phones in their phonological analyses, that they
regard the phoneme as a class of phones, and that they do not operate
with neutralization, let alone with archiphonemes. In an example
like German *und* they will thus on the basis of phonetic similarity
assign the final phone to the class /t/, i.e. they will propose a phonetically based either–or analysis and consider /d/ absent in word–final
position. In this and the following section I shall briefly discuss why
there is no room for the concept of neutralization in the theories
of these Anglo–American phonologists.

In the case of Daniel Jones this attitude results from the limited
goals he has proposed for himself. According to Jones a phoneme
analysis serves three practical purposes: it aids the acquisition of a
good pronunciation of a foreign language (for this purpose a broad
transcription is well suited); it forms the basis for the description of
grammar and semantics; and it enables us to construct adequate
systems of writing (1962, p. 218f). With such ends in view it is unnecessary, for example, to regard the postinitial stop consonant of
an English word like *spill* as anything more than, or different from, a
representative of the class /p/, or possibly of the class /b/. That [p]
and [b] do not form a distinctive opposition in this environment is
immaterial for Jones, since 'distinctive function' is not part of his
physical–generic phoneme definition, which runs as follows: "a
family of sounds in a given language which are related in character
and are used in such a way that no one member ever occurs in the
same phonetic context as any other member" (1962, p. 10).[7] It is
a corollary to this definition, and of decidedly secondary importance,
that phonemes have a semantic function. If one were to ask Jones
why the stop consonant of *spill* should be assigned to either /p/ or
/b/ when [p] and [b] are never distinctively opposed to each other

---

7) Jones ignores free variants in his definition, for "language" is taken to
   mean "the speech of one individual pronouncing in a definite and consistent style" (cf. Jones 1962, p. 9 and Fischer–Jørgensen 1975, p. 52).

after initial *s* in English (where two structural places have been reduced to one), he would probably have answered that this solution simplifies the transcription and thereby makes the teaching of pronunciation more effective, that it is compatible with an adequate description of grammar and semantics, and that it optimizes the orthographic system. When a phone occurs in a certain phonetic context to the exclusion of two related phones, one should, according to Jones, assign it to that phoneme which the phonetically more closely related of these two phones is a member of. If no phonetic grounds can be found for preferring one of the two phonemes to the other, the most practical solution is to make an arbitrary choice between these phonemes (1962, p. 100). Only in very exceptional cases is it perhaps permissible to recognize overlapping in the same context — for example, if the relationship between words is otherwise unnecessarily obscured.

It would not be unreasonable to object that Jones's goals are too limited and that his particular type of phonemic analysis does not lead to any profound insight about the relations which exist between the phonological units of a language. But if the analyst is primarily interested in devising a simple system of transcription and an adequate orthography, one must agree with Jones that the concept of neutralization becomes nearly irrelevant. On the other hand, Jones may be criticized on one of his own premises — that of the optimal orthographic system — for neglecting morphophonology.

3.4. American Structuralism

The American post–Bloomfieldians have not lowered their sights quite as much as Jones; they are not as practical-minded nor as preoccupied with substance. Although they are far more interested in syntagmatic than in paradigmatic relations, 'contrast' is a relatively important concept for them, as it also was for Bloomfield himself. If contrast, however, occupies a far less important position in American than in European structuralism, it is because of the theoretical misgivings which the Americans had about including semantic criteria in the linguistic analysis. Bloomfield had been sceptical about the possibility of describing meaning scientifically: "The statement of meanings is ... the weak point in language–study, and will remain so until human knowledge advances very far beyond its present state" (1933, p. 140). Accordingly, his successors endeavoured to exclude practically the whole of semantics from the linguistic description proper (microlinguistics) and to relegate it to 'metalinguistics' (which was largely neglected).[8] The typical post–Bloomfieldian phoneme description from the 1940's was therefore based on a number of heuristic principles, and although contrast was one of these ('differential meaning' being the only aspect of semantics which it was permissible to include in the linguistic description proper), it was not considered crucial. According to Hockett (1955, p. 155; 1958, p. 107–110) there were four generally accepted principles: (i) contrast and complementation, (ii) phonetic realism, (iii) pattern congruity, and (iv) economy. Contrast corresponds to European 'opposition', although it does not presuppose the existence of minimal pairs; in English, for example, /ʃ/ and /ʒ/ contrast not only in *mesher* : *measure*, but also in the subminimal pair *pressure* : *pleasure*.

As contrast is included among their phonemic principles, it would not have been unnatural for the Americans to recognize the concept of neutralization, even though such a solution is less obvious in a phone–based analysis than in an analysis which starts from commutation series. For example, it would be quite possible to reach the conclusion that in an English word like *spill* the phone [p], which is in complementary distribution with both [ph] (*pill*) and [b] (*bill*), belongs to the class /p/ as well as to the class /b/; this is phonetically perfectly realistic, and it does not conflict with the criteria of symmetry and economy. Even in a case like German *Rad*, a <t/d> analysis would not conflict with the demand for phonetic realism, for the voicelessness of the final phone may be attributed to the environment (occurrence before a boundary). In this connection it may be mentioned that Bloomfield considered [ə] in English a variant of all the stressed vowel phonemes, i.e. of /æ/ in *at*, of /e/ in *them*, etc. Nevertheless such a both–and analysis is rejected by practically all American structuralists, and in this connection it is important to discuss an article dating from 1941 by B. Bloch, in which some crucial methodological views were put forward.

In this article Bloch recognizes overlapping in different contexts, for example, of English /r/ and /t/, which are represented by the phone [ɾ] after dental fricatives and between vowels respectively (*three, butter*). In other words, he allows overlapping if the context differs. On the other hand he rejects overlapping *in the same context*,

---

8) Cf. Trager and Smith 1951 for the terms 'microlinguistics' and 'metalinguistics'.

of e.g. English /p/ and /b/ after initial *s*, or of English /æ/, /e/, etc. in unstressed syllables. The reason why this type of overlapping should be rejected is that it leads to analytic indeterminacy and thereby violates "sound phonemic method." When we come across an [ə] in English, for example, we have no way of knowing, except by including morphological criteria, which class this phone should be assigned to:

> a system in which successive occurrences of a given sound x under the same conditions must be assigned to different phonemes necessarily breaks down, because there can be nothing in the facts of pronunciation — the only data relevant to phonemic analysis — to tell us which kind of x we are dealing with in any particular utterance (1941 (1957, p. 95)).

Bloch's rejection of overlapping in the same context met with general acceptance in the US and resulted in the maxim "once a phoneme, always a phoneme". Thus Pike states the following: "Once two segments are proved to be phonemically distinct it is assumed that they remain phonemically distinct" (1947, p. 62). If it has been demonstrated, for example, that /t/ and /d/ are different phonemes in German, then each occurrence of [t] (also in *Bund, Rad,* etc.) must be assigned to the class /t/. It must be possible to infer not only which sequence of phones corresponds to a given sequence of phonemes, but also *vice versa* (the biuniqueness condition). In other words, given any phone in any phonetic context it must be possible to assign it uniquely to one phoneme.

Bloch's biuniqueness condition has subsequently been criticized severely, among others by Chomsky (1964, p. 100), who points out that it has unnecessarily complicating effects, and who in this connection refers to Halle's discussion of the Russian obstruent voicing assimilation (Halle 1959): since e.g. /k/ and /g/ contrast in Russian, the [g] which occurs in an example like [mog bi] 'were (he) getting wet' must according to Bloch's condition be assigned to /g/, in spite of the fact that the opposition /k/ : /g/ is not found before obstruents. As a result of such an analysis, however, one general assimilation rule must be broken down into two specific ones, a phonemic–phonetic rule and a morphophonemic–phonemic rule, as exemplified by respectively /žeč bi/ → [žej̆ bi] 'were one to burn' and |mok bi| → /mog bi/ (notice that [č] and [j̆] are variants of the same phoneme in Russian). Although this criticism is certainly not unjustified, two things should be pointed out: first, it applies only to the post–Bloomfieldians and not, as claimed by Chomsky, to other structuralist phonologists; secondly, it is not, in fact, the bi-uniqueness condition which prevents a general and adequate description of the assimilation rule, but the rejection of the concept of neutralization (cf. Lockwood 1972, p. 658, and chapter 7 of this book). In Prague phonology, where [mog bi] would be analysed as /moK bi/, the relation between the phonetic and phonemic levels is for any given environment still biunique (cf. Fischer–Jørgensen 1975, p. 285).Derwing (1973, p.183ff) also criticizes the biuniqueness condition and regards Bloch's concern over indeterminacy as exaggerated and unwarranted. For one thing, indeterminacy is sometimes inherent in the data, and furthermore this condition frequently forces the analyst to make completely arbitrary decisions — for example, when the postinitial consonant of an English word like *stop* is assigned to /t/ rather than to /d/.

As mentioned above, Bloch only recognizes a phonemic analysis which is based exclusively on phonetic data. The widespread acceptance of the condition that grammatical criteria should be excluded from the phonological analysis also helps to explain why the concept of neutralization failed to find a place in the taxonomic theory of the American descriptivists. The fact that the [t] of German *Rad* is replaced by [d] in *Rade* would for many phonologists be a hint that the final phone of the uninflected form should perhaps not be analysed as /t/. But such reasoning was anathema to practically all American structuralists.

Chapter 4

GLOSSEMATICS

It has been pointed out by Martinet (1968) that the concept of neutralization finds its justification only within the framework of functionalist linguistics, where phonological opposition is regarded as being of primary importance. In glossematics, as in the Prague school, linguistic function is the focus of the analyst's attention, and consequently neutralization plays an important part in this theory of language as well.

Louis Hjelmslev discussed the concept of neutralization for the first time in an article dating from 1939 — 'Note sur les oppositions supprimables'. As regards the special conceptual apparatus employed in glossematics it should be mentioned that a distinction is drawn — in this article as well as in Hjelmslev's subsequent works — between two linguistic planes, that of *content* and that of *expression*, and that within each plane a further distinction is drawn between *form* and *substance*. Substance presupposes form but is not presupposed by it. The glossematist studies both homoplane functions, by which is meant functions within the form of each plane, and heteroplane functions, thus, for example, the manifestation of expression form in expression substance. *Commutation* is a central concept, and the commutation test is performed not only on the plane of expression (as in the Prague school) but also on the plane of content. The linguistic chain is broken down into progressively smaller units, and at each stage of this analysis the inventory of commutable entities is established. On the plane of expression one arrives in this way via modulations, stress groups and syllables at *pre-taxemes*, i.e. at a preliminary inventory of commutable sound segments. These pretaxemes are subsequently reduced to (*expression*) *taxemes*, which are also termed *cenemes* (since these entities are purely formal, Hjelmslev does not wish to call them 'phonemes'). The glossematic analysis is followed by a synthesis, in which the units uncovered are assigned to various categories.

It often turns out to be the case that two sound segments under certain conditions are commutable and thus constitute pre-taxemes, while under certain other conditions they are non-commutable. An example is provided by [t] and [d] in German, which are commutable initially and medially but not finally in words, cf. *Tusche* ≠ *Dusche*, *Rate* ≠ *Rade*, and *Rad* = *Rad*. The difference between the German pre-taxemes /t/ and /d/ may therefore be said to be suspended, or suppressed, in final position. According to Hjelmslev it is only possible to speak of (true) *opposition* if a difference between pre-taxemes can be suspended. Otherwise, i.e. if no suspension is involved, one should only speak of a *difference*. In German, /t/ and /d/ thus form an opposition while /t/ and /p/, for example, do not. It will be seen that whereas 'neutralization' according to the Prague phonologists presupposes 'opposition', the opposite is assumed to be the case in Hjelmslev's theory. Solely the suspension of a difference is something purely formal, since it is characterized by a coalescence of two forms irrespective of the specific substance in which the manifestation takes place, and Hjelmslev criticizes the Prague phonologists for establishing — inductively, *a priori*, and on the basis of substance — pseudo-oppositions of different types, e.g. privative, gradual, proportional, and isolated. However, he does appreciate the fact that both Trubetzkoy and Martinet attach special importance to suppressible "oppositions", and he believes that this insight ought to bring about a revolution in phonology (1939, p. 93):

> La phonologie s'était placée dès le début sur le terrain de la méthode inductive, en se proposant de monter graduellement de la substance à la forme, des faits concrets aux faits de plus en plus abstraits. Mais le rôle particulier joué par la suppression par rapport à l'opposition suffit pour faire voir qu'il y aura lieu de renverser les termes, et de se placer de prime abord sur le terrain de la forme et de la fonction pure pour en déduire après coup les faits de substance.

The planes of content and expression — also termed the *plerematic* plane and the *cenematic* plane respectively — are considered to be analogously structured, and they should therefore be analysed according to the same principles. A striking example of this parallelism is provided by the suspension of differences, and by way of illustration Hjelmslev cites the following: in Latin the difference between the plerematic units 'nominative' and 'accusative' is suspended under the dominance of the neuter. On the plane of expression the result of this suspension is that two cenematic units, whose function is to express two plerematic units which only differ as regards the opposition 'nominative' : 'accusative', coalesce and become structurally identical, cf. for example, 'nominative' and 'accusative' in the neuter word *templum,* as compared with the feminine forms *domus* (nominative) and *domum* (accusative). In Russian the difference between the cenematic units /t/ and /d/ is suspended under the dominance of final position. On the plane of content the result of this is that two plerematic units, expressed by means of two cenematic units which differ only as regards the opposition /t/ : /d/, merge and become structurally identical, cf. for example, /ro<t/d>/ 'race' and /ro<t/d>/ 'mouth'. In each of these cases a suspension of two units has taken place on one plane which has repercussions on the opposite plane. It should be added, though, that in order for neutralization to be recognized it is not a condition that such a repercussion on the opposite plane can be observed in each separate case. For example, Hjelmslev recognizes suspension in the Russian word /na<t/d>/ 'above', where there is no repercussion on the plerematic plane. But in order for the <t/d> neutralization to be recognized it is naturally a condition that there are repercussions on the opposite plane in *some* cases, cf. /ro<t/d>/.[1]

In *Prolegomena to a Theory of Language* (henceforth referred to as *Prolegomena*), which was first published in Danish in 1943, Hjelmslev returns to the concept of neutralization. A number of new ideas are introduced along with a partly changed terminology.[2] A suspended commutation between two units is called an *overlapping,* and the category which is established in this way is on both

---

1) Hjelmslev's theory that suspension of opposition may be found on both planes and that expression–neutralizations and content–neutralizations should be given parallel treatment has been criticized convincingly by Siertsema (1965, p. 186ff). According to Siertsema neutralization is exclusively an expression–phenomenon; to operate with "suppression" of the difference between, for example, the plerematic units 'nominative' and 'accusative' in Latin is "a clear instance of a transfer of expression-phenomena into the plane of content" (p. 186).

2) The terminology used in the remainder of this chapter (overlapping, syncretism, fusion, implication, latency, facultativity, etc.) corresponds to the one which is used in the revised edition of *Prolegomena,* in the original Danish version of the same book, and in the English translation 'Outline of the Danish expression system with special reference to the *stød*'. In the other works referred to (Hjelmslev 1939, 1951, 1953) the terminology is somewhat different.

planes termed a *syncretism*. In Danish, for example, there is commutation between /p/ and /b/ initially, cf. *pære* ≠ *bære* ('pear',
'carry'), but suspension of commutation finally, cf. *lap* = *lab* ('patch',
'paw'), both of which may be pronounced either [lap] or [lab], and
/p/ and /b/ together with their overlapping thus constitute a syncretism. Since the difference between /t/ and /d/ and between /k/
and /g/ is also suspended finally in Danish, it is the case in this
language that /p/ and /b/, /t/ and /d/, /k/ and /g/, are invariants
initially, but that they are variants finally, where only the syncretisms <p/b>, <t/d>, and <k/g> are invariants. (See below as
regards Hjelmslev's further analysis of these syncretisms as /h/ +
/b d g/).[3]

A syncretism may be either *obligatory* or *optional*. An example
of the former type is <t/d> finally in German (*Rad, Rat, Bund,
bunt, und,* etc.). The latter type may be exemplified with <ɣ/v>
after /ɔ: o: ɑ:/ in Danish (cf. Fischer-Jørgensen 1973, p. 145);
words like *love* 'laws' and *låge* 'gate' can be pronounced respectively
['lɔ:və] and ['lɔ:ɣə], but both of them can also be pronounced
['lɔ:uə], i.e. /ɣ/ and /v/ overlap, but not obligatorily.

Syncretisms can be manifested in different ways. A *fusion* is a
manifestation of a syncretism which is identical with all or none of
the members that enter into the syncretism. This type of syncretism
can be exemplified with <p/b> in Danish, which in final position is
manifested as either [p] or [b], or with <a/o> in Russian, which in
unaccented non-pretonic syllables is manifested as [ə]. An implication is a manifestation of a syncretism which is identical with one
or more of the members that enter into the syncretism but not with
all. An example is <t/d> in German, which in final position is manifested as [t]. On the plane of content we find an example of fusion
in German: after the preposition *längs* the opposition between the
genitive and the dative is syncretized, and here both members are
manifested – cf. *längs des Strandes* and *längs dem Strande*, which
have the same semantic content ('along the beach'). A plerematic
implication is found in French. In this language a distinction is made
between the emphatic pronoun *moi* and the non-emphatic pronoun
me; when governed by a preposition, however, only *moi* occurs. The
opposition of emphasis is thus in this environment syncretized and
manifested as one of the members; it can here be said that 'emphasis',

---

3) In order to regard <t/d> and <k/g> as syncretisms finally in Danish it
   is necessary to interpret [ð] and [ɣ] as separate phonemes, cf. chapter 1,
   note 3, and note 5 below.

which to Hjelmslev is a plerematic category, implies 'absence of emphasis'.

Hjelmslev also recognizes syncretism between an explicit unit and zero. If a syncretism of this type is obligatory it is termed *latency*. By way of example it can be mentioned that finally in French there is syncretism between a consonant and zero, cf. *sot* /so<t/Ø>/, *pot* /po<t/Ø>/, etc. (words like *sotte* (fem.) and *acte*, which are pronounced with a final consonant, are interpreted by Hjelmslev as /sotə, aktə/). If a syncretism involving zero is not obligatory it is termed *facultativity*. In Danish there is syncretism between /ɣ/ and zero after close vowels; thus *tiger* 'tiger' and *tier* 'keeps silent' are both pronounced ['tiːɒ], and *luger* 'trap–doors' and *luer* 'flames' are both pronounced ['luːɒ], but *tiger* and *luger* may also be pronounced respectively ['tiːɣɒ] and ['luːɣɒ], and the syncretism <ɣ/Ø> is therefore not obligatory (cf. Fischer–Jørgensen 1973, p. 146).

A syncretism can often be *resolved* by introducing analogically the member which does not contract the overlapping that establishes the syncretism. In an example like German /bun<t/d>/ (which represents both *Bund* and *bunt*) it is possible from the inflected forms /'bundə/ (*Bunde*) and /'buntə/ (*bunte*) to introduce respectively /d/ and /t/ and in this way to arrive at the forms /bund/ (*Bund*) and /bunt/ (*bunt*) with resolved syncretisms. Similarly, we can resolve the latency <t/Ø> in French words like *sot* and *pot* by analogy with feminine forms and liaison forms such as *sotte*, *pot au lait*, and in this way proceed from /so<t/Ø>, po<t/Ø>/ to /sot, pot/. If such an analogical inference is not possible, as in the case of the overlapping of /p/ and /b/ finally in Danish words like *kop* 'cup' and *top* 'top', the syncretism is *irresoluble*. – As an example of a resoluble plerematic syncretism Hjelmslev mentions <nominative/accusative> in Latin under the dominance of the neuter (*templum*). Here we can resolve the syncretism either by introducing 'nominative' on the analogy of the feminine word *domus* or by introducing 'accusative' by analogy with *domum*.

A notation with resolved resoluble syncretisms, e.g. /bunt, bund/ in German and /sot, pot/ in French, is called *ideal*. A notation with unrevolved resoluble syncretisms, e.g. German /bun<t/d>/ and French /so<t/Ø>/, is termed *actualized*.

On the basis of the above description, and bearing in mind that pre-taxemes are set up by means of the commutation test, the reader will be inclined to assume that Hjelmslev operates with syncretism extensively and that it is thus a very powerful concept in glossematics. But if one examines 'Outline of the Danish expression system with special reference to the *stød*' (henceforth *Outline*), which was first published in Danish in 1951, and which represents Hjelmslev's only real application of his theory of expression, one observes that the concept of syncretism is delimited and that *defective distribution* is recognized as well. For example, *sp, st, sk* in Danish are analysed as /sb sd sg/ in spite of the fact that there is not commutation between /sb/ and /sp/, etc. In *Prolegomena* Hjelmslev defines overlapping, which is presupposed by syncretism, as a suspended (com)-mutation between two functives and *suspension* is in its turn defined in the following way (p. 88):

> given a functive that is present under certain conditions and absent under certain other conditions, then, under the conditions where the functive is ... absent there is said to be *suspension* or *absence* of the functive, so that the functive is said to be *suspended* or *absent* under these conditions.

By a function is understood any type of dependence and by a functive an element that enters into a function (cf. Uldall 1957, p. 36f). It should by added that "under certain conditions" cannot be construed as "in certain positions". If this were the case Hjelmslev would necessarily have to operate with suspension of the functives /p t k/ after *s* in Danish, cf. that the functive /p/ in the function /p/ : /b/ by this interpretation would have to be considered present under certain conditions, viz. initially (*pil* 'arrow' ≠ *bil* 'car'), but absent under certain other conditions, viz. postinitially (*spil* 'play'). As mentioned above, however, Hjelmslev does not operate with syncretism after *s* in Danish, but with defective distribution of /p t k/ instead. In a German example like *Rad, Rade* [rɑːt, 'rɑːdə], on the other hand, the conditions for operating with suspension are fulfilled. Here the functive /d/ in the function /t/ : /d/ is present in the dative form, cf. *Rate* ['rɑːtə], but absent — in the same position in the morpheme — in the nominative and accusative form, cf. *Rat* [rɑːt]. In the nominative/accusative form the functive is thus suspended, and consequently overlapping and syncretism must be recognized: /rɑː<t/d>/. In this case it is a *grammatical alternation* which enables Hjelmslev to operate with syncretism. However, he also recognizes syncretism in some cases where no alternation occurs, thus, for example, the one between /p/ and /b/ finally in a Danish word like *top* 'top'. Here the speaker is free to use either [p] or [b], and it is therefore possible to claim also in this case that the functive /p/, for example, is present under certain conditions and absent under certain other conditions. (In more precise terms it may be said that [p] or [b] are used word-finally before a pause, and that [b] occurs in word-final position otherwise, thus, for example, in *en top i hånden* 'a top in one's hand'). On the other hand it appears from *Outline* that Hjelmslev operates with defective distribution of /p t k/ after *s* in Danish, cf. ideal notations like /'sbreng, 'sdɒi, 'sgib, 'blɒmsd, 'ɛlsg/ (*spring* 'jump', *støj* 'noise', *skib* 'ship', *blomst* 'flower', *elsk* 'love'). The reason for this must be that the functives /p t k/ are always absent in this position, and that the conditions for operating with suspension are therefore not fulfilled. Whereas a preceding central part of a syllable according to Hjelmslev syncretizes homo-syllabic /p/ and /b/ in Danish, a preceding *s* defectivates homo-syllabic /p t k/. In German examples such as *ab* [ap] and *und* [unt] the functives /b/ and /d/ are always absent, and one would therefore expect Hjelmslev to operate with defectiveness in this case. However, by analogy with forms like *lieb* [li:p] – *liebe* ['li:bə] and *Bund* [bunt] – *Bunde* ['bundə] he recognizes the syncretisms <p/b> and <t/d> in non-alternating words of this type.

Hjelmslev's reason for delimiting the concept of syncretism – on the plane of expression chiefly by means of alternations – is un-doubtedly that he does not want it to become too powerful and to exclude defectiveness entirely. Unlike the Prague phonologists he cannot accomplish this by demanding that in order for neutralization to be recognized two or more phonemes should share phonetic properties which separate them from all other phonemes of the lan-guage in question, for as mentioned before he does not operate with phonemes, but with cenemes, i.e. with empty formal entities, and he does not wish to take substance into consideration. Consequently he demands alternation instead, and this seems relatively formal since the only substance phenomena which have to be taken into consideration are the ones connected with the commutation test, cf. for example German *Rade*, *Rate* (commutation) and *Rad*, *Rat* (non-commutation). But when faced with oscillating manifestation and absence of alternation, e.g. with a case like [p] and [b] finally in Danish, Hjelmslev is in trouble, for since both members of the opposition occur he cannot operate with defectiveness. Here he operates with syncretism instead, but the reason for his recognition of syncretism in this particular case, as compared with his non-recognition of syncretism in the postinitial position of a Danish word like *spand* 'bucket', is exclusively that he is taking *phonetic substance* into account. It can be seen, then, that Hjelmslev in addition to considering substance when performing the commutation test and when identifying segments in different position (as he himself admits after having been criticized on this point, cf. Hjelmslev 1954, p. 171) makes allowance for phonetic substance when distinguishing between syncretism and defective distribution. Such a substance contamination of linguistic form is at variance with his own theoretical principles, but if cenematic syncretism can only be recognized in the case of alternation the question naturally arises how one should then analyse oscillating manifestation combined with absence of alternation (and of commutation). This would be a case of neither syncretism nor defectiveness, and since it is not a case of opposition either, it constitutes an apparently insoluble problem.

In the case of oscillating manifestation, then, Hjelmslev is forced into recognizing syncretism, also in those cases where there is no alternation, and his position on this point is clear, although theoretically open to criticism. However, it is not clear what he proposes to do about the type of fusion in which the manifestation is identical with none of the members that enter into the syncretism and where there is no alternation (as there is in the case of [ə] in English words like *saucepan, commercial,* cf. *pan, commerce*). An example of this is found in English, where the stops after initial *s* are unaspirated and voiceless, where initial *p, t, k* are aspirated and voiceless, and where initial *b, d, g* are unaspirated and (optionally) voiced. Here it can hardly be claimed, as it can in Danish, that one set of functives is present, while the other is absent and therefore rendered defective by *s*. Since it appears just as unfeasible to interpret these data as an instance of defective distribution as in the case of oscillating manifestation, it seems probable that Hjelmslev would recognize syncretism on the basis of substance in this case as well. If this surmise is correct, then Hjelmslev's insistence on alternation as a prerequisite for recognizing cenematic syncretism refers exclusively to the type of manifestation called implication.

It is difficult to know precisely to what extent Hjelmslev's system is capable of resolving syncretisms. As mentioned before he is able to resolve the syncretism <t/d> in a German example like *bunt* by analogy with *bunte* and in this way to set up the ideal form /bunt/. But in German *ab* and *und* he considers the syncretisms irresoluble, for both alternations of the type *lieb-liebe, Bund-Bunde* and of the type *Lump-Lumpe, bunt-bunte* occur, and any preference for introducing /b d/ rather then /p t/, or *vice versa*, therefore cannot be given. In *Prolegomena* Hjelmslev claims that the syncretism <p/b> in a Danish word like *top* 'top' is irresoluble. Apparently he has over-looked alternations like *galop-galopere* ('gallop' n. and v.), *attrap-attrapere* ('fake' n., 'catch' v.) where the derived verbs are pro-nounced with a [p], and on the basis of which it would seem possible to resolve the syncretism in *top*.[4] (As examples of analogous alter-nations involving <t/d> and <k/g> *vat-vatere* ('cotton wool', 'wad' v.) and *lak-lakere* ('lacquer' n. and v.) can be given.) However, one does find an isolated alternation in Danish where it is a [b] which occurs in the derived form, viz. *klaustrofob-klaustrofobi* ('claus-trophobe', 'claustrophobia'), and it must therefore be assumed that the syncretism <p/b> in *kop, top*, etc. cannot be resolved after all.

The syncretisms found in Hjelmslev's analyses of the expression systems of individual languages are most often *latencies* and *facultati-vities*. In the analysis of Danish this is a consequence of the fact that in order to restrict the taxeme inventory as much as possible he analyses [p t k] as /hb hd hg/ or as /bh dh gh/ (where the choice be-tween the former and latter interpretation is governed by phono-tactic considerations). In *Outline* one therefore finds ideally re-presented forms like /'bang(h)/ *bank* 'knock' and /bɒld(h)/ *bold* 'ball' instead of /'ban<k/g>/, /'bɒl<t/d>/.[5] In the description of French (Hjelmslev 1970) there are many latent consonants, e.g. /p t d g/ finally in words like *trop, sot, chaud, sang*. Hjelmslev's ideal notations, where syncretisms have been resolved on the basis of alternations, have a strong resemblance to the underlying forms

---

4) It should be pointed out, however, that *galop-galopere* is mentioned in Uldall 1936, and that Uldall wrote this paper in close collaboration with Hjelmslev.

5) Hjelmslev's analysis of Danish in *Outline* has been criticized convincingly by Basbøll (1971, 1973) and by Fischer-Jørgensen (1973). Basbøll points out that Hjelmslev's interpretation of the final stops as syncretisms is inconsistent with his interpretation of the pre-taxemes [ð], [ɣ], and [u] — diphthongs as respectively (syllable-final) /d/, /g/, and vowel + /b/. If words like *led* [leð] 'joint' and *rug* [ruɣ] 'rye' are analysed as /'led, 'rug/, it is impossible to analyse *lidt* [let] 'little' and *RUC* [ruk] 'R(oskilde) U(niversity) C(entre)' as /'le(h)d, 'ru(h)g/, i.e., /h/ cannot be considered optional in these words. And if a word like *døv* [døʔu] 'deaf' is to be inter-preted as /'døb/, one cannot interpret *døb* [døʔp] 'christen' as /'dø(h)b/, nor is it possible to analyse it as /'døhb/, since this form must be reserved for *dyp* [døp] 'dip'.

found in generative phonology — compare, for example, the ideal form /ynə pətitə amiə/ (*une petite amie*) and the underlying form /pətit+ə+S#ami+ə+S#/ (*petites amies*) found in Schane 1968. Like the generativists Hjelmslev tries to set up the lowest possible number of expression units, and he states that a French word like *fenêtre* should have only one form, from which the phonetic manifestations [fnɛ tR, fə'nɛ tR, 'fnɛ tRə, fə'nɛ tRə] are derived by means of mechanical rules.

Finally, we must discuss a concept which Hjelmslev has transferred from the analysis of content to the analysis of expression, and which is closely related to the Prague distinction between 'marked' and 'unmarked'. In *La catégorie des cas* (1935) he makes a distinction in the case paradigm between on one hand an intensive case, characterized by a tendency towards concentration of its semantic content, and on the other hand one or more *extensive* cases, characterized by a tendency towards expansion of their semantic content to the remaining cases. A simple example is found in English: if the linguistic context is disregarded and nouns are considered in isolation, the 'subjective', 'dative' and 'translative' cases — which appear in this order of succession in a sentence like *The boy sent his mother a letter* — are syncretized. For nouns referring to persons there are therefore only two cases: genitive and non-genitive. Of the two the genitive is the intensive case as its semantic content is restricted and well-defined (possession), and the non-genitive is the extensive case. In Hjelmslev's conceptual system the semantic value of the genitive is, in the directional dimension, one of 'éloignement'. As compared with this the non-genitive may represent 'éloignement' as well as 'rapprochement' and 'repos', and if the linguistic context is taken into consideration it may transform itself into the subjective ('éloignement'), the dative ('rapprochement'), or the translative ('repos'). — As an example of transference of the concepts of intensiveness and extensiveness to the expression analysis it may be mentioned that the two modulations (intonations) which according to Hjelmslev are found in Danish, viz. /ˋ/, which is manifested as falling tone, and /ˊ/, which is manifested as non-falling tone, are classified in *Outline* as respectively intensive and extensive. The reason for considering /ˊ/ the extensive member of the pair is that it can replace /ˋ/, e.g. in non-suspensive (complete) utterances, whereas the reverse is not the case, and /ˋ/ is therefore the more restricted of the two modulations. It can now be seen that in a German opposition like /t/ : /d/ the former member, which by the Prague phonologists is considered

unmarked because it is [t] which occurs in the position of neutralization, constitutes the extensive member, for [t] appears not only
initially and medially (*Tusche, bunte*) but also in the position of
overlapping (*bunt, Bund*). Since [d], on the other hand, is of more
restricted occurrence (*Dusche, Bunde*) /d/ constitutes the intensive
(marked) member.

The distinction between extensive and intensive plays an important part in *Knud Togeby*'s description of French. In this book
(1951, p. 81ff) the French phonemes are classified according to (i)
syllabicity ("indépendance dans la syllabe"), (ii) position (into initial,
final, final-initial, and central units), (iii) possibilities of combination
(e.g. into vocalic consonants, which always occur next to a vowel,
and consonantal consonants, which can be separated from the vowel
by another consonant), (iv) syncretism, and (v) extension. In this
system of classification /b/ in French is (i) a consonant ("dépendance
dans la syllabe"), (ii) initial-final, cf. *bas, rob*, (iii) consonantal, cf.
bruit, where it occupies the outermost position in the consonantal
margin, (iv) a unit which enters into syncretism with /p/, cf. *obtenir*,
(v) the intensive (marked) member of the opposition /p/ : /b/, since
it is [p] which appears in the position of neutralization before a
voiceless consonant, cf. [ɔptəni:r]. In the French syncretisms <g/k>,
<d/t>, <e/ɛ>, and <ɑ/a> (where the last two phonemes are syn-
cretized before a nasal and manifested as [ɑ̃] cf. *blanc*), the former
members are considered intensive and the latter extensive for the
following reasons: it is [k] and [t] which occur in the case of liaison,
cf. *un sang impur* and *un grand enfant*; /ɛ/ appears in both open and
closed syllables, whereas /e/ occurs in open syllables only; /a/ is far
more frequent than /ɑ/, which chiefly occurs before /s/. Phonemes
are also classified according to extension when no syncretism takes
place. In the opposition /l/ : /r/ the former member is considered
intensive because it does not occur after /t/ and /d/. Extension is
also an important criterion of classification in Togeby's grammatical
description.

In Hjelmslev's theory of syncretism there are a number of insuffi-
ciently clarified points. It must be remembered, though, that
Prolegomena was intended as the introduction to a complete theory
of language, as the title implies. Hjelmslev and Uldall worked for
many years on a comprehensive book on glossematics, the first part
of which was published in 1957. It was written by Uldall, entitled
Outline of Glossematics, and deals with the general aspects of the
theory. Hjelmslev attempted to write the second part, but owing to

ill-health he was unable to finish it, and *Prolegomena* can therefore be likened to the portal of a colossal cathedral which was never to be built.

Chapter 5

ROMAN JAKOBSON'S THEORY OF DISTINCTIVE FEATURES

The theory of distinctive features, which was worked out by Roman Jakobson in the thirties and forties and presented in detail in *Preliminaries to Speech Analysis* (Jakobson, Fant, and Halle 1952), originated from the realization that phonemes cannot be regarded as the smallest distinctive units on the plane of expression. According to Jakobson it is possible to pursue the analysis one step further and to penetrate to a level lower than that of phonemes. In this way he reaches the distinctive features, i.e. the "ultimate components, capable of differentiating morphemes from each other" (Jakobson and Halle 1956, p. 4). The importance of phonemes, which can no longer be considered the basic units of phonology, is hereby reduced somewhat, but the decomposition of phonemes into features (splitting the atom of phonology) in no way necessitates a rejection of phonemes as such. These units are now regarded as "bundles of concurrent features" (ibid., p. 5), as they were by Bloomfield. If there is still room for phonemes, it also still makes sense to operate with suspension of phonemic oppositions, i.e. with neutralization and archiphonemes.

Schane points out that in the phonological representations of the Prague school the exact status of the archiphoneme is not always clear, but that this vagueness has since then been eliminated. "With the advent of distinctive features, the notion of the archiphoneme was made explicit" (1968, p. 711). By way of illustration he mentions English *pin, bin, spin*. In the first of these words the stop consonant is [– compact, + grave, + tense], in the second it is [– compact, + grave, – tense], and in the third it is [– compact, + grave, 0 tense]. In *spin* neutralization as well as the archiphoneme are in this way shown explicitly by leaving the stop consonant after *s* unspecified for tenseness. What we find post–initially in this word is a phoneme which can be broken down into the distinctive (commutable) features [+ consonantal, – vocalic, – continuant, –nasal, – compact, + grave], cf. examples like *spear, sphere, smear, steer* and *spy, sky, sly*. The same point is made by Roman Jakobson himself (1962,

p. 646): "The embarrassing problem of the so–called "neutralized" phonemes and their assignment disappears on the level of distinctive features, and the concept termed "archiphoneme" finds its new and true foundation." As an example Jakobson mentions the suspension of the opposition /f/ : /f'/ in a Russian word like *devki* 'girls'. This word may be pronounced [d'éf'k'i] (with assimilatory palatalization of the labial before [k']), [d'ɛ fˣk'i] (where the labial is not assimilated by [k'], and is velarized), or [d'éfk'i] (where the labial is partly assimilated by [k'] and thus non–velarized). While the phonemic identification of the labial is controversial, the distribution of features is unambiguously clear: the feature sharp/non–sharp is absent, i.e. it has lost its relevance, in the labial. In Jakobson 1959, similarly, it is pointed out that all complications resulting from neutralization of phonemes disappear once the level of features is reached.

It is quite true that neutralization is shown explicitly in the analytic transcriptions where distinctive features are arranged vertically and phonemes horizontally, namely, by assigning the value 0 to a particular feature, or by bracketing it. Nevertheless such a manner of presentation also partly obscures neutralization. Although neutralization is always shown with 0, this symbol is used for other purposes as well, viz. in the case of what has subsequently been termed 'segment redundancy' and in the case of defective distribution. In other words, any type of redundancy is shown by means of 0.[1] In Jakobson, Fant, and Halle 1952 (p. 45) the following is said about the omission of redundant feature values in analytic transcription: " If we consistently follow this principle by bracketing any feature predictable from other features of the same phoneme or from other phonemes of the same sequence, the amount of actually distinctive features in a sequence proves to be very restricted." In order to illustrate this principle the authors transcribe the Russian word *velosiped* 'bicycle':

---

1) Fischer-Jørgensen points out (1975, p. 166) that the assignment of 0 to a feature may signify (1) that an opposition does not apply to a particular phoneme, cf. [0 compact] in /h/, (2) that the manifestation of a given phoneme is intermediate between + and -, cf. [0 grave] in Italian /a/, or (3) that the manifestation of a given phoneme is sometimes + and sometimes -, cf. [0 grave] in Danish /a:/.

	v'	i	l	a	s'	i	p'	'e	t
vocalic/consonantal	(-)	+	±	+	(-)	+	(-)	(+)	(-)
compact/diffuse	(-)	(-)		+	(-)	(-)	-	±	-
grave/acute	+	(-)			-	-	+	-	-
nasal/oral	(-)				(-)		(-)		(-)
sharp/plain	+		(-)		+		(+)		-
continuant/interrupt.	+		+		+		-		-
voiced/voiceless	+				-		-		(-)
stressed/unstressed		(-)		(-)		(-)		(+)	

In order to explain the bracketing and omission of some of the feature values in this matrix the following comments are necessary (some of these, viz. the first and third as well as the remarks on neutralization in (4) and (8) have been taken from Jakobson, Fant, and Halle 1952):

1) In Russian no unstressed /e/ exists, and a Russian word carries not more than one stressed vowel. Consequently /e/ is stressed and all the remaining vowels are unstressed.
2) The only voiced palatalized grave continuant in Russian is /v'/, i.e. in a segment which in this language is [+ grave, + sharp, + continuant, + voiced] all the remaining feature values are redundant (segment redundancy).
3) After /v'/ the only possible unstressed vowel is /i/. (It seems likely that Jakobson would regard this as defective distribution of /a/ and possibly of /u/).
4) The only Russian phonemes which are [± vocalic] are /r r' l l'/, the former two of which are interrupted (segment redundancy). Of the latter two phonemes, /l'/ does not occur before unstressed /a/ (neutralization of the opposition /l/ : /l'/).
5) The only compact vowel in Russian is /a/ (segment redundancy — /e/ and /o/ are [± compact]).

6) The only voiceless palatalized acute continuant in Russian is /s'/ (segment redundancy).

7) The only unstressed acute vowel in Russian is /i/ (segment redundancy + stress conditions).

8) The only voiceless stops in Russian which are grave and diffuse are /p/ and /p'/ (segment redundancy). Before /e/ only palatalized consonants occur (neutralization of the opposition /p/ : /p'/).

9) The only Russian vowel which is [± compact] and [– grave] is /e/ (segment redundancy).

10) In Russian, /t/ and /d/ are the only nonpalatalized stops which are diffuse and acute (segment redundancy — note that nasals are normally considered neutral as regards the continuousness feature). In word-final position the opposition of voice is suspended (neutralization of /t/ : /d/).

In an alphabetical representation the word *velosiped* can thus be written /v'i$\lessdot$l/l'$\gtrdot$ as 'i$\lessdot$p/p'$\gtrdot$ e$\lessdot$t/d$\gtrdot$/, i.e. with three neutralizations indicated. Such a representation, it may be added, corresponds to Hjelmslev's actualized notation.

   A question which naturally arises is whether a distinction should still be made — within the framework of Jakobson's theory — between neutralization and defective distribution, or whether one should operate with one general type of sequence redundancy only. The answer to this question is found in Jakobson and Lotz 1949 (reprinted in Jakobson 1962, p. 427), where it is stated that neutralization is not identical with defective distribution. Neutralization is here defined in the following way: "When in well-defined situations two opposite features cannot alternate, we speak of *neutralization*."[2] According to this definition there is thus neutralization finally in Russian, where 'voiced' and 'voiceless' cannot alternate. It follows from the definition that there is not neutralization, first, when two opposite features cannot alternate in situations which are not well-defined, i.e. if one dichotomous feature loses its relevance in such situations, and, secondly, when more dichotomous features than one lose their relevance, whether in well-defined situations or not. It is difficult to know how "well-defined situations" should be

2) As pointed out by Fischer-Jørgensen (1975, p. 146f), Jakobson's use of the term 'feature' is ambiguous, since it may refer both to components (as it does here) and to dimensions. Thus 'voiced/voiceless', for example, can be understood both as two opposite features and as one dichotomous feature.

understood precisely, but it seems likely that the former of the situations outlined above can be illustrated by means of the following example: after initial /st-/ in British English the opposite features 'grave' and 'acute' cannot alternate in non-consonantal and non-vocalic phonemes; for example, there are English words beginning with [stj-] (*stew, steward*, etc.), but not with [stw-]. These conditions can hardly be considered well-defined, for both /tw-/ and /dw-/ occur, and the lack of *stw*-words is probably accidental (note that only five current *dw*-words exist: *dwarf, dwell(ing), dwindle, Dwight, Dwina*). As yet another example it can be mentioned that in the frame [h＿t] in English the opposite features 'compact' and 'diffuse' cannot alternate in acute vowels; thus *hit* happens to occur but not **het* (in Jakobson, Fant, and Halle 1952 only six English vowels are set up, and of these the only acute ones are /i/ and /e/). But in this case the situation cannot be regarded as well-defined either; and consequently the opposition between 'compact' and 'diffuse' should not be considered neutralized. If more than two opposite features cannot alternate, i.e. if more dichotomous features than one lose their relevance, one should not (according to Jakobson) speak of neutralization, but probably of defective distribution instead. In English, for example, there is no opposition between consonant phonemes initially before phonemes which are characterized by the feature specification [+ consonantal, - vocalic], since only [s] occurs in this environment (cf. examples like *spill, still, skill, sphere, smile, snail*). In this case more features than one lose their relevance, namely all except 'consonantal'. Consequently we can here state that a post-initial consonant phoneme renders defective all English consonant phonemes apart from /s/ in the position preceding it. The conception of neutralization as the inability of two opposite features to alternate is shared by Martinet, who as early as 1946 (p. 48) put forward the following view (cf. 2.4 above):

> Transportée du plan des oppositions de phonèmes sur lequel on l'avait tout d'abord placée, sur celui des caractéristiques pertinentes, la neutralisation signifie qu'un trait, différenciatif dans certaines complexes, perd cette qualité lorsque ces complexes se retrouvent dans des positions déterminées.

Like Jakobson, then, Martinet is of the opinion that phonemes can be broken down into 'caractéristiques pertinentes' (or 'traits différenciatifs'), and that neutralization can be regarded as contextually determined loss of the validity of one (dichotomous) feature. According to this view the suspension of the opposition /p/ : /b/ word-finally in Russian, cf. *lob* [lop] 'front' and *pop* 'pope', can be described as [± voiced] → [0 voiced] in final position.

In connection with the distinction between neutralization and defective distribution discussed above, one particular type of sequence redundancy must be commented on. In Russian, palatalization is sequentially predictable before dentals (cf. 2.2) and voicing in obstruents is predictable before obstruents (cf. 2.4). In examples like [s't'in'a] 'wall' and ['aist] 'stork' both these contexts occur, and both sharp vs. plain and voiced vs. voiceless are therefore irrelevant in the sibilant. Here *two* dichotomous features have lost their validity, but nevertheless it must be a case of neutralization, not of defective distribution. The reason why such a solution has to be adopted is that we are faced with two contextually determined losses of feature relevance each of which can be observed separately, and which in this case act together. In [s't'in'a] and ['aist] two neutralizations coincide in the sibilant, which may consequently be interpreted as the archiphoneme <s/s' /z/z'>. In the English example of defective distribution mentioned in the preceding paragraph (*spill*, etc.) no such combination of neutralizations is found. To be sure more features than one lose their validity as in the Russian example, but this is not a result of a number of coinciding contextually determined losses each of which can be observed separately.

Although a distinction between neutralization (understood as contextually determined reduction of distinctive components by one) and defective distribution is possible, it is natural to ask if it is justified. What reasons can be adduced for regarding the preconsonantal [s] in English, which is represented simply as [+ consonantal] in an analytic transcription, as a manifestation of the phoneme /s/ rather than of an archiconsonant? A possible answer to this question might be that if a phonemic representation is meant to be not only descriptively adequate but also psycholinguistically plausible it seems reasonable to distinguish between neutralization and defective distribution and to regard the example quoted as an instance of the latter. Experiments with slips of the tongue suggest that speakers of English after initial *s* encode stop consonants which are unspecified for voice, i.e. neutralization products, or archiphonemes (cf. Davidsen–Nielsen 1975). Analogously, it seems likely that speakers of Spanish and Italian encode in preconsonantal position a nasal consonant which is unspecified as regards place of articulation — cf. Spanish examples like *un beso* 'a kiss', *un tonto* 'a fool', *un gato* 'a cat', where the occurrence of [m], [n], and [ŋ] respectively is automatically determined by the following consonant; and Italian examples like *impossibile* 'impossible', *insolito* 'unusual', and *incolto* 'uncultivated', where the same distribution is in evidence.[3] On the other hand nothing suggests that the speaker of English encodes the initial segment of a word like *scholastic* as anything but an /s/. For whereas a slip of the tongue like [skə'læstɪk] → [gə'slæstɪk] is a distinct possibility (cf. Davidsen-Nielsen 1975, where it is shown that an English nonsense word like [skə'meɪt] may through a speech lapse be transformed into [gə'smeɪt]), slips like [gə'plæstɪk, gə'klæstɪk, gə'blæstɪk, gə'glæstɪk, gə'flæstɪk] have never been recorded and are quite inconceivable. From a psycholinguistic/neurolinguistic viewpoint it may therefore be argued that the features which distinguish *s* from other English consonants retain their validity in preconsonantal position: although they are irrelevant from a (primary) contrastive point of view, they have a 'secondary relevance'. In the post–initial segment of *scholastic,* on the other hand, the feature 'voiced' is both primarily and secondarily irrelevant. It could be argued that the dimension of voice is absent after initial *s* in English stop phonemes in the same way that the dimension of glottalicness, for example, is absent in English vowels.

This argument is, of course, largely speculative, but in principle it can be verified or falsified by means of performance investigations. And before it is rejected it should be remembered that Trubetzkoy introduced the concept of neutralization on the basis of linguistic consciousness (cf. the discussion of his monograph on Polabian in 2.2). According to Trubetzkoy (1929) there is an important psycho-

---

3) Fromkin (1973, p. 250) gives examples of slips of the tongue in English words containing [ŋ], and these errors may be interpreted archiphonemically (i.e. as containing the sequences /Ng/ and /Nk/) at the level of encoding. In a slip like *the rank* [ræŋk] *order of the subjects* → *the rand* [rænd] *orker of the subjects* it cannot be a velar nasal which is encoded since [ŋk] ... [d] is changed to [nd] ... [k], not to [ŋd] ... [k] (/rænd/ is clearly a pronounceable sound sequence in English, cf. *hanged, fanged,* etc.). However, an /ng, nk/ interpretation is also possible here, i.e. an error such as *sink* [sĩŋk] *a ship* → [sĩmp] *a* [ʃɪk] can be analysed either as /Nk ↲ p/ or as /nk ... p/. According to Hans Basbøll (personal communication) Danish [n] may be assimilated to a following consonant across a boundary between the elements of a compound and across a weak word boundary, whereas [m] and [ŋ] may not; this would seem to support an /n/-analysis rather than an /N/-analysis.

logical difference between neutralization and segment redundancy (cf. 2.2). This assumption is quite plausible, and it seems reasonable to presume that there is a psychological difference between two different types of contextually determined redundancy as well, viz. neutralization and defective distribution.

Returning to Roman Jakobson's theory it should be pointed out that due to the nature of the proposed features it is possible to operate with neutralization in certain cases where the Prague phonologists would operate with defective distribution instead. As mentioned in 2.2 Trubetzkoy does not operate with neutralization of /b/ : /d/ (or of /p/ : /t/) initially before /l/ in German and similarly, as mentioned in 2.4, Martinet does not operate with neutralization of /p/ : /t/ (or of /b/ : /d/) initially before /l/ in English. The reason underlying this non-recognition is that the labial and dental stop consonants do not have in common a set of distinctive features which the velar stop consonants do not share with them, and consequently there is no way of knowing whether it is the oppositions /b/ : /d/ and /p/ : /t/ or the oppositions /d/ : /g/ and /t/ : /k/ which are suspended (cf. *Blatt, glatt* but not **dlatt* in German; and *play, clay* but not **tlay* in English). Given the new features, however, an argument in favour of one of these possible solutions can be adduced. In English the stop consonants are characterized by the following feature specifications (cf. Jakobson, Fant, and Halle 1952, p. 43):[4]

	p	t	k	b	d	g
continuant/ interrupted	–	–	–	–	–	–
compact/diffuse	–	–	+	–	–	+
grave/acute	+	–	0	+	–	0
tense/lax	+	+	+	–	–	–

The distribution of the compactness and gravity features can also be shown by means of the following triangular patterns:

---

4) In this matrix [0 grave] signifies that the phonemes in question are manifested as [+ grave] but that gravity is not in this case distinctive (cf. footnote 1 above).

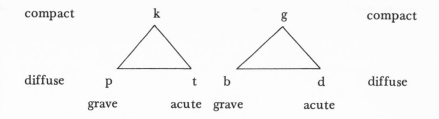

	compact						compact	

diffuse p t b d diffuse

grave acute grave acute

It appears that /p/ and /t/ as well as /b/ and /d/ have in common the
features 'diffuse' and 'interrupted'. As opposed to this the feature
shared by /k/ and /t/ and by /g/ and /d/, viz. 'interrupted', is shared
by /p/ and /b/ as well.[5] A neutralization rule can therefore be formulated according to which the feature 'gravity' loses its relevance
initially before /l/ in stop consonants. In words like *play, blue, clay,
glue* the initial consonants can then be analysed in the following
way:

	<p/t>(leɪ)	<b/d> (luː)	k(leɪ)	g(luː)
continuant/ interrupted	–	–	–	–
compact/diffuse	–	–	+	+
grave/acute	0	0	0	0
tense/lax	+	–	+	–

This solution, however, is not convincing. In the pronunciation of
many speakers of English, for one thing, there is free variation between [t] and [k] and between [d] and [g] initially before /l/, i.e.
pronunciations like [tlaɪm] (*climb*) and [dlʌv] (*glove*) coexist with
[klaɪm] and [glʌv] (as opposed to this, pronunciations like [tleɪ] (of
play) and [dluː] (of *blue*) do not occur). Sound changes like later
Latin *vetlum* > Italian *vecchio* 'old' and substitutions in the speech of
children involving dentals and velars also tell against the <p/t>,

---

5) Bazell (1956, p. 28) points out that /k/ and /t/ (and /g/ and /d/) have a
common base which /p/ (and /b/) does not share with them, namely
'nongrave stop consonant' (where 'nongrave' is not identical with 'acute').
However, such a common base can only be established if the feature 'grave/
acute' is subdivided into the features 'grave/nongrave' and 'acute/nonacute'.

<b/d> analysis. Furthermore, attention may be directed to the following French graffiti from the Second World War: *à bas icler* (*Hitler*) (A. Martinet, personal communication). This particular type of vacillation and substitution points towards neutralization of the oppositions /t/ : /k/ and /d/ : /g/ instead; but with the features which have been proposed so far (Jakobson, Fant, and Halle 1952; Chomsky and Halle 1968; Ladefoged 1971) it is not possible to establish a common base for the members of these oppositions which is not shared by /p/ and /b/ as well. If, like Ladefoged, we operate with a multivalued feature called 'articulatory place' it becomes impossible to recognize neutralization even of /p/ : /t/ and /b/ : /d/, for since there are minimal pairs such as *play* ≠ *clay* and *blue* ≠ *glue* we cannot claim that the place–feature loses its relevance initially before /l/ in stop consonants. Within the framework of such a feature system it must be said that a post–initial /l/ renders defective the phonemes /t/ and /d/ in the preceding position. Only if the opposition between all places of articulation is suspended, as in the case of nasal consonants before obstruents in many languages, is it possible to claim that the feature of place loses its relevance, i.e. is neutralized.

In conclusion it should be emphasized that the inception of the theory of distinctive features does not automatically rule out the concept of neutralization. Neutralization may now be regarded as contextually determined loss of the relevance of one (dichotomous) feature, and neutralization rules may be formulated of the type [± voiced] → [0 voiced] finally in Russian/German, and [± sharp] → [0 sharp] before dentals in Russian. Neutralization differs from another type of sequence redundancy — defective distribution — in that only one feature loses its relevance, i.e. only minimal oppositions may be neutralized. Just as, according to Trubetzkoy, there is a psychological difference between segment redundancy and neutralization, a distinction between neutralization and defective distribution seems justified on psychological grounds. On the level of phonemes there is nothing which prevents the analyst from recognizing neutralization products, or archiphonemes, and in accordance with such a recognition employing transcriptions like Russian /v'i<l/l'>as'i<p/p'>e<t/d>/, English /s<t/d>ıl/, and Spanish /uN beso/.

Chapter 6

PHONOLOGICAL THEORY IN THE SOVIET UNION

6.1. The Leningrad School

Until 1962, the year Šaumjan's *Problems of Theoretical Phonology* was published in its original Russian version, Soviet phonology was dominated by two major schools: the Leningrad school and the Moscow school. Both of these were strongly influenced by the Polish linguist *J. Baudouin de Courtenay*. The founder of the Leningrad school was *L.V. Ščerba*, who in the twenties and thirties was the most influential phonetician in the Soviet Union. Ščerba was strongly influenced by Baudouin (who had taught at St. Petersburg university from 1910 to 1918), but he had also studied in Paris under *Passy* (1908-1909). In accordance with both these scholars Ščerba emphasized the distinctive function of the phoneme (1911, p. 2). Under the influence of Baudouin's theory of the psycho-phoneme ("ein psychischer Aequivalent des Sprachlautes") he furthermore regarded phonemes as psychological entities, i.e. as sound types which the speaker, as a result of their distinctive function, is consciously aware of. However, after having been criticized by Marxist linguists for subjective idealism, Ščerba stopped referring to the linguistic feeling of the speaker-hearer. In 1937 he defined phonemes as "the sound types capable of differentiating words and their forms" (cf. Krámský 1974, p. 127). By characterizing the phoneme as a 'sound type' Ščerba comes close to the generic phoneme definitions of Daniel Jones and the post-Bloomfieldians. Within the class (family, type) of sounds comprising a phoneme he regards one member as the "fundamental variant".

When working out the phonological system of a given language, Ščerba uses the two criteria of psychological and phonetic resemblance to equate phonemes in one position with those in other positions (cf. Kortlandt 1972, p. 20). Due to the charge of subjective idealism mentioned above, however, the second of these criteria has gradually become more important. This means that phonemes in different positions are identified according to the same principle — phonetic similarity — as in the London school of Daniel Jones and the American structuralist school. As morphophonemic problems are regarded by Ščerba and his followers as outside the scope of phonology (cf. Halle 1963, p. 11), identification based on alternations is not allowed.

Neutralization is not recognized and no archiphonemes are set up. In a Russian word like [xot] 'motion' Ščerba identifies the stop consonant with the phoneme /t/, in spite of the systematic absence of [d] in final position, and in spite of the occurrence of /d/ in alternants like [xoda] (cf. Fischer-Jørgensen 1975, p. 326). A similar example is mentioned by Halle (1963, p. 9): in Russian /a/ and /o/ must be distinguished as different phonemes in stressed position, but in unstressed position after nonpalatalized and nonpalatal consonants there is only a single nonhigh vowel phoneme, which in pretonic position is realized as [ʌ] and in all other positions as [ə]. Ščerba assigns not only unstressed [ʌ] but also [ə] to the phoneme /a/, rather than to /o/, since in distinct pronunciation [ə] is frequently replaced by [a].

Since Ščerba's death in 1944, *L.R. Zinder* has become the most prominent member of the Leningrad school. Like Ščerba, Zinder rejects neutralization, which he considers nothing more than a case of defective distribution, as well as the archiphoneme, which he regards simply as a relation between phonemes (cf. Fischer-Jørgensen 1975, p. 328f). In *Obščaja fonetika* Zinder identifies phonemes in different positions on the basis of phonetic similarity and points out that this criterion requires that the segments in question share a number of distinctive features.[1] Every sound is assigned unambiguously to a given phoneme; i.e. like the post-Bloomfieldians the members of the Leningrad school insist on the biuniqueness condition (cf. Halle 1963, p. 10).

6.2. The Moscow School

Like Ščerba and his followers in Leningrad the adherents of the Moscow school of phonology have been strongly influenced by J. Baudouin de Courtenay. The direct forerunner of the Moscow school, however, is the Causasist *N.J. Jakovlev*, who tried to avoid psychologism on the one hand and phoneticism on the other by identifying phonemes in different positions on the basis of alter-

---

1) As I do not read Russian, this chapter is based on works written in English, French, and German. Nevertheless some references to books and papers written in Russian have been included in the bibliography.

nations (an idea which also goes back to Baudouin). Jakovlev actually defines the phoneme as a set of alternating sounds in different positions (cf. Kortlandt 1972, p. 21).

The most prominent first-generation members of the Moscow school are *R.I. Avanesov, V.N. Sidorov, P.S. Kuznecov*, and, in particular, *A.A. Reformatskij*. One of the characteristics of the Moscow theory, which was worked out in the twenties and thirties, is a distinction drawn between *strong position*, in which the maximum number of distinctions is operative, and *weak position*, where some of these oppositions are neutralized and where, consequently, a smaller number of distinctions is operative. To the Muscovites neutralization is thus a central concept. The sounds occurring in weak position are termed *variants*. Reformatskij (1970), however, has proposed a broader conception of 'weak position', which in his view refers not only to significatively weak position, where there is neutralization and where variants occur, but also to perceptually weak position, where the phoneme does not appear in its basic shape but is strongly modified by the surroundings. Sounds occurring in perceptually weak position are called *variations*, and unlike variants they can always be referred to one definite phoneme.

The distinctive units which occur in the positions which are weak in respect of significative function are termed *hyperphonemes*. The concept of hyperphoneme, which was introduced by Kuznecov and subsequently developed by Sidorov in the early thirties, is thus closely related to the Praguian concept of archiphoneme, particularly in the sense of Martinet ("unité phonologique simple susceptible, en certaines positions, de se dissocier en deux ou plusieurs éléments phonologiquement distincts", Martinet 1936, p. 54). The hyperphoneme, however, is said to differ from the archiphoneme in two respects. Whereas an archiphoneme, according to Postowalowa (1975, p. 149), is regarded by the Prague circle primarily as the coalescence in a given (weak) position of two phonemes occurring in other (strong) positions, the Muscovites stress the fact that a hyperphoneme is opposed as a unit to other hyperphonemes occurring in weak position.[2] It should be pointed out, though, that this

---

2) Notice in this connection that M.V. Panov, a second-generation member of the Moscow school, has characterized Trubetzkoy and his fellow Praguists as "founders of syntagmatic phonology" (cf. Kortlandt 1972, p. 22). According to Kortlandt this characterization is unreasonable, since the cornerstone of Trubetzkoy's theory is distinctiveness, which is a paradigmatic relationship.

seems to constitute not a notional difference but only a difference in where the emphasis is put. Secondly, unlike the archiphoneme, the hyperphoneme does not necessarily presuppose more than one phoneme:

> Quant à l'unité phonologique qui se trouve au-dessus du phonème dans la structure des étages, les opinions ne sont pas identiques et je crois que l'opinion de Martinet sur l'archiphonème ne coïncide pas avec la terminologie phonologique praguoise; l'école phonologique de Moscou a dégagé la notion d'"hyperphonème" qui ne coïncide pas avec celle d'archiphonème, puisque l'hyperphonème ne présuppose pas obligatoirement un ensemble de phonèmes mais peut se limiter à un seul phonème. Par exemple en russe on distingue à un niveau (voyelles accentuées) cinq unités, i, e, a, u, o, mais à un autre niveau (voyelles inaccentuées) après les consonnes dures, i/e et a/o forment des unités indifférenciées et il reste une opposition entre trois hyperphonèmes: i/e, a/o et u: les hyperphonèmes comprennent la neutralisation des phonèmes i et e, a et o, mais u reste identique à lui-même, cependant à ce niveau, ce n'est plus un phonème mais l'hyperphonème u (Reformatskij 1957, p. 105f).

Once again, this can hardly be regarded as a basic difference but rather as a terminological difference. According to the Prague phonologists it is the archiphonemes /I/, /A/ and the phoneme /u/ which are opposed to each other in weak position in Russian, and according to the Muscovites it is the hyperphonemes <i/e>, <a/o> and <u> which contrast here. It seems clear, therefore, that the concepts of the archiphoneme and of the hyperphoneme are very closely related indeed.

In the Moscow theory grammar and phonetics form an integrated whole, and identification from one position to another may therefore be based on the comparison of morphemes (cf. Jakovlev). For example, the unstressed vowel in *sadú* [sʌ'du] 'garden' (locative case) can be identified with the phoneme /a/, rather than with /o/, since /a/ occurs in the alternant *sad* (nominative case). In *vodá* [vʌ'da] 'water' (nominative case), on the other hand, [ʌ] is identified with /o/ because of alternants like *vódu* (accusative case) (cf. Fischer-Jørgensen 1975, p. 333). The variant [ʌ] thus represents the phoneme /a/ in *sadú* and the phoneme /o/ in *vodá*. At the same time, however, it represents the hyperphoneme $<a/o>$ in both these words. This is possible since the hyperphoneme analysis is carried out at the first stage of the phonological description and precedes the phoneme analysis proper. In the Moscow school the phonological analysis thus consists of two stages: 1) the hyperphonemic analysis, whereby the inventory of hyperphonemes is established in different (weak) positions, and 2) the phonemic analysis proper, in which the operation of identification is performed on the basis of alternations (cf. Postowalowa 1975, p. 153). In this way [sʌˈdu], for example, is interpreted at the first stage as /s$<a/o>$ˈdu/ and at the next stage as /saˈdu/. Notice that this method of recognizing and subsequently resolving neutralizations is strikingly similar to that of Hjelmslev, according to which a distinction is drawn between actualized and ideal notation (cf. chapter 4).

The term hyperphoneme is also used in a different and more restricted sense from the one outlined above, namely to refer to the cases where a unit in weak position cannot be identified with one definite phoneme due to the lack of alternations. As examples the Russian words *barán* 'ram' and *koróva* 'cow' may be mentioned. Here it cannot be decided whether [ʌ] in the first syllable should be identified with /a/ or with /o/, since in all forms of these words the first syllable is invariably unstressed. 'Hyperphoneme' is used in this restricted sense by Kuznecov. In the wider sense of the term, it may be added, it is not possible in these cases to go beyond the hyperphonemic analysis $<a/o>$.

In the Soviet Union the fifties were characterized linguistically by a search for a synthesis between the theories advanced by the Muscovites and by Ščerba and his followers. Kuznecov attempted to restate the Leningrad definition of the phoneme in terms of the Moscow school, and Avanesov tried to restate the Moscow definition in terms of the Leningrad school. In 1962 *S.I. Bernštejn*, a member of the Leningrad school who moved to Moscow in the thirties, tried to devise a neutral terminology in which both kinds of phoneme could find their place (cf. Kortlandt 1972, p. 26). In his attempt to bridge the gap between the two Soviet theories of phonology *Avanesov* (1955), according to Postowalowa, does not utilize the concept of neutralization, and this particular synthesis therefore calls for some comment.

As mentioned in the section on the Leningrad school, Ščerba and his followers assign unstressed [ʌ] in Russian to the phoneme /a/, rather than to /o/, on phonetic grounds. To Avanesov such a solu-

7*

tion is unacceptable since it "fails to take into account the fundamental difference in the functioning of sound units in strong position, on the one hand, and in weak position, on the other" (cf.
Halle 1963, p. 12). Avanesov interprets the vowel occurring in this
position as the *weak phoneme* /α/. Similarly, in a Russian word like
vod 'water' (nominative case), the final consonant is analyzed not
as /t/, on phonetic grounds, but as $/t_2/$, where the subscript indicates
that this is a weak phoneme, viz. the equivalent of the two strong
phonemes /t/ and /d/. When the opposition of palatalization is inoperative Avanesov uses the subscript $_1$, and in the cases where both
the palatalization and the voicing opposition are inoperative the
subscript $_3$ is used. This graphic method is in principle identical
with that of Trubetzkoy, who also used special symbols (capital or
Greek letters) in significatively weak position. However, whereas
both the Prague phonologists and the adherents of the original
Moscow theory identify a unit occurring in weak position with two
units occurring in strong position — an identification which in the
Moscow school is shown explicitly by notations like <a/o>, <t/d>,
etc. — Avanesov refrains from performing this operation. Although,
for example, the weak phoneme $/t_2/$ is regarded as the equivalent of
the strong phonemes /t/ and /d/, Avanesov does not — according to
Postowalowa — identify them with these phonemes. We here note
a certain affinity to Twaddell's and Firth's theories, where as a result
of the polysystemic approach there is no room for the concept of
neutralization. It must be because of this absence of identification
that Postowalowa describes Avanesov's approach to the units occurring in significatively weak position as characterized by non–utili-
zation of the concept of neutralization ("ohne Verwendung des Auf-
hebungsbegriffs", 1975, p. 153). In my opinion it seems very doubtful whether it is possible to regard a weak phoneme as the equivalent
of two strong phonemes without at the same time recognizing and
using the concept of neutralization. Anyhow, Avanesov operates
with different inventories in different positions, and the presence of
weak phonemes like /α/ and $/t_2/$ in addition to strong phonemes
would seem to enlarge and complicate the total inventory. However,
the inventory of phonemes is considered equal to the inventory of
strong phonemes, weak phonemes occupying in the system a subordinate role with respect to the strong ones (cf. Halle 1963, p. 12).
This solution has been criticized as inconsistent by Kuznecov, who
finds the original Moscow theory simpler (cf. Fischer–Jørgensen
1975, p. 340).

For the description of Russian, Avanesov sets up a gliding scale of four positions: 1) completely strong, where both the distinction 'voiced/voiceless' and the distinction 'palatalized/unpalatalized' are operative; 2) completely weak, where neither of these distinctions is operative; 3) relatively strong (weak) in the sense that only the distinction 'voiced/voiceless' is operative; and 4) relatively strong (weak) in the sense that only the distinction 'palatalized/unpalatalized' is operative (cf. Postowalowa 1975, p. 135f).[3] Another characteristic of Avanesov's theory is his proposal to establish three types of transcription for representing utterances in an increasingly abstract manner: 1) a *phonetic* transcription, which indicates contextual variants; 2) a *phonemic* transcription, in which redundant information has been eliminated, and in which not only strong but also weak phonemes occur; and 3) a *morphophonemic* transcription, in which a given morpheme is always represented by the same sequence of symbols (Avanesov 1956). The task of devising three types of scientific linguistic transcription is regarded as being of great importance by Šaumjan (1968, p. 105), to whom we must now turn our attention.

6.3. Šaumjan's Two-level Theory of Phonology

1962 may be regarded as a milestone in Soviet linguistics (cf. Kortlandt 1972, p. 28), since this year saw the publication not only of Bernštejn's article, which put an end to the discussion between Ščerba's followers and the Muscovites, but also Šaumjan's *Problemy teoretičeskoj fonologii* (translated into the English in 1968). In this book, which represents a complete break with the Russian tradition, Šaumjan gives a full account of a mathematically oriented phonological theory which he had worked out over a period of several years. Šaumjan is strongly influenced by western structuralism, in particular by Hjelmslev, and like Hjelmslev he regards the hypothetico-deductive method as the basic tool of linguistic theory. In contradistinction to other Soviet linguists, he is of the opinion that phonetics and phonology should be kept strictly apart. As in contemporary logic of science, a distinction must be drawn between two levels of abstraction: the *level of observation* and the *level of constructs*. "Constructs are concepts which deal with unobservable

---

3) For Russian vowels under stress Avanesov distinguishes eight positions, cf. Šaumjan 1968, p. 54.

entities that are postulated for the explanation of facts given through direct observation" (Šaumjan 1968, p. 7). It is because of this strict demarcation of two abstraction levels that Šaumjan's approach is characterized as the two-level theory of phonology.

In Šaumjan's theory the term 'phoneme' refers to a hypothetical unit belonging to the level of constructs. Phonemes do not correspond directly with sounds, i.e. with primitive, undifferentiated physical concepts, but are embodied as relational-physical elements called *phonemoids*. These phonemoids belong to the level of observation and are, in their turn, embodied as sounds. Šaumjan's phoneme has thus been elevated to a relatively high level of abstraction (cf. Hjelmslev's 'expression taxemes'), whereas his concept of phonemoid is fairly similar to the traditional Praguian phoneme concept, although probably somewhat less abstract. Šaumjan now introduces a distinction between *concrete phonemes*, which are bound to definite positions, and *abstract phonemes*, which are classes of concrete phonemes (cf. the Moscow-concept of position and Twaddell's micro- and macrophonemes). On the level of observation a corresponding distinction is made between concrete and abstract phonemoids and between concrete and abstract sounds. Features are also recognized. On the level of constructs they are termed *differentors* and on the level of observation *differentoids* (relational-physical concepts) and *acoustic properties* (purely physical concepts). The system of concepts belonging to Šaumjan's theory of phonology is summed up in the following table (Šaumjan 1968, p. 109):

Level of constructs	Constructs	Concrete differentor	Abstract differentor	Concrete phoneme	Abstract phoneme
Level of observation	Relational physical concepts	Concrete differentoid	Abstract differentoid	Concrete phonemoid	Abstract phonemoid
	Purely physical concepts	Concrete acoustic property	Abstract acoustic property	Concrete sound	Abstract sound (sound type)

In the establishment of phonological oppositions and phonemes Šaumjan feels forced to eliminate semantic criteria, for one thing because of the existence in every language of lexical doublets. Semantic criteria are replaced by criteria of linguistic behaviour; i.e.

Šaumjan adopts the same method as Twaddell and Hockett (cf. 3.1). If, according to the native informant, there is not identity but difference between two 'signifiant segments' there is, in Šaumjan's terminology, a relationship of *contrast* between them. If in a Russian word like *palka* 'stick', the vowel [a] is replaced by [o] the informant will say that the two signifiant segments are different (cf. *polka* 'shelf'). Since there is at least one sound to which [a] is in a relationship of contrast, it can be concluded that the individual sound [a] is a substratum of the individual phoneme /a/. On the basis of such tests with informants a limited number of individual phonemes may be established in each position. The question now arises how the transition from individual (concrete) phonemes to classes of individual phonemes (abstract phonemes) takes place. In other words, how should the operation of identification be performed?

In order to solve this problem Šaumjan proposes the *operator method*, which consists of the following steps: 1) selection of a standard, 2) establishment of homogeneous sets of sounds, 3) measurement of the action of positional operators, and 4) establishment of paired sounds. This method is explained by means of the following example: in stressed syllables Russian vowels have a minimal palatal shading between plain consonants (position P_1), stronger palatal shading following a plain and preceding a sharp consonant (position P_2) as well as following a sharp and preceding a plain consonant (position P_3), and maximal palatal shading between sharp consonants (position P_4). Examples are *palka* 'stick', *tačka* 'wheelbarrow', *trjapka* 'rag' and *Ljal'ka* (a proper name). As standard, Šaumjan selects the set of sounds occurring in position P_1: $M_1 - a_1$, o_1, u_1, i_1, e_1. Secondly, the following homogeneous sets of sounds are established: $M_2 - a_2$, o_2, u_2, i_2, e_2 (in position P_2), $M_3 - a_3$, o_3, u_3, i_3, e_3 (in position P_3) and $M_4 - a_4$, o_4, u_4, i_4, e_4 (in position P_4), the criterion of homogeneity being the dependence of sound changes on the influence of positional conditions. If, by means of a mental experiment, the influence of positional conditions is removed, the sets M_2, M_3 and M_4 coincide with their standard M_1. Thirdly, the action of the positional operators P_1, P_2-P_3, P_4 is measured and expressed as first, second and third degree of palatalization respectively (the difference between P_2 and P_3 being that the former operator affects the final phase and the latter the initial phase of the vowel). Finally, paired sounds are established by means of the so-called *law of reduction*:

if a given set of sounds M_i is taken as a standard, then for
every sound a_i of this set one can find a corresponding
sound a_j of the set M_j, whose difference from the sound
a_i can be attributed solely to the action of the positional
operator P_j (Šaumjan 1968, p. 118).

In this way, then, the *a*-vowels of *tačka, trjapka* and *Ljal'ka* can be
identified with the *a*-vowel of *palka,* since the difference between
the vowels has been reduced to the actions of the positional operators.
As pointed out by Fischer-Jørgensen (1975, p. 353) this is actually a
complicated way of saying that instead of basing identification on
phonetic similarity it is required that the phonetic difference between units occurring in different positions can be explained as an
influence of the environment.

Šaumjan's operator method, however, does not shed new light on
the problem of neutralization. If, for example, the set of initial stop
consonants is selected as a standard in German, then for the sound
[th] of this set we can find a corresponding sound [t^h] of the set of
final stops whose difference from [th] can be attributed to the
positional operator. However, for the sound [d] of the set of initial
stops the sound in final position, whose difference from [d] can be
attributed to the positional operator, will also be [t^h]. Furthermore,
as pointed out by Kortlandt (1972, p. 39), the law of reduction is
not reversible. Given final [t^h] in German we cannot select just one
initial sound which together with [t^h] constitutes a pair. Although
this problem is not discussed explicitly in his book, it is clear that
Šaumjan recognizes the concept of neutralization and that in
position of neutralization he operates with archiphonemes (1968,
p. 103). In the Russian words *luk* 'bow' and *lug* 'meadow', for
example, he interprets the final stop as an archiphoneme which
differs fundamentally from both the /k/ of *kust* 'bush' and the /g/
of *gust* 'thick' by containing a smaller number of differentors:
whereas 'voicelessness' belongs among the differentors of /k/ and
'voicedness' among the differentors of /g/, the archiphoneme /K/
comprises neither of these differentors. Šaumjan's analysis is thus on
this point identical with that proposed by Trubetzkoy. Due to
alternants like *luka, luku, lukom* and *luga, lugu, lugom,* however, the
final stops of *luk* and *lug* are on a higher plane of abstraction referred
to the *morpho-phonemes* |k| and |g| respectively. Morpho-phonemes
(and morpho-differentors) are characterized as constructs of a
second plane which relates phonology to grammar.

The approach to neutralization and archiphonemes in *Problems of Theoretical Phonology* is thus quite traditional. In an article of 1967, however, Šaumjan puts forward the revised view (recall that his book on phonology was published in its original Russian version already in 1962) that neutralization takes place not at the level of constructs but at the level of observation (p. 134f):

> ... nun darf man fragen, wieweit überhaupt die Neutralisierung sinnvollerweise als Erscheinung zu betrachten ist, die dem idealisierten phonologischen System zugehört. Eher scheint sie, um einen Ausdruck der Informationstheorie zu benutzen, Geräusch, also eine Störung der Funktion des idealisierten phonologischen Systems, zu sein und als solche zum Niveau der akustischen Substanz zu gehören. Wir können postulieren, dass die Neutralisierung im idealisierten phonologischen System überhaupt nicht stattfindet.

In the Russian words *luk* and *lug*, for example, it is no longer a neutralization of phonemes which is assumed to take place, but a neutralization of *phonemoids*. In the idealized phonological system, i.e. on the level of constructs, the two words are now interpreted as /luk/ and /lug/ respectively. This analysis has the advantage of integrating phonology with grammar (to which phonology should be considered subordinate) and at the same time recognizing neutralization, which is not swept under the carpet as in strongly grammatically oriented phonological theories (generative phonology). Furthermore, the concept of archiphoneme may now be dispensed with. Although he himself emphasizes that as a result of neutralization a new type of unit arises which is fundamentally different from both members of an opposition, Šaumjan does not, however, point out that as a result of shifting neutralization to the level of observation a new concept of *archiphonemoid* will necessarily have to be introduced. At the level of relational–physical concepts the final unit of Russian *luk* and *lug*, for example, must now be an archiphonemoid containing a smaller number of differentoids than the corresponding phonemoids. Therefore no overall saving is obtained. Whereas Šaumjan's original approach to neutralization is practically identical with Trubetzkoy's, his revised approach is quite similar to that of Hjelmslev, who distinguishes between actualized notation, where neutralizations are indicated, and ideal notation, where they have been resolved on the basis of alternations (cf. chapter 4). It may therefore be concluded that although neutralization is an important concept in the two-level theory of phonology, Šaumjan can hardly be said to have contributed in any original way to the elucidation of this particular problem.[4]

---

4) In his article of 1967, Šaumjan mentions that he intends to write a separate paper on the concept of neutralization.

Chapter 7
GENERATIVE PHONOLOGY

7.1. Morris Halle

As the reader undoubtedly knows, it is above all Morris Halle who has worked out the theory of generative phonology, and *The Sound Pattern of Russian* (Halle 1959) is the first major treatise in which a number of the new principles are introduced. For each morpheme Halle sets up one underlying form, and from this form the morpheme variants are derived by means of rules; i.e. in the phonological representation a morpheme appears "in the form from which all other forms of the same morpheme can be derived in the simplest fashion" (Halle 1959, p. 56). In a generative description of the sound pattern of any language only two levels of representation are recognized — the phonetic level and the morphonemic level (subsequently termed 'phonological' or 'systematic phonemic' in generative studies) — and these are connected by means of ordered rules. One does not operate with, or recognize, a level reflecting the surface (i.e. phonemic) contrasts of the language under investigation. The reason for rejecting such a level is that it prevents the formulation of the simplest set of rules connecting the morphonemic and phonetic representations. For example, Halle claims (ibid., p. 22f) that the presence of a phonemic level implies that the rule of voicing assimilation in Russian, according to which the voicing of an obstruent is determined by that of a following obstruent, has to be broken up into two subrules: a phonemic rule and a subphonemic rule. For example, the morphonemic sequences |m'ok bi| "were (he) getting wet" and |ž'eč bi| "were one to burn" are manifested phonetically as [m'og bi] and [ž'eǯ bi], but whereas /k/ and /g/ are different phonemes in Russian (cf. minimal pairs like /k'ol/ 'stake' vs. /g'ol/ 'naked'), [č] and [ǯ] are variants of the same phoneme, viz. /č/. Retention of a phonemic level therefore necessitates two assimilation rules:

Morphonemic	Phonemic	Phonetic
|m'ok bi| $\longrightarrow$	/m'og bi/ - - - $\rightarrow$	[m'og bi]
|ž'eč bi| - - - $\rightarrow$	/ž'eč bi/ $\longrightarrow$	[ž'eǯ bi]

It is due to difficulties of this type that Halle rejects a phonemic
level. It is worth pointing out immediately, however, that this argument is only valid if by 'phonemes' one has in mind the kind of
units which the post-Bloomfieldians and Daniel Jones operate .with.
In those phonological schools where neutralization is recognized, the
above example causes no difficulties, a fact which has frequently
been pointed out (cf. Householder 1967, p. 942f; Johns 1969, p.
374f; Derwing 1973, p. 186; Linell 1974, p. 105; and Fischer-Jørgensen 1975, p. 285). If neutralization is indicated in the phonemic
representation, the Russian assimilation rule is purely phonetic:
in the example cited it has the effect that the archiphoneme $<$k/g$>$
and the phoneme /č/ are manifested as [g] and [ǯ] respectively. It
should be added, though, that an extra neutralization rule connecting
the third morphoneme of |m'ok bi| with the archiphoneme of
/m'o$<$k/g$>$ bi/ will be necessary. A case which is analogous to the
Russian one is described by Matthews (1974, p. 200ff): in Italian
the negative prefix written *in-*, *im-* has the phonetic realizations
[im, im̦, in, iņ, iŋ] ([ŋ] symbolizes an alveopalatal nasal). As examples
the words *impossibile* 'impossible', *infelice* 'unhappy', *insolito*
'unusual', *ingiusto* 'unjust', and *incolto* 'uncultivated' may be mentioned. If a phonemic level is to be retained, and if neutralization is
not recognized, the rule according to which the articulatory place of
a final nasal consonant is determined by that of a following consonant has to be broken up into two subrules:

Morphonemic		Phonemic		Phonetic	
|in|	⟶	/im/	- - -→	[im]	(in *impossibile*)
|in|	⟶	/im/	⟶	[im̦]	(in *infelice*)
|in|	- - - →	/in/	- - -→	[in]	(in *insolito*)
|in|	- - - →	/in/	⟶	[iņ]	(in *ingiusto*)
|in|	- - - →	/in/	⟶	[iŋ]	(in *incolto*)

It can be seen that phonemic assimilation takes place in *impossibile*,
infelice and that subphonemic assimilation takes place in *ingiusto*,
incolto, *infelice* (according to Matthews [n], [ņ] and [ŋ] are different
allophones of /n/; and [m] and [m̦] are different allophones /m/). If
neutralization is recognized, however, only one subphonemic rule is
required, which connects the archiphoneme $<$N$>$ with the variants
[m, m̦, n, ņ, ŋ].[1]

The rejection of a phonemic level in generative phonology obviously implies that the only neutralizations which can be recognized are the ones which remain in force on the morphonemic level, i.e. those which cannot be resolved on the basis of morphological alternations. In an English word like *spill* the neutralization in the stop consonant will thus be recognized and shown in the morphonemic representation by assigning the value '0' (= zero) to the feature 'voiced' in this segment. In a German example like *Rad*, on the other hand, no neutralization of voicing can be recognized in the final segment on any level. On the morphonemic level the value '+' will be assigned to the feature 'voiced' in the stop consonant (cf. *Rade, Rades*, etc.), and on the phonetic level this value is changed to '-' by the rule of final devoicing in German. It should be added that Halle uses zeroes also for other purposes than that of neutralization. Like Jakobson, he expresses segment redundancy and defective distribution in this way as well; i.e., in the original version of generative phonology any type of redundancy on the morphonemic level is shown by means of zero.

In *The Sound Pattern of Russian* a distinction is made between *fully specified morphonemes* (p. 32) and *incompletely specified morphonemes* (p. 37). With these terms Halle refers respectively to morphonemes in which only segmental redundancies have been extracted, and morphonemes in which both segmental and sequential redundancies have been extracted. By way of illustration Russian |brod| 'ford' can be mentioned (ibid., p. 33). In this word the post-initial morphoneme is characterized as [+ vocalic, + consonantal, - continuant, - sharped], and as the remaining feature specifications within this morphoneme can be predicted from these values, it is fully specified. On the other hand the initial morphoneme of the same word is characterized as [- vocalic, + consonantal, - compact, + low tonality, - strident, - nasal, + voiced], and as these pluses and minuses in themselves do not uniquely define one segment, this morphoneme is incompletely specified: the feature 'sharped', the value of which is sequentially, but not segmentally, predictable

---

1) In this case, unlike the Russian one, it seems likely that an extra neutralization rule converting the morphoneme |n| into the archiphoneme <N> is unnecessary. Morpheme-finally in normal Italian words only "n" occurs, and in the lexicon it is therefore possible to leave all morpheme-final nasals unspecified for place of articulation (Hans Basbøll, personal communication).

(non–compact consonants being unpalatalized before |r|), has been left unspecified. Halle now claims that his fully specified morphonemes "are the analogs of 'phonemes' and 'morphophonemes' in other linguistic theories" (ibid., p. 32) and that his incompletely specified morphonemes are analogous to the archiphonemes of the Prague school (ibid., p. 39):

> It will have been noticed that incompletely specified morphonemes are analogous to the Prague school's "archiphonemes". Although Trubetzkoy defined the latter as "the set of distinctive features shared by two phonemes", in his practice — as exemplified, for instance, in his *Das morphonologische System der russischen Sprache* — he operated with "archi–phonemes" in which there was more than one neutralized (unspecified) feature.

This parallel is somewhat forced, as will appear from the following example. In Russian the only sequence of four initial consonants is the one found in |fstr'et'i| 'to encounter, meet' (ibid., p. 57), and consequently each of these four morphonemes is incompletely specified (only the features 'vocalic' and 'consonantal' need be given '-' and '+' respectively). However, since it is not a case of suspension of minimal oppositions, no Prague phonologist would here operate with four archiconsonants. In Halle 1962 (1964, p. 341), it is pointed out once again "that the idea of representing segments in a given form by less than their normal complement of features is essentially identical with the "archiphoneme" concept ... ." The parallel between archiphonemes and incompletely specified morphonemes is here drawn in connection with a discussion of initial consonant clusters in English whose first segment can only be |s|. In such clusters |s| need only be specified for the features 'vocalic' and 'consonantal'. But once again the Prague phonologist would operate not with an initial archiconsonant, but rather with defective distribution of all consonants except *s* (see chapter 5). In spite of the considerable difference between archiphonemes and incompletely specified morphonemes the same parallel is drawn in Chomsky and Halle 1968 (p. 64), where the term *archi–segment* is used to refer to a unit which is not fully specified.

In Halle's phonological description it is the purpose of the morpheme structure rules (henceforth MS rules) to ensure "that all distinctive feature segments appearing in the representation be either fully or incompletely specified morphonemes" (1959, p. 38). In the |fstr'et'i|-example, however, the four initial consonants are incompletely specified even before the application of the MS rules, since already at this stage they fulfil the conditions which, according to Halle, must be imposed on incompletely specified morphonemes, namely, that they begin at the initial node ('vocalic/nonvocalic') in his tree diagram (p. 46), that they terminate at an intermediate node (in this case that of 'compact/noncompact'), and that all features lower in the diagram are unspecified. Frequently, however, segments will be incompletely specified only after they have gone through the MS rules. Before the application of the MS rules, the post-initial segment of a Russian word like |fčir'a| *včera* 'yesterday' is neither fully specified nor incompletely specified since it is [0 compact] and since features lower in the hierarchy than that of compactness must be given '+' or '−' in the morphonemic representation. By means of an MS rule according to which a consonant is compact after a grave non-compact consonant, [0 compact] is now changed to [+ compact] (p. 60). When all the MS rules have been applied, the post-initial morphoneme of *včera* is fully specified, and the initial morphoneme is incompletely specified since neither voicing nor palatalization is specified in this segment. The initial morphoneme thus covers [f], [f'], [v] and [v'], and not until the phonological rules are reached is the value '−' assigned to the features 'voiced' and 'sharped'. Halle now points out that those morphonemes which are incompletely specified *after* the application of the MS rules are practically identical with the archiphonemes of the Prague school (p. 39):

> As a matter of fact, the MS rules given in Chapter II insure that the (transformational) rules of Russian morphology will operate with incompletely specified morphonemes that are substantially identical with the "archi-phonemes" postulated by Trubetzkoy in the last mentioned work [Trubetzkoy 1934; NDN].

These 'post-MS' incompletely specified morphonemes are considerably more closely related to the Prague school's archiphonemes than the 'pre-MS' ones. In this case, therefore, it seems justifiable to draw the analogy. In Russian examples such as |pjan| and |brod| the initial segments are incompletely specified since the feature 'sharped' is here given the value '0', and consequently they correspond to the archiphonemes ⟨p/p'⟩ and ⟨b/b'⟩. Halle is also right in pointing out that Trubetzkoy in his description of Russian morphonology (1934) operates with archiphonemes which are not in agreement with his own definition ("the set of distinctive features shared by two phonemes"): in transcriptions such as /vjeST/ 'entrance', /leST'/ 'flattery', /iSd'oxnuT/ 'kick the bucket', 'die', and /j'eSd'iT'/ 'ride', Trubetzkoy uses the capital letter S as a symbol of the 'archiphoneme' <s/s'/z/z'>, which in the words quoted is realized as [s], [s'], [z] and [z'] respectively (cf. chapter 5).

It seems reasonable, then, to draw an analogy between archiphonemes and incompletely specified morphonemes only if by the latter one has in mind the type of units which appear after the application of the MS rules. Furthermore, the latter units obviously differ from the former in that they are archi*mor*phonemes. Finally, it should be mentioned that even disregarding these differences there are Prague school archiphonemes which are not matched by incompletely specified morphonemes. Stanley has pointed out that one of the motives for representing the morphonemes (systematic phonemes) of a given language with a branching diagram is that such a diagram "gives a way of formalizing the notion of archiphoneme" (1967, p. 408). But tree diagrams necessitate a hierarchic arrangement of features, and in his description of Russian Halle has chosen to place the feature 'voiced' higher in the hierarchy than 'sharped'. Whereas it is thus possible to capture archiphonemes such as <f/f'> (a palatalization–irrelevant segment) and <f/f'/v/v'> (a palatalization– and voicing–irrelevant segment) with Halle's tree diagram, there are no incompletely specified morphonemes in his system corresponding to Prague school archiphonemes such as <s/z> and <f/v>, where the feature voiced has been extracted. Stanley is therefore perfectly right in pointing out that "branching diagrams fail to capture the notion of archiphoneme because of a quite basic and unavoidable fact of their structure" (ibid., p. 409).

In conclusion it may be said that there is a certain fundamental similarity between Halle's incompletely specified morphonemes and the Prague school's archiphonemes in so far as both types of units are characterized by a reduced number of feature specifications. But in several important respects the two concepts differ from each other, and consequently the analogy which may be drawn between them must be regarded as relatively weak.

7.2. Richard Stanley

We have seen that in *The Sound Pattern of Russian* those neutralizations which cannot be resolved on the basis of alternations are recognized and shown in the phonological representation by assigning the value '0' to the neutralized feature. The same method is used in the lexical representation, which in Halle's descriptive system is virtually identical with the phonological representation. However, the use of zeroes in underlying representations has met with considerable opposition in generative phonology. In a short paper dating from 1963 *T.M. Lightner* raised objections to the use of blanks because of difficulties which arise when rules are applied to unspecified matrices. In an important article of 1967 by *Richard Stanley* it is pointed out that in certain cases blanks create a third value (i.e. neither plus nor minus), and this obviously conflicts with the binary principle. Such an improper use of blanks occurs, for example, if the only difference between two matrices is that one of them has a plus or minus where the other has a zero. Suppose that we have the following morpheme structure rules (cf. Stanley 1967, p. 413f; 'f' and 'g' refer to features):

$$
\begin{array}{cccc}
\text{(i)} & \text{(ii)} & \text{(iii)} & \text{(iv)} \\[4pt]
[\ \ ] & [+\,f] & [-\,f] & [-g] \\
\downarrow & \downarrow & \downarrow & \downarrow \\
[-\,g] & [+\,g] & [+\,g] & [+\,f]
\end{array}
$$

Let us further suppose that we have the following matrices, the only difference between them being that the first has a zero where the second and third have plus and minus respectively:

$$
\begin{array}{ccc}
\text{(a)} & \text{(b)} & \text{(c)} \\[4pt]
\begin{bmatrix} 0\,f \\ 0\,g \end{bmatrix} &
\begin{bmatrix} +\,f \\ 0\,g \end{bmatrix} &
\begin{bmatrix} -\,f \\ 0\,g \end{bmatrix}
\end{array}
$$

Matrix (a) will be changed by rule (i) to $\left[\begin{smallmatrix} 0\ f \\ -\ g \end{smallmatrix}\right]$ and by rule (iv) further to $\left[\begin{smallmatrix} +\ f \\ -\ g \end{smallmatrix}\right]$ (since morpheme structure rules, as opposed to phonological rules, cannot reassign values to specified features, no further changes will take place). Matrix (b) will be changed by rule (ii) to $\left[\begin{smallmatrix} +\ f \\ +\ g \end{smallmatrix}\right]$, and matrix (c) will be changed by rule (iii) to $\left[\begin{smallmatrix} -\ f \\ +\ g \end{smallmatrix}\right]$. It can be seen that '0' has been used with a third value, namely to keep matrix (a) apart from both (b) and (c). But this is a specious simplification, and it conflicts with the binary principle. Stanley therefore argues that "when rules have to recognize blanks in any way, the road is open for these blanks to function as a third value" (ibid., p. 414).

However, it is quite possible to avoid the improper use of blanks in phonological representation. For example, the analyst may observe the *well-formedness condition*, according to which the situation must not arise that a phonological representation in which there is an unspecified feature is subjected to an MS rule in whose structural description this feature appears. But Stanley considers the well-formedness condition unnecessarily complicated and also too strong, and consequently he replaces it with the *true generalization condition*. This condition is fulfilled if every MS rule expresses a true generalization about the fully specified systematic phonemic matrices of the language. If the analyst had observed this condition, the above misuse of '0' could not have taken place, for rule (ii) ($[+ f] \rightarrow [+ g]$) is not a true generalization about occurring matrices, as witnessed by the fully specified form of (a), which is $[\begin{smallmatrix} + & f \\ - & g \end{smallmatrix}]$.

It is quite possible, then, to use blanks properly. Nevertheless Stanley is of the opinion that the use of blanks in phonological representations is neither necessary nor desirable. Instead of (like Halle) having MS rules some of which — the sequence structure rules — are placed initially in the phonological component and others of which — the segment structure rules — are not kept apart from the remaining phonological rules, Stanley operates with (unordered) *MS conditions* which are placed in the *lexicon*. Such a placement is considered preferable since a sharp distinction is hereby made between MS conditions (which express redundancies on a certain level, viz. the phonological one) and phonological rules (which map one level onto another), and since it is easier and more natural to formulate phonological rules which operate on fully specified matrices. The MS conditions account for any type of segmental and sequential constraint, and they thus filter out all those sequences which are not possible morphemes in the language. But this rejection of impossible morphemes is not effected by replacing zeroes in lexical matrices with pluses and minuses, for even lexical representations should, according to Stanley, be fully specified. To be sure this approach implies that we lose the evaluation measure which tells us that the best set of MS conditions is "the shortest set ... that allows us to leave the greatest number of blanks in dictionary matrices" (ibid., p. 434). It is possible, however, to define an alternative evaluation measure which does not count zeroes in lexical matrices. According to this alternative measure an MS condition should be included in the grammar if its 'statement cost' is less than its 'generality index' (ibid., p. 435).[2] By disallowing blanks in lexical representations as well, a number of arbitrary decisions can be avoided. For example, if in a given environment the value [+ f] implies the value [+ g] and the value [+ g] implies the value [+ f], then the choice between writing [+̥ f/g] or writing [0̥ f/g] in the lexical representation is arbitrary.

In Halle's original version of generative phonology there was still room for the notions of neutralization and archi(mor)phoneme on the systematic phonemic level. In the type of phonological description proposed by Stanley, however, incompletely specified segments are nowhere to be found, and in this theory archiphonemes have thus disappeared completely. On the other hand those neutralizations which remain in force on the systematic phonemic level, i.e. which are not resoluble on the basis of alternations, are expressed by means of MS conditions, but as in the theories of Jakobson and Halle they are not kept apart from other types of redundancy. As an example of an MS condition Stanley adduces the following 'if–then' condition (ibid., p. 426), which states that the first of two initial true consonants in English is [s] and that the second is a stop ([p, t, k, m, n]):

$$
\text{I} \quad (C) \quad + \quad [\,+ \text{Consonantal}\,] \quad
\begin{bmatrix} + \text{Consonantal} \\ - \text{Vocalic} \end{bmatrix}
$$

$$\downarrow$$

$$
\text{T} \quad (C) \quad
\begin{bmatrix} - \text{Vocalic} \\ - \text{Grave} \\ - \text{Compact} \\ + \text{Continuant} \end{bmatrix}
\quad [\,- \text{Continuant}\,]
$$

This redundancy condition, whose function is to account for a sequential constraint in fully specified morphemes, not to fill in blanks, would be regarded by the Prague phonologists and by Jakobson as a rule about defective distribution (cf. chapter 5). But neutralization in the narrow sense of the word will also be expressed with MS conditions of this type in Stanley's theory.

Like Halle, Stanley operates with two levels of representation only, and consequently he cannot recognize those traditional phonemic neutralizations which do not remain in force on the systematic phonemic level, e.g. the one between /t/ and /d/ in German *Rad*.

---

2) "Suppose we have a language L with the set SP of systematic phonemic matrices and with a proposed MS condition C. Define the GENERALITY INDEX of C with respect to SP as the sum of the weights of C with respect to each member of SP. Also, define the STATEMENT COST of C as the number of feature values needed to state C" (Stanley 1967, p. 435).

However, he points out in his paper that there are possibly rules which state redundancies at the systematic *phonetic* level and that the formulation of such rules might enable the analyst "to capture something resembling a phonemic system" (ibid., p. 397). But rules of this type are not contained in Stanley's theory; due to the complexity and depth of ordering of the phonological rules they would, in his opinion, be very difficult to construct (ibid., p. 405).

7.3. The Sound Pattern of English

The reader of this book — the principal work about generative phonology — cannot help noticing that its authors are very uncertain as to where the redundancy rules are to be placed and, accordingly, as to which levels are to be considered imcompletely specified and which fully specified. At the beginning of the book the redundancy rules are placed in the phonological component (as they were in Halle 1959). This implies that phonological representation is incompletely specified, that irresoluble neutralizations, like any other kind of redundancy, are expressed by means of zeroes in the phonological matrices, and that archi(mor)phonemes are recognized:[3] "Phonological matrices typically consist of archi–segments. Thus, an important difference between phonological and phonetic matrices is that the latter are fully specified while the former are not" (Chomsky and Halle 1968, p. 166). In Chomsky and Halle's informal alphabetical notation archi–segments are symbolized with capital letters; for example, one finds phonological forms with archi–vowels and archi–nasals such as /siNg#ly/ *singly* and /king#lVt/ *kinglet* (ibid., p. 85). Subsequently, however, it is stated that as a matter of fact ("strictly speaking", "really", "actually") the redundancy rules do not belong in the phonological component but in the readjustment component. As a result of this shift the phonological representation becomes fully specified, and redundancy can now be shown in the lexical representation only. There is still room for irresoluble neutralizations and archi–segments, but they can no longer be expressed in the phonological forms. Later on in the book (p. 382ff) Chomsky and Halle accept Stanley's proposal (1967) and put forward a third solution. The redundancy rules are now moved from the readjust-

---

3) Chomsky and Halle use the term *archi–segment*, which refers to a partly specified segment and corresponds to "incompletely specified morphoneme" in Halle 1959.

ment component to the lexicon and are made unordered. Unlike Stanley, however, Chomsky and Halle still consider the lexical representation incompletely specified, and they are therefore able to retain an evaluation measure which consists in counting zeroes ("we can require that each redundancy condition result in a saving of features in the lexical representation that is larger than the number of features required to state the condition itself", ibid., p. 389). According to this method irresoluble neutralizations are then still shown in the lexical representation, and there is still room for archi(mor)phonemes.

This way of tackling the problem, however, is regarded as an interim solution, and in the final chapter a fourth, and this time very radical, revision is made. Instead of operating with '+', '-', and '0' in lexical matrices, Chomsky and Halle adopt the Prague theory of (naturally) marked and unmarked feature values and accordingly now assign the letter *u* (unmarked) to any feature whose value is universally predictable and the letter *m* (marked) to any feature whose value is the opposite of the one which is to be expected. To a certain extent, moreover, Chomsky and Halle use pluses and minuses, which like *m*'s, and in contrast to *u*'s, contribute to complexity, but there are no zeroes. In the lexical representation of an English word like *stun* practically all features are unmarked. It is only necessary to state that the post–initial segment is [m vocalic, + coronal], that the pre-final segment is [+ back], that the final segment is [m nasal], and that all four segments are [m segment].[4] That the only consonant which may occur initially before a consonant is /s/, is no longer an English redundancy rule but a distributional fact which is universally to be expected. The same goes for the voicing neutralization in the stop consonant. Similarly, Chomsky and Halle no longer operate with an archi-nasal in English, but instead with an unmarked nasal consonant, which through a marking convention is specified as /n/, and which by late phonological rules is changed to [m], [n], and [ŋ] in words like *lamp, wind, sink*. The consequence of operating with fully specified lexical matrices and universal marking conventions is that archiphonemes are nowhere to be found and that a large number of (irresoluble) neutralizations are omitted from the phonological description.

---

4) The appearance of /s/ initially in this word results from a questionable marking convention according to which [+ continuant] is considered unmarked before a consonant and after a boundary, i.e. in the environment +__C (Hans Basbøll, personal communication).

7.4. C.E. Cairns

Chomsky and Halle's theory of M/U representation of lexical items
has in principle been endorsed by *P.M. Postal* (1968); but Postal adds
that the establishment of universal marking conventions is a "vast
undertaking" and that our knowledge about these matters is still
very limited. In his opinion one of the advantages of the M/U
theory is that a large number of language specific morpheme structure rules can now be dispensed with (cf. the discussion of *stun* in
7.3.):

> One of the crucial additional contributions made by this
> new theory is that it serves to eliminate a large proportion
> of previously required morpheme structure rules. Each
> such rule in a language was, in effect, a representation of
> one or more neutralizations of one kind or another. But in
> the new theory neutralizations will be treated by U markings
> in the dictionary and these will be converted to 'normal'
> values by completely universal rules (Postal 1968, p. 172).

But even if |+ st|, for example, is more 'natural' (predictable) than
|+ ʃt| and |+ sd| and may therefore be analysed as [U anterior, U
high] (first segment) and [U voiced] (second segment), it ought to
appear from a description of English, for instance, that [M anterior,
M high] (first segment) and [M voiced] (second segment) are ruled
out, i.e. that |+ ʃt| and |+ sd| are impossible in this language. An at-
tempt at solving this problem has been made by *C.E. Cairns* in an
important paper dating from 1969. Like Postal, Cairns accepts the
theory of lexical M/U representation, but in order to exclude the
impossible (morphonemic) sequences he operates with neutralization rules (N-rules) which place constraints on the distribution of
M's in the lexicon and which thus account for any type of lexical
redundancy. ("An N-rule specifies that a particular feature or set
of features may not have the marked value in given environments",
Cairns 1969, p. 866.)[5] On the basis of certain universal implications
concerning initial consonant clusters, which have been demonstrated
by Greenberg, Cairns sets up a number of universal and hierarchically
ordered neutralization rules. From these rules each language makes a

---

5) According to Cairns the term 'neutralization' covers more than the loss
of one feature's relevance: "we use the term neutralization to cover all
cases of restrictions on the appearance of phoneme classes in certain environments" (Cairns 1969, p. 864).

selection, and if it does not possess a given N-rule it does not possess the preceding rules either. By way of illustration the following neutralization rule may be mentioned:

(N 2)   N (nas)   /   + [M cns] _____

This rule states that the nasality feature is neutralized, i.e. may only assume its unmarked value (which according to the universal marking conventions is '-'), if a preceding morpheme initial segment is marked with respect to the feature 'consonantal', i.e. is [+ cns]. A language which possesses this neutralization rule therefore permits the sequence + CLV (where C = voiceless obstruent, L = liquid, V = vowel) but not the sequence + CNV (where N = nasal consonant). Applying this method to the example discussed in 7.3 (*stun*), we must establish a neutralization rule which is used in English and which blocks the clusters |+ ʃt| and |+ sd|. Cairns furthermore puts forward the hypothesis that the explanation of the universal redundancy rules must be sought for in articulatory and perceptual limitations in the speaker-hearer. There exists an archetypal phonetic pattern, and each M represents "either a complication in the program for driving the vocal tract, or some attenuation of perceptual distinctions" (ibid., p. 878). For example, the neutralization rule which excludes + CcV (where c = voiced obstruent) but not + CCV and + ccV must be related to the physiological fact that the first cluster requires three different glottal states (involved in the pronunciation of voiceless obstruents, voiced obstruents, and vowels), whereas the second and third clusters require only two different glottal states. Cairns furthermore theorizes that a child possesses all the universal N-rules from birth, and that part of the acquisition of a particular language consists in abandoning some of these and in introducing marked feature values in lexical matrices.

Although neutralization rules have thus been built into the M/U version of generative phonology, a number of problems remain to be solved. Due to the placing of the neutralization rules in the lexicon, those neutralizations which have the word, or higher units, as their domain are not taken into consideration.[6] According to Cairns

_____

6) One problem connected with Cairns's theory is that his N-rules apply on an abstract level whereas his data (taken from Greenberg) derive from a relatively concrete level. Consequently, it would probably be more reasonable to regard the N-rules as concrete, in which case they would have the word (or higher units) as their domain (Hans Basbøll, personal communication).

these neutralizations may possibly be handled by means of Chomsky and Halle's 'linking conventions'. We are not told explicitly how this is to be done, but the following example from Russian may probably serve to illustrate this method. In the morpheme *včera* [fčira] 'yesterday' the initial segment will be [U voiced], and by a marking convention it will be specified as [- voiced]. Furthermore, there will be an N-rule (placed in the lexicon) which excludes [M voiced] in this position, i.e. which rules out the sequence |+ vč|. In the di-morphemic word *rybka* [rɨpka] 'little fish' the labial will be [M voiced] (cf. *ryba* [rɨba] 'fish'); by a marking convention it will be specified as [+ voiced], and by a phonological rule it will be changed further to [- voiced]. By a linking convention the above N-rule could now be extended and permitted to apply at word level, i.e. it could be included among the phonological rules, thereby excluding the sequence /b + k/. Another problem is posed by those neutralizations in which neither the marked nor the unmarked feature value occurs, but rather a third value (recall, for example, Russian <a/o>, which in unstressed, non-pretonic syllables is manifested as [ə], not as [a]). In cases like these, Cairns considers the possibility of operating with the feature value 'N' in addition to M and U. He does not, however, discuss the problem of oscillating manifestation, as exemplified by the realization of <t/d> as [t] or [d] in a Danish word like *hat* 'hat'. It is an open question, then, how neutralizations which are not manifested by the unmarked feature value should be dealt with. Finally, it should be mentioned that neutralization in its original narrow sense is not kept apart from other types of redundancy.

7.5. S.A. Schane

A significant contribution to the discussion of the concept of neutralization in generative phonology has been given by S.A. Schane (1968) in a paper dealing with the problem of non-unique phonological representations. Like the generative phonologists mentioned above Schane operates with two levels only — that of underlying representations and that of phonetic representations — and consequently resoluble neutralizations are not recognized in his phonological description. For example, he interprets German *bunt* and *Bund* as respectively |bunt| and |bund|. In the morpheme *und*, which unlike *bunt* and *Bund* is incapable of alternation, Schane considers the possibility of interpreting the dental stop as [0 voiced], i.e. of recognizing neutralization here and regarding the final segment as a voicing-irrelevant dental occlusive archi(mor)phoneme. According to the German rule of word-final devoicing of non-nasal consonants, [- voiced], [+ voiced], [0 voiced] in respectively *bunt, Bund, und* will then be changed to [- voiced]. Such a procedure is quite possible here, but Schane points out that there are other cases where a zero-solution is not feasible. In French the [ã] of *paysan* [peizã] and the [ã] of *genre* [ʒãr] must be interpreted as respectively |an| and |en| because of alternating forms like *paysanne* [peizan] and *générique* [ʒenerik] (Schane analyses any nasal vowel in French as an oral vowel followed by a nasal consonant). Similarly, the [ɛ̃] of *fin* [fɛ̃] and the [ɛ̃] of *américain* [amerikɛ̃] must be interpreted as respectively |in| and |ɛn| because of alternants like *fine* [fin] and *américaine* [amerikɛn]. However, in a word like *vendre* [vãdr], which like German *und* is incapable of alternation, we have no way of knowing whether the nasal vowel should be analysed as |an| or |en|. In this case, moreover, a zero solution is impossible, for the 'archiphoneme' <e/a> is characterized by the feature specifications [- diffuse, - flat, 0 grave, 0 compact], and it thus includes |ɛ| as well. Since this is unacceptable, the analyst has to choose between |vandr| and |vendr|, and this choice is arbitrary:[7]

> In other words, there is no archiphoneme (that is, no partially specified segment) which would include both |en| and |an| to the exclusion of |ɛn|. Similarly, there is no partially specified segment which would include both |in| and |ɛn| to the exclusion of |en|. Hence, in the case of *vendre* one is forced to make a choice between |an| and |en|, the choice being completely arbitrary. Within the framework of generative phonology, *vendre* thus requires a non-unique phonological representation (Schane 1968, p. 714).

It is not always possible, then, to account for neutralization by means of zeroes in the phonological representation, and consequently the analyst must search for another line of approach. Like Chomsky, Halle, Postal and Cairns, Schane turns his attention to marked-

---

7) It is a serious weakness in Schane's example that the alternation with [en] (*genre-générique*) is limited to learned words, which cannot be connected with native words by acceptable rules anyway (Hans Basbøll, personal communication). Consequently, [ã]'s possibility of alternating with [en] may safely be ignored, and in this way the problem disappears.

ness. Among related segments which differ from each other as regards markedness, the unmarked segment is the most frequent one, the one which is acquired first by children, the one found in most languages, and the one which usually occurs in positions of neutralization. Since |a| is less marked than |e|, we may non-arbitrarily select |vandr| as the form underlying French [vãdr]. Furthermore, the final segment of German *und* may now be interpreted as |t|, rather than as $<t/d>$, since this segment is unmarked with respect to voicing. The consequence of this approach — a fully specified underlying M/U notation and a fully specified phonetic surface notation — has already been pointed out: the concept of neutralization, the importance of which was greatly reduced with the advent of Halle's 1959-theory, is on its way out of generative phonology.

It should be pointed out that German *und* and French *vendre* are not completely analogous examples. Only the former word exemplifies neutralization in the Praguian and Jakobsonean sense of the word, since one feature only ('voiced') has here lost its relevance. In *vendre*, on the other hand, two features are irrelevant ('grave', 'compact'), and in contradistinction to German |t| : |d|, French |e| : |a| is not a minimal opposition; consequently $<e/a>$ is not an archiphoneme in the traditional sense of the word. In those cases where there is neutralization in the narrow sense (= contextually determined loss of the relevance of one feature), a zero-solution like the one considered by Schane raises no problems, for archiphonemes established in this way can never intersect with any other phonemes, and consequently the analyst will not be forced into making arbitrary decisions. It would be possible to argue, therefore, that the problem of non-unique representation in generative phonology could be solved by means of a zero-notation in cases like German *und*, where one feature only is neutralized, and by means of an M/U notation in cases like *vendre*, where more features than one have lost their relevance. Like other generativists, however, Schane is not prepared to distinguish between two types of sequence redundancy (cf. his definition of the archiphoneme as a "partially specified segment").

7.6. M. Shibatani and J. Crothers

In an article dating from 1972 Shibatani and Crothers advance the view that to a certain extent — more precisely in those cases where the choice between '+' and '−' is arbitrary — it is permissible to use blanks for expressing redundancies in lexical representations. In the first place, the abuse of blanks pointed out by Lightner and Stanley may be avoided by observing the well-formedness condition. To be sure Stanley and Chomsky/Halle are not wrong in claiming that this condition is extremely complex, but Shibatani and Crothers argue that since it is going to be difficult to control the well-formedness of a grammar in any case this objection is hardly justified. As an example of a lexical form which ought to contain blanks they mention the first person affix in Tereno, which is realized as a nasal homorganic with a following consonant, but drops out before a vowel or glide or word boundary, leaving nasality in the preceding vowel. In this case the choice between |m|, |n|, and |ŋ| in the underlying form is arbitrary. An analogous example is found in Turkish, where in suffixes a high vowel is realized as [i], [ü], [u], or [ɨ] and a low vowel as [a] or [e], and where the occurrence of these vowels is entirely determined by the preceding vowels. In the case of these harmonizing vowels the choice of underlying form is also in part arbitrary.

Such problems cannot be solved by resorting to the concept of markedness. According to Chomsky and Halle the unmarked nasal consonant is |n|, but recent work by Matthew Chen suggests that |ŋ| is the least marked nasal in morpheme final position. Shibatani and Crothers also mention that in Japanese a morpheme final nasal is homorganic with a following consonant but is realized as [ŋ] before vowels and in word final position, and that in this case the underlying form must be |ŋ|. In Turkish, similarly, one cannot postulate a single unmarked high vowel in the suffix syllable, for according to Chomsky and Halle's marking conventions |i| and |u| have the same degree of complexity.

Since problems like these cannot be solved (with our present limited knowledge) on the basis of markedness, Shibatani and Crothers cannot advocate an M/U type of lexical representation. Instead they adopt Stanley's model, where lexical matrices contain pluses and minuses and where there are MS conditions that express true generalizations about fully specified representations, but with one important modification: in examples of the above type they accept blanks:

> (1) lexical entries are specified for all features in so far as those features can be determined, with MS conditions expressing whatever redundancies there are; (2) but if there is no way to determine from the phonetic alternants of a form the basic value of some feature, it is acceptable, in

fact desirable, to leave the feature blank (Shibatani and Crothers 1972, p. 75).

This proposal marks a partial return to Halle's model (1959), where irresoluble neutralizations are symbolized with zeroes in underlying representations. However, blanks are not used to nearly the same extent as in Halle's original theory. If neither a '+' or '–' interpretation nor a '0' interpretation leads to arbitrary decisions, Shibatani and Crothers prefer the former interpretation. In those cases, furthermore, where it is not clear which of two features should be considered distinctive (e.g. in the case of backness vs. rounding in vowels in languages with the standard system *i, e, a, u, o*), they follow Stanley and specify the values of both features. Here one should not use blanks and make an arbitrary choice between distinctive and redundant: "It remains true that in many instances of redundancy the use of blank features is not desirable, due to the arbitrariness in the choice of redundant and non-redundant features. The suggestion here is that blanks be avoided generally, but that there is no real objection to their use in certain well-defined situations" (ibid., p. 71).

7.7. *Jørgen Rischel*

In his *Topics in West Greenlandic Phonology* (1974) Jørgen Rischel arrives at basically the same conclusion as Shibatani and Crothers (but independently of them), namely that it is sometimes necessary to recognize ambiguously specified (ambivalent) morphophonemes. In a large number of cases it is possible to operate with unambiguously specified morphophonemes and set up unidirectional replacement rules. In Italian, for example, |(i)n| may be selected as the basic alternant in the negative prefix *in-, im-*, for although the place of articulation of the nasal is determined automatically by a following consonant, e.g. in *impossibile, insolito, incolto*, |n| always occurs before vowels, e.g. in *inelegante* (my example, not Rischel's).[8] But in those cases where there is insufficient evidence for regarding one alternant as "basic" and the other(s) as "derived" this solution cannot be adopted. For example, most stops and continuants in West Greenlandic may be involved in phonologically conditioned

---

8) As an example of this type Rischel mentions the West Greenlandic alternation /u/ ∼ /i/, which is represented as |u| at the underlying level and converted into /i/ by a unidirectional replacement rule.

alternation, and here there is no valid evaluation measure for deciding between 'strengthening' and 'weakening' rules; i.e. there is no decisive synchronic evidence for regarding one group of obstruents as basic and the other as derived. In examples like /sinik+kalu^{w}a^{r}ppuq/ 'he sleeps, it is true' and /matu+galu^{w}a^{r}ppuq/ 'it is closed, it is true', where the occurrence of the stop /k/ and of the continuant /g/ is determined by the preceding segment (consonant versus vowel), Rischel therefore recognizes an ambiguous morphophoneme initially in the suffix /kalu^{w}aCq/ ~/galu^{w}aCq/.

In contradistinction to Shibatani and Crothers, Rischel does not in such cases operate with blanks, which, because they are distinct from pluses and minuses, raise problems for the application of phonological rules.[9] Instead he proposes a positive specification of plus and minus simultaneously; i.e. he operates with ambivalent segments where ± is a marker of alternating status. In the suffix mentioned above the initial segment is thus represented as [± continuant]. Unless there are statements to the contrary, rules apply maximally, i.e. a rule which applies to persistent stops (or persistent continuants) also applies to segments which are [± continuant]. Plus–minus notations are disambiguated by rules. In some cases the rule that spells out ± is not crucially ordered with respect to other rules, but in other cases it must precede certain rules. For example, the disambiguation in West Greenlandic of [± high] "must precede affrication of /t/, since affrication occurs both in front of invariant and alternating /i/ but not when the latter is eventually specified as /a/ : /kiguȼ+ga/ 'my tooth' versus /kiguta+a/ 'his tooth' " (p. 347).

When a segment alternates with zero it may also be necessary to recognize ambivalent morphophonemes. Frequently it is possible to set up unidirectional rules of deletion or insertion, but sometimes there is insufficient evidence for selecting a segmental alternant as basic and a zero alternant as derived or *vice versa*; i.e. there is no criterion for choosing either a deletion rule or an insertion rule rather than the opposite. In such cases Rischel operates with latent morphophonemes, e.g. in /igala(ṣ)aq/ 'window', and these must also be disambiguated by rules.

---

9) Rischel also rejects underlying representations in the form of marked and unmarked feature values: "In its present, highly tentative shape marking theory has met with much scepticism ... , which I fully share. The concept of "universal" is used both too loosely and too ambitiously, and the conventions involved are of widely different kinds" (p. 343).

Rischel's solution is clearly a costly one. He argues, however, that it has the advantage of stating only how much determinacy there is in the pattern, nothing more. The phonological description is not 'simplified' by postulating plus or minus in genuine cases of indeterminacy, for as the choice of either value is in these cases arbitrary such a simplification would be spurious. Furthermore, he points out, this indeterminacy might well turn out to be real; i.e. the status of alternations like West Greenlandic /i/ ∼/a/ and /k/ ∼/g/ in language change, language acquisition, etc. may be different from that of alternations like West Greenlandic /i/ ∼ /u/ which can be dealt with by means of unidirectional rules. Within the framework of current generative phonology Rischel's conception of ambivalence must be said to be well-founded and perfectly sensible.

7.8. *Joan B. Hooper*

In a 1974 article by Joan B. Hooper, yet another aspect of Halle's 1959 model (cf. 7.6) is revived. Hooper works within the framework of Stampe's and Vennemann's theories of *natural generative phonology*, but unlike these phonologists, both of whom demand fully specified underlying representations, she wishes to reintroduce the archi-segment ("NGP reformulated to allow archi-segmental lexical representation", Hooper 1974, p. 27). In Hooper's model the lexical representation of a non-alternating morpheme is identical to its surface form, apart from the fact that all naturally derivable redundant features have been removed. The lexical representation of an alternating morpheme consists of segments which actually occur in one or more of the surface allomorphs, and also in this case all naturally derivable redundant features have been removed. By 'naturally derivable' is understood 'derivable by unordered, phonetically motivated rules'; and by 'phonetically motivated rules' is meant rules which may be formulated in purely phonetic terms, i.e. which operate exclusively with phonological features, syllable boundaries, and pauses (in contradistinction to such rules, morpho-syntactically motivated rules require non-phonetic information). In Hooper's model a non-alternating morpheme like English *stun* will thus consist of four archi-segments: in the initial segment all features will be unspecified except 'consonantal'; in the post-initial segment a number of features will be unspecified, among these 'voiced'; and in the last two segments there will also be a number of blanks. An alternating morpheme such as American English *write* (cf. *writer*,

writing pronounced with an intervocalic voiced flap) will also consist of archi-segments: in the initial segment all features except 'consonantal', 'vocalic', 'anterior' are unspecified, and in the remaining
segments there are also a number of blanks, although not in the case
of 'voiced' in the *t*-segment, which in this word must be specified as
'–' (unlike the stop segment of *stun*). Hooper's rules are not used
until the morphemes have been inserted into syntactic surface structures and combined into words, and all rules apply at this point. In
conformity with Stampe's and Venneman's theories, she does not
keep redundancy rules apart from other phonological rules; on the
other hand, a fundamental distinction is made between phonetically
motivated rules and rules that have a morpho-syntactic motivation.[10]
At this point, then, both morphophonemic rules (which on the basis
of grammatical information convert, for example, |k| to [s] is an
English word like *electricity*) and phonological rules apply. One of
the functions of the latter rules is to fill in blanks, i.e. to insert
pluses and minuses whenever features values are segmentally or sequentially redundant, as in the case of English *stun, latter, ladder*
(where the opposition between 'voiced' and 'voiceless' is neutralized in the stop consonant). The other function of the phonological
rules is to change feature values, e.g. in the stop segment of *writer,
writing* (the flapping rule in American English is thus capable both
of filling in a blank and of changing a feature value). Hooper accepts
Vennemann's 'no ordering condition'; i.e. her rules are not ordered
(as they are in the standard version of generative phonology), but
are random sequential. In defense of amalgamating redundancy rules
and phonological rules she argues that so far strong evidence for
keeping them apart has not been adduced, and she concludes a
lengthy discussion of this problem in the following way (ibid., p. 9):

> Until and unless strong evidence to the contrary is adduced,
> we must conclude that there is no significant difference
> between types of phonetically motivated rules, and that
> divisions of rules into those that change feature values and
> those that do not, and those that apply within morpheme
> boundaries and those that apply across them, are accidental,
> not systematic divisions.

---

10) It seems unfortunate to speak of morpho-syntactically vs. phonetically
   motivated rules if by this one understands simply rules in which reference
   is or is not made to non-phonological features (Hans Basbøll, personal
   communication).

In Hooper's theory sequence structure rules have the syllable as their domain, and she adduces a number of weighty arguments in support of this choice (for instance, it is simpler to account for the distribution of segments in relation to the syllable than to the morpheme, due to the fact that morphemes are often polysyllabic). The rule which replaces [0 voiced] with [- voiced] in the syllable-final segment of an English word like *mist* will thus also change [+ voiced] into [- voiced] in the syllable-final segment of *missed*.

The advantage of reintroducing archi-segments in the underlying representation is that their "indeterminacy obviates the problem of making arbitrary choices in positions of neutralization" (ibid., p. 21). To this Hooper adds that the objections which have been raised against archi-segments can be refuted. In the first place there can be no abuse of blanks if no distinction is made between redundancy rules and phonological rules (i.e. if the rules are permitted both to fill in blanks and to reassign values) and if the rules apply in random sequential order. In Stanley's example (cf. 7.2) the matrix $\begin{bmatrix} 0 & f \\ 0 & g \end{bmatrix}$ was replaced by $\begin{bmatrix} + & f \\ - & g \end{bmatrix}$ according to rules (i) and (iv) and was thus incorrectly kept apart from both $\begin{bmatrix} 0 & f \\ 0 & g \end{bmatrix}$ and $\begin{bmatrix} \bar{0} & f \\ 0 & g \end{bmatrix}$. But $\begin{bmatrix} + & f \\ - & g \end{bmatrix}$ would in Hooper's type of description be changed further by rule (ii) to $\begin{bmatrix} \ddagger & f \\ & g \end{bmatrix}$, and as the realization of the matrix $\begin{bmatrix} 0 & f \\ 0 & g \end{bmatrix}$ hereby becomes identical with the realization of the matrix $\begin{bmatrix} + & f \\ 0 & g \end{bmatrix}$, blanks are no longer used improperly. Hooper accepts the use of blanks also in those cases where it seems arbitrary which of two features one should regard as distinctive and which as redundant (as in the case of backness vs. rounding in vowels in languages with the standard system *i, e, a, o, u*). The reason why we find it difficult to make a decision in such cases is that we still know too little ("I believe that the question of which of two features is redundant is an empirical question that may be answered with increased knowledge about perception and production", ibid., p. 19). Finally, Hooper is not convinced by some objections against archiphonemes which Stampe has raised in his doctoral dissertation (1973) and which are of a more substantial type. In this dissertation Stampe claims (p. 36f) that it is not the 'archiphoneme' <p/b> which occurs after /s/ in an English word like *spin* but the phoneme /p/ instead:

> But there is abundant evidence that the *p*'s of *spin* and *pin* are phonologically identical, as opposed to the *b* of *bin*, and that in general stops after /s/ are phonologically voiceless. There is the persistent orthographic tradition in Eng-

lish (and comparable languages) of writing *p t k* rather than
b d g after *s*. There are the spontaneous spellings of children
with little knowledge of English orthography - - WISPRT
whispered, SCICHTAP *Scotch tape*, MOSTR *monster*,
SKEEIG *skiing*, STARTID *started* (Read 1971). There are
the voiceless stops which appear when /s/ is transposed in
slips of the tongue, e.g. [hwipsr̩] (not [hwibsr̩]) for *whisper*
(Fromkin 1971). There is the fact that intensive /s/ in
crunch/scrunch,   trample/strample,   mash/smash, etc.,
. . . is never added to words with voiced stops: *bash* but not
spash, grouch but not *scrouch*, etc.

Hooper is not convinced by these arguments. In the first place, orthography is largely conventional and possibly does not reflect underlying
forms. Therefore it should perhaps not be used as phonological
evidence; but if it is taken into consideration after all, it is worth
remembering that in Middle and Early Modern Irish, where there is
also neutralization after /s/, the spellings *sb, sd, sg* are used rather
than *sp, st, sk*, a convention which survives in Scots Gaelic, cf. *sdair*
'history'. Secondly, children's spellings cannot be regarded as reliable
evidence either, since such spellings are strongly influenced by phonetics. Finally, it should be remembered that there are languages (in
which the opposition of voicing is suspended after *s*), where an
intensive /s/ is added to words beginning in /b d g/, cf. Scots Gaelic
where *beach* is in this way changed to *sbeach* 'wasp'. In continuation
of Hooper's criticism the following objections may be raised to
Stampe's arguments: (1) in Old High German manuscripts the
spellings *sb, sd, sg, (fd, hd)* are not infrequently found in addition to
the normal spellings *sp, st, sk, (ft, ht)* (cf. Davidsen–Nielsen 1976,
p. 49). (2) Slips of the tongue do not, in fact, weaken the theory of
archiphonemes; they strengthen it. In Davidsen–Nielsen 1975 (pp.
15ff) it is shown that when slips of the tongue affect English (as
well as German and Danish) *sp, st, sk* in such a way that the stop
consonants move out of the position of neutralization and are thereby disambiguated, these stops surface sometimes as [b d g] and
sometimes as [p t k]. If the interfering segment (i.e. the segment
which attracts the stop or is interchanged with it) is voiced, [b d g]
emerge, and if it is voiceless, [p t k] emerge. For example, English
words like *speedometer* and *spittoon* will characteristically be
changed by a slip of the tongue to [bɪ'stɒmɪtə] and [pɪ'stu:n]. The
example quoted by Stampe, where the stop consonant occurs in an

obstruent cluster also after the speech error, can hardly be regarded as a genuine case of disambiguation (even if the syllable boundary is positioned between the stop and the sibilant, i.e. *whip-ser*, it is difficult to hear whether it is a [p] or a [b] which is pronounced). (3) In Danish, where the opposition between /p t k/ and /b d g/ is also suspended after /s/, children who are in the process of learning to write frequently use the misspellings *sb, sd, sg*. It must therefore be concluded that Stampe has not in fact adduced 'abundant evidence' in favour of the interpretation /sp (st sk)/, but rather that none of his arguments against the archiphoneme are convincing.

Hooper's underlying representations are set up according to practically the same principles as the ones advanced in Halle's *The Sound Pattern of Russian*, so in this respect one may almost speak of *status quo ante* in generative phonology. It is only irresoluble neutralization which is recognized and expressed by means of '0', and neutralization is not kept apart from other types of redundancy on the morphonemic level. On the other hand Hooper's rules are widely different from Halle's original ones. Like other adherents of natural generative phonology she attaches great importance to the construction of a theory which reflects the act of speech production, and like Vennemann she regards the phonetic level as the only level which has psychological reality. "The model I have proposed also reflects the reality of the phonetic level, since the archi-segmental underlying forms are completely meaningless without the rules that apply to them" (ibid., p. 25). It is not the underlying representation, then, which is assumed to reflect the speaker-hearer's linguistic capabilities, but the phonetic representation and the rules. The neural commands to the vocal organs are governed by rules, and as these rules also apply to nonsense words, they must, according to Hooper, apply outside the lexicon.

7.9. S. Bolozky

In a short paper published in 1975 S. Bolozky discusses Hooper's proposal (as well as a similar proposal made by G. Hudson, 1974) to reintroduce archi-segments in lexical representation. In Bolozky's opinion such a solution is connected with serious difficulties. If the Russian word for 'bread' is interpreted as /xleB/, we can easily and automatically derive [- voiced] in the stop segment of [xlep] by the rule of final devoicing. But given /xleB/ how is it possible to arrive at the [+ voiced] specification for alternants like [xleba] 'bread, gen. sing.'?

131

Since voicing is here unpredictable this seems to constitute a very difficult 'otherwise' problem. Bolozky discusses some alternative possibilities of solving it, but concludes that each of them is unsatisfactory.

I believe that Bolozky has misunderstood Hooper and that Hooper would interpret [xlep] not as /xleB/ but as /xleb/, i.e. she would specify the final segment of this morpheme as [+ voiced]. She states (1974, p. 23) that the "lexical representations of alternating morphemes consist of non-redundant representations of segments actually occurring in one or more surface allomorphs (where ... only naturally derivable redundancies are removed)." This implies that she is free to choose (the non-redundant feature specification of) /xleb/ as the form which underlies the alternants [xlep] and [xleb(a)]. Now Hooper's analysis of the words *write, writer, writing* in American English seems to show that this is indeed what she would do. In *writer, writing* the voicing opposition is (in some dialects) suspended in the alveolar stop, i.e. these words are pronounced in the same way as *rider, riding*, and the value of voicing can here be automatically derived by the English flapping rule. Nevertheless Hooper operates with /t/ in these words and not /T/, i.e. she interprets the stop segment as [- voiced]: "the English flapping rule will fill in the blank value for voice in *ladder* and *latter*, and it will change the value of voice in the final consonant of *write* when a suffix such as -*er* or -*ing* is added to this verb" (Hooper 1974, p. 21). It will be seen that the Russian example and the English example are analogous. Since voicelessness is distinctive and unpredictable in English [raɪt], the stop segment must be interpreted on the underlying level as [- voiced], and by the flapping rule this value is changed to [+ voiced] in [raɪɾə̆, raɪɾɪŋ]. Similarly, since voice is distinctive and unpredictable in Russian [xleba], the stop segment must be analysed as [+ voiced] in the underlying representation, and by the rule of final devoicing this value is changed to [- voiced] in [xlep]. It seems, then, that Bolozky's criticism of Hooper is here based on a misinterpretation and can be dismissed as irrelevant.[11]

11) At one point in her article (p. 23) Hooper sets up an underlying form which may possibly have induced Bolozky to raise his 'otherwise' objection: in Andalusian Spanish [trẽŋ] ~ [trẹnẹ] 'train(s)' and [melõŋ]~ [mẹlọnẹ] 'melon(s)' she analyses the allomorphs as /treN/, /meloN/. Now if [n] could not be predicted in the plural form of nouns ending in a nasal the way that [ŋ] can be predicted finally, i.e. if there were examples of final [ŋ] alternating with, say, intervocalic [m], Hooper's analysis would indeed be highly problematic. As a matter of fact, however, [n] can be
cont.

9⁺

Besides drawing attention to the above-mentioned 'otherwise' difficulty Bolozky adduces three arguments which are meant to show that the archi-segment is not always supported empirically.

1) He refers to an experiment which he carried out with Russian informants and which is claimed to indicate that there can be no archisegments underlying morpheme-final pre-pausal obstruents in Russian.

> One can show, for instance, that native speakers of Russian consistently interpret allomorphs containing morpheme-final devoiced obstruents as if they ended in voiced ones. I read aloud nonsense 'allomorphs' with morpheme-final voiced obstruents before vowel-initial suffixes, paired with their alternants with voiceless obstruents before a pause (nonsense 'meanings' were suggested for each item) and asked my Russian informants to orally repeat and then write down what they heard. In about ninety per cent of the cases, speakers transcribed both 'allomorphs' with an identical *voiced* obstruent, though they actually pronounced them with a voicing distinction. I believe that had these speakers had underlying archi-segments, spelling in pre-pause position would have been less consistent (Bolozky 1975, p. 256).

In my opinion this is not a valid argument against underlying voicing-irrelevant archiphonemes in Russian. What has taken place is undoubtedly the following: in about ninety per cent of the cases the informants performed a morphemic identification between the alternant with voiceless pre-pausal obstruent and the corresponding alternant with voiced prevocalic obstruent. According to their internalized graphemic rules they then wrote the morpheme-final obstruent in the two alternants with the same letter, viz. the one symbolizing the voiced obstruent.[12] When confronted with a nonsense pair such as [pop] ~ [poba] 'lampoon' (my example), a Russian informant will spontaneously equate the two forms and accordingly write them with a *b*. Such behaviour seems perfectly

---

cont.

> predicted intervocalicly, even in a plural form like *albumes* (Sven Skydsgaard, personal communication). Consequently, the interpretation /treN, meloN/ does not present any 'otherwise' difficulties.

12) Bolozky does not overlook the possibility of graphemic interference, but he takes up the following inconsistent attitude: "Even if the results of this test are attributed to habits of spelling, they cannot be completely dismissed as linguistic evidence" (p. 256-257).

natural, and I therefore disagree with Bolozky when he writes that
if speakers of Russian had underlying archiphonemes "one would
expect [them] to opt for voiceless representation before a pause in
more than just ten per cent of the cases" (p. 256). In my opinion
it is more surprising that the informants did not, by using the same
letter, make the connection between the alternants in more than
ninety per cent of the cases.

2) According to Bolozky most of the arguments adduced by Stampe
(1973) in favour of interpreting the stops after initial *s* in English as
phonologically voiceless are quite convincing. This problem has been
discussed in 7.8, where it was demonstrated that none of Stampe's
arguments are cogent.

3) As a third instance of empirical evidence against the archiphoneme Bolozky gives the following example: if a German word like
[unt] is pluralized, then this is done (so he claims, citing Barkai in
support) in the shape of [undə], not [untə]. This allegedly points
towards underlying /und/ rather then /unT/. Now in the first place,
it is simply not normal for a speaker of German to pluralize *und* as
[undə]. The form which he is likely to use is either [unts] or [unt].
For example, a sentence like *There are many 'ands' in the text* will
be translated by Germans into *Es sind viele 'unds' im Text* or *Es sind
viele 'und' im Text*. I have checked this with seven German informants. All of them spontaneously used [unts] or [unt], and only
one of them suggested [undə] after having proposed [unts] first.
When confronted with the form [undə] the other six informants
said that it was very odd and that they had never heard it used.
Secondly, even granting that a few speakers of German might use
this form, I do not think that it can be used as empirical evidence
against the phonological interpretation /unT/. If a schwa-vowel is
added to /unT/, the dental stop will necessarily have to be disambiguated as either /t/ or /d/. Since /d/ is far more frequent in the
context /Vn_ə/ than /t/ — note that there are scores of words like
Bunde, Hunde, gesunde, Bande, Rinde but relatively few words like
Bunte, Kante, unter, Mantel, and that /d/ occurs in inflected present
participles (*fliegende, liegende* etc.) — it would not be surprising if
an underlying /T/ were here disambiguated as /d/.
 Bolozky concludes that the concept of the archi-segment needs
further clarification and that the use of blanks in lexical forms
should not go beyond that proposed by Shibatani and Crothers

(cf. 7.6). Within the framework of generative phonology such a solution may perhaps be justified, but I do not think that Bolozky has presented any arguments in support of it.

7.10. Blair A. Rudes

In a recent paper on lexical representation in natural generative phonology an even more extensive use of blanks than that suggested by Hooper has been proposed (Rudes 1976). Like Vennemann, but unlike Hooper, Rudes regards the word, not the morpheme, as the basic unit of the lexicon. According to the method of representation which he advocates there will in English not only be lexical entries such as *write* and *ride* but also separate entries like *writer* and *rider*, i.e. the last two words are represented in the lexicon in their totality. Secondly, only those features whose values are unpredictable and which therefore cannot be considered redundant are specified with pluses or minuses in lexical representations; otherwise blanks are used. Consequently, not only irresoluble neutralizations, e.g. [0 voiced] in the second segment of English *stun*, but also resoluble neutralizations are recognized and expressed in lexical representations by means of blanks. In those American dialects, for example, where *writer* and *rider* are pronounced alike, Rudes sets up the same lexical representation for both words, namely /RÁITR/ (syllable boundary is also shown). This form consists of five archi-segments since each segment is only partly specified (cf. note 3 to this chapter). For example, the feature 'syllabic' is unspecified in the initial segment, in the final segment, and in /I/. In the stop consonant, which is realized phonetically as a voiced flap, the neutralization of the voicing opposition is shown by leaving the feature 'voiced' unspecified. In other words, the neutralization of the opposition /t/ : /d/, which other generativists would resolve on the basis of *write* : *ride*, is indicated in the lexical representation in the same way as it is in e.g. *stun*. In Rudes's lexical representation any type of redundancy is expressed with blanks, i.e. neutralization is not kept apart from other types of redundancy. By means of phonological rules which are unordered and exclusively phonetically motivated these blanks are subsequently filled in with pluses or minuses.

In 7.8 it was pointed out that the underlying forms proposed by Hooper are of basically the same type as those proposed by Halle (1959) and that one may in this respect speak of a return to the original version of generative phonology. Rudes's theory of lexical representation marks a return to an even earlier type of phonological representation, namely the one proposed by Roman Jakobson in the early fifties before the advent of generative phonology (cf. chapter 5), i.e. a return to a model in which surface contrasts are shown and where any feature predictable from other features in the same segment or from other segments of the same sequence is bracketed. In conclusion, therefore, it may be said that this version of natural generative phonology, in which surface contrasts are characterized directly in lexical representation, is closely related to Praguian and Neo-Praguian phonology.

7.11. Concluding Overview

The elimination in generative phonology of a level reflecting the surface contrasts of a language (Halle 1959), implies that resoluble neutralizations can no longer be recognized. In German *Rad*, for example, the final segment cannot be interpreted phonologically as [0 voiced] since the neutralization of /t/ and /d/ is resolved in *Rade*. On the other hand the rejection of an autonomous phonemic level does not preclude the recognition of irresoluble neutralization. Thus the stop consonants which are found post-initially in English *spill, still, skill* and finally in German *ab* and *und* may still be analyzed as [0 voiced] the way they were by most Prague phonologists.

In generative phonology neutralization is not kept apart from other types of redundancy. In Halle's 'incompletely specified morphonemes' and Chomsky and Halle's 'archi-segments' both segmentally and sequentially redundant features are left unspecified, and any type of sequential redundancy is shown in this way. The important difference between the Prague school's archiphoneme and the generativists' archi-segment is that only one sequentially redundant feature is left unspecified in the former, whereas all redundant features are left unspecified in the latter. In this way the Praguian concept of neutralization is absorbed by the more comprehensive concept of redundancy.

The legitimacy of operating with blanks and thus of recognizing archi-segments is a question which has been discussed at great length in generative phonology. In Halle's original theory archi-segments were recognized, but they have subsequently been rejected by some generativists. These phonologists point out that problems may arise when phonological rules are applied to matrices which contain zeroes in addition to pluses and minuses (Lightner 1963; Stanley

1967), and they therefore argue that lexical matrices should be fully specified. Nor can archi-segments be recognized in the markedness version of generative phonology, since any feature in a lexical matrix must be specified as M, U, '+', or '-'. On the other hand irresoluble neutralizations may be captured by means of Cairns's N-rules, which place constraints on the distribution of M's in the lexicon. In some recent works (Shibatani and Crothers 1972; Rischel 1974), where it is suggested that underlying representations in the form of marked and unmarked feature values should be ruled out until the markedness theory becomes more definitive, it is argued that unspecified or ambivalent segments may to a certain extent be used in underlying representations. If evidence cannot be adduced in favour of regarding one alternant as basic and another as derived, i.e. if it is impossible to argue in favour of unidirectional replacement rules, such segments are not only permissible but also desirable. Within the framework of natural generative phonology a more extensive use of archi-segments has recently been proposed (Hooper 1974 and Rudes 1976).

Chapter 8
STRATIFICATIONAL PHONOLOGY

The concept of neutralization plays an important part in stratificational linguistics. It does not, however, cover exactly the same ground in this theory as in Prague phonology. In an article of 1964 by *Sidney Lamb* it is proposed that the term 'neutralization' should be used to refer to the situation in which two or more entities of one level have an identical realization at a lower level. In an example like English *sp, st, sk,* consequently, where it is not a case of a higher (morphophonemic) contrast being lost on a lower level, there is no neutralization in the sense discussed by Lamb. In order for neutralization to be recognized in stratificational linguistics it should, in other words, be resoluble, as in German *Bund-Bunde, bunt-bunte.* It may be pointed out immediately, however, that practically any Praguian neutralization is expressed in stratificational description. But it is only termed 'neutralization' if it can be resolved by means of an alternation.

The stratificational conception of neutralization is described in detail in an article of 1972 by *David G. Lockwood.* Lockwood argues that not only is neutralization compatible with stratificational theory, it is actually necessary in order to arrive (within this framework) at a maximally simple description of the linguistic facts. According to Lockwood, most instances of phonological neutralization are to be dealt with in the *hypophonotactic* portion of a stratificational description, i.e. that part in which the distribution of phonological components termed *hypophonemes* (features like 'closed', 'labial', 'voiced', etc.) is accounted for.

By means of a hypothetical example Lockwood demonstrates that the Neo-Bloomfieldian conception of non-suspendability is incompatible (or poorly compatible) with stratificational theory. Assume that in a given language the following obstruents occur phonetically:

Initially: [p t k b d g f s x]
Medially: [b d g v z ɣ]
Finally: [p t k f s x]

138

As there are no cases of free variation, the Neo–Bloomfieldian pho-
nemicist will set up nine phonemes — /p t k b d g f s x/ — all of
which occur initially. Medially he will state that only /b d g f s x/
occur and finally that only /p t k f s x/ occur ("once a phoneme,
always a phoneme"). In stratificational linguistics these nine phonemes are broken down componentially in the following way (the
abbreviations symbolize 'closed', 'spirant', 'labial', 'apical', 'dorsal'
and 'voiced'; notice that voicelessness is treated as equivalent to
absence of voicing):

/ p	t	k	b	d	g	f	s	x /
Cl	Cl	Cl	Cl	Cl	Cl	Sp	Sp	Sp
Lb	Ap	Do	Lb	Ap	Do	Lb	Ap	Do
			Vd	Vd	Vd			

In order to account for the distribution (tactics) of these hypophonemes the following diagram is set up. In this diagram triangular
nodes symbolize *and*-relations, and nodes resembling brackets lying
on their sides symbolize *or*-relations; notice that there are both
upward and downward or's.

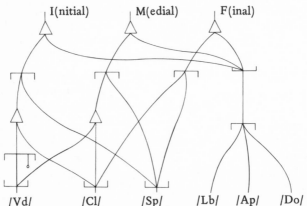

In the diagram any obstruent is shown to be either labial, apical or
dorsal and either closed or spirant. If closed, an initial obstruent is
either voiced or not (the latter situation being symbolized by means
of a line ending in a zero) and a medial obstruent obligatorily voiced.
In no case is a final obstruent voiced. It is when this hypophonotactic pattern is connected with the stratum above it that difficulties
arise. Each hypophoneme has an upward connection not only to the
tactic pattern but also to one or more phonons (i.e. morphophonemic

components) which it realizes, and which belong to the phonemic stratum. These upward connections are made with *diamond nodes* (see Lockwood, *Introduction to Stratificational Linguistics*, p. 226f):

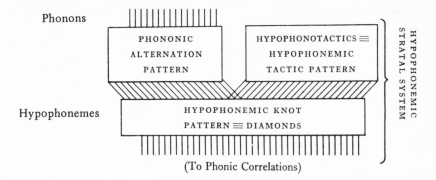

The problem which arises is that the hypophoneme /Vd/ is not always a realization of the phonon (morphophonemic component) |Vd|: medially this is the case only if there is neutralization in the stratificational sense, e.g. if a morpheme with a medial stop consonant has an alternant with a corresponding initial voiced stop (say, [udin] ~ [din]). In other words, /Vd/ will be realized medially whether or not |Vd| is signalled. In order to account for this fact the diamond at the bottom of the branch marked /Vd/ must lead upward to either |Vd| or zero, as shown in the following figure (in which the dashed line marks the boundary between the lower level of hypophonemes and the higher level of phonons):

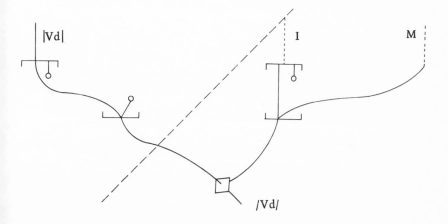

140

In this way the problem is claimed to be solved medially. However, /Vd/ will now be realized also *initially* whether or not the corresponding phonon |Vd| has been selected, and this does not correctly represent the facts of the language. "An upward *or* with one branch to zero in this case would mean that the component down to which it leads, namely, /Vd/, will be realized wherever the tactics permits it to occur, regardless of the specifications of the upper stratum" (Lockwood 1972a, p. 661).

By the Prague phonologist the hypothetical data under discussion would be analysed in the following way: he would recognize the same obstruent phonemes as the Neo–Bloomfieldian — /p t k b d g f s x/ — but in medial and final position he would consider the voicing contrast neutralized, i.e. he would in these positions operate with the archiphonemes ⟨p/b⟩, ⟨t/d⟩, ⟨k/g⟩. Transferred to stratificational phonology such a recognition of suspendability implies that the line leading from M down to /Vd/ must bypass the diamond:

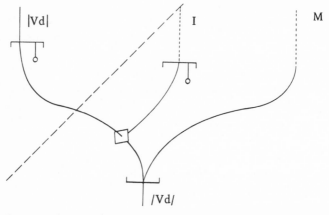

Lockwood now draws a distinction between hypophonemes and *hypophonemic signs*. Hypophonemes are signalled from the upper (phonemic) stratum by the activation of a diamond and are distinctive. Hypophonemic signs, which are nondistinctive, are not signalled from the phonemic stratum by the activation of a diamond (note the neural net analogy) but are determined by the tactics of the hypophonemic stratum. An occurrence of the phonon |Vd| will now fail to be realized medially in the same way that it fails to be realized finally, and its signal will take the path to zero. But medially, unlike finally, voicing will be determined by the occurrence of the hypophonemic sign /Vd/. Lockwood concludes his discussion of how the hypothetical example is described most adequately like this (p. 663):

This account ... represents the type of analysis favored by the Prague School, since it incorporates P-neutralization [i.e. Prague neutralization; NDN] in the same places as the Prague phonologist would. It states that /Vd/ is distinctive for initial obstruents in this language, but nondistinctive for medial and final obstruents. The hypophonemic sign /Vd/ is, however, determined for all obstruents in medial position, while it is obligatorily absent for final obstruents and all nonmedial spirants. It therefore appears that, in this and similar cases, phonological analyses incorporating P-neutralization are preferable under stratificational assumptions to the competing neo-Bloomfieldian treatments of the same data. Furtheremore, this solution ... still meets the biuniqueness condition, like the Praguian analysis of which it is a formalization.

Lockwood accepts Trubetzkoy's principle that the member of a contrast occurring in the position of neutralization is the *unmarked member*. On the basis of examples from North Fork Monachi and Bulgarian this solution is shown to be the simplest alternative according to the stratificational simplicity measure. He furthermore points out that the most common situation in which Praguian neutralization is represented in stratificational phonology is that in which a component contrasts with its absence in some environments and in which only the segment without this component occurs in the position of neutralization. Here the assignment of markedness is quite straightforward, but in other situations it is difficult to decide between marked and unmarked on the basis of occurrence in position of neutralization. This is the case, for example, when one member of the contrast is realized in one set of neutralized positions whereas another occurs in the remaining ones, as in the hypothetical example where [b d g] are found medially and [p t k] finally. The same difficulty arises if there is free variation between two or more members in the position of neutralization, or if the sound realized here is intermediary between the two members. In such cases the choice of unmarked must be determined according to the simplicity measure. If neutralization in the stratificational sense (S-neutralization) is involved, i.e. if there is a morphophonemic alternation, it is according to Lockwood simpler to select that member as unmarked which appears in the alternant without neutralization. In a language where, say, [p] and [b] are in free variation in word-final position, [p] can be regarded as unmarked if it is this member which occurs in the corresponding (but nonfinal) position in alternants. Although this solution seems sensible, it should be borne in mind that in Danish, for example, where [p] and [b] occur in free variation word-finally, [p] emerges in some instances of alternation and [b] in others, cf. examples like *galop* [-p, -b] 'gallop' (noun) ~ *galopere* [-p-] 'gallop' (verb) and *klaustrofob* [-p, -b] 'claustrophobe' ~ *klaustrofobi* [-b-] 'claustrophobia'. In such cases, therefore, the choice of unmarked member cannot be based on alternations. If S-neutralization is *not* involved, and if it is not a phonetically clear case of one member occurring in the position(s) of neutralization, Lockwood is apparently prepared to recognize *universal* marking and to select one member of a contrast as inherently unmarked. For one thing he refers to Lamb, who has suggested that 'dorsal' is inherently unmarked as compared with 'labial' and 'dental', and in an article of 1969 Lockwood argues (p. 307) that although the marked vs. unmarked distinction is almost exclusively a matter which must be decided individually for each language, the notion of universal markedness should not be ruled out completely.[1] In order for a member to be selected as inherently unmarked, however, a set of universal conventions is required, and unlike some generative phonologists the stratificationalists have not attempted to work out any such set, however tentative. It seems clear, therefore, that there are some unsolved problems concerning the determination of unmarked values within stratificational phonology.

Unlike neutralization the concept of the *archiphoneme* is not accepted by Lockwood. In his opinion archiphonemes are only appropriate in a theory where a distinction is drawn between the unmarked member of an opposition and the irrelevance of this opposition. In stratificational phonology such a distinction is not made. In the hypothetical data discussed above the initial voiceless labial stop, for example, is composed only of the hypophonemes 'labial' and 'closure' (/p/ is unmarked as compared with /b/), and it is therefore identical with both the medial voiced labial stop and the final voiceless labial stop. In terms of hypophonemes, in other words, there is no difference between these three consonants. At the level of hypo-

---

1) Lamb's choice of 'dorsal' as unmarked is a surprising one (cf. Jakobson 1941, where it is pointed out that velars and palatals are acquired at a later stage by children and lost at an earlier stage by aphasiacs than labials and dentals).

phonemic signs, on the other hand, there is no such identity since the medial stop differs from the others in containing the hypophonemic sign 'voiced'. By drawing no distinction, at the level of hypophonemes, between the unmarked entity occurring in the position of contrast and the entity occurring in the position of neutralization, Lockwood occupies a position, as he himself points out, which is close to that occupied by Trubetzkoy around 1931 (cf. 2.1):[2]

> In den Stellungen, wo die korrelative Eigenschaft eines Phonems seine phonologische Gültigkeit verliert, wird dieses Phonem mit dem merkmallosen Korrelationsglied identifiziert, selbst wenn es objektiv mit dem merkmalhaltigen Korrelationsglied identisch ist (Trubetzkoy 1931, p. 98).

Markedness is incorporated in stratificational phonology in order to arrive at the simplest possible description, and consequently there is (according to Lockwood) no room for archiphonemes. Neutralization, on the other hand, is accepted as a necessary concept. Such a solution may perhaps sound attractive, but it presupposes that the unmarked member of a contrast can always be determined, and as pointed out above such a determination will frequently be problematic. Until a satisfactory theory of marking has been worked out, therefore, it does not seem possible to recognize neutralization without at the same time recognizing archiphonemes. It seems psychologically unconvincing, it might be added, that a neutralized segment is (always) identified by the speaker–hearer with the unmarked member of an opposition.

Neutralization in stratificational phonology has also been discussed by *William J. Sullivan* (1974). Like Lockwood, Sullivan is of the opinion that the concept of neutralization must be incorporated in a stratificational description, and like Lockwood he accepts the view (suggested by Trubetzkoy in 1931) that the segment occurring in the position of neutralization should be interpreted phonologically as the unmarked member of a distinctive opposition, rather than as an entity which differs from both the marked and unmarked member. It is "a unitary member of a distinctive disjoint opposition which, in some environments, serves as well to represent either member of the opposition"(p. 288). In a Russian word like *podbirát'*

---

2) On the other hand Lockwood differs from Trubetzkoy in allowing neutralization for contrast of more than two terms, e.g. labial, apical and dorsal.

'choose (imperfective)', consequently, Sullivan analyses the neutralized preconsonantal segment, not as *Cl • Ap • 0 Vd*, but as *Cl • Ap*, i.e. as composed of the same phonons as the unneutralized intervocalic segment of a word like *otobrát'* 'select (perfective)'. Sullivan operates, in other words, with a mark 'voice' which is present in the intervocalic stop of Russian *podobrát'* 'choose (perfective)' but absent in the dental stops of *otobrát'*, *podbirát'*, and *otbirát'* 'select (imperfective)'. "A separate level for '0 voice' would ... be wasteful" (p. 297).

Unlike Lockwood, on the other hand, Sullivan deals with neutralization in the description of the *phonemic* stratal system, not the hypophonemic system, and in contradistinction to Lockwood he recognizes the concept of the *archiphoneme*: "It is the aim of this study to show that stratificational phonology incorporates the archiphoneme" (p. 289). Before a given entity can be designated an archiphoneme, however, two conditions, both of which are mentioned in Trubetzkoy 1939, must be met. First, it should fulfil the *feature definition*; i.e. it should consist of distinctive features held in common by two phonemes. Secondly, it should fulfil the *neutralizing definition*; i.e. there should be a suspension of opposition. As understood by Sullivan, however, the latter definition also implies that the entity occurring in the position of neutralization is interpreted as the unmarked member of the opposition. In the preconsonantal segment of a Russian word like *podbirát'* both definitions are fulfilled: (i) the features (phonons) *Cl • Ap* are shared by the phonemes /t/ and /d/;[3] (ii) the opposition /t/ : /d/ is neutralized before /b/, and *Cl • Ap* constitute the unmarked member of this opposition.

Sullivan's conception of the archiphoneme, it should be pointed out, is much wider than that of the Prague phonologists. If I have understood him correctly, his archiphoneme is the phonological entity which remains when the 'mark' has been removed from a minimal neutralizable opposition. This implies that not only are the preconsonantal stops in words like *otbirát'* and *podbirát'* archiphonemes, but also the intervocalic stop in a word like *otobrát'* is an archiphoneme. In the first place this segment (*T*) fulfils the feature definition, since the phonons *Cl • Ap* are shared by /t/ and /d/.

---

3) Actually, these features are also shared by /t'/ and /d'/, and it therefore seems highly questionable whether the feature definition is really fulfilled. In his discussion of the Russian obstruents, however, Sullivan excludes the palatalized consonants.

145

Secondly, *T* in *otobrāt'* fulfils the neutralizing definition, since it is a unitary member of an opposition which, in some environments, serves to represent either member of the opposition (cf. *otbirât'*). Such a conception of the archiphoneme is not really in the spirit of Trubetzkoy, who would at least never have regarded the intervocalic stop of *otobrat'* as anything but the phoneme /t/. It is clear, however, that Sullivan in his description of the neutralizing definition leans heavily on Trubetzkoy's theory of the *archiphoneme representative*. He refers to the place in *Grundzüge* where it is stated that the unmarked member of an opposition is the one which functions as the archiphoneme in the position of neutralization, and on page 288 he points out that a dental stop consonant which is unspecified for voice does not fulfil the neutralizing definition since it is neither *t* nor *d*, and since either *t* or *d* is required. It should be borne in mind, though, that the archiphoneme representative is a highly problematic concept, which has been critized convincingly by Akamatsu (cf. 2.10). Ultimately, it is a notion which is inconsistent with Trubetzkoy's own theory of neutralization and which implies that contrast cannot be regarded as a fundamental principle.

We have seen that stratificationalists disagree on the status of the archiphoneme, and on the choice of stratal system where phonological neutralization ought to be represented. But they agree in accepting, indeed in attaching great importance to, the concept of neutralization, particularly where higher contrasts are lost on a lower level. In holding this view, which is rather atypical among American linguists, they have clearly been influenced by the Prague phonologists (and by Hjelmslev).

10

146

Chapter 9
OTHER CONTRIBUTIONS

9.1. C.E. Bazell

A noteworthy contribution to the understanding of neutralization has been given by the British linguist *Charles E. Bazell*. According to Bazell, linguistic units and categories should be established on the basis of several different criteria, and such a convergence of criteria is also called for when dealing with neutralization. In his book of 1953 (p. 20) the most typical instances of neutralization are said to fulfil the following conditions: (i) inclusive distribution; (ii)a single feature shared by the including and the included member;[1] (iii) the distributional positions from which one member is excluded permit that member which from other points of view also may be considered unmarked; (iv) morphological emergence of the excluded member in permitted positions. German *Bund* [bunt], consequently, is a typical case of neutralization: the distribution of [t] includes that of [d]; [t] and [d] share a single feature (in fact all but one); [t] is unmarked as compared with [d] also from other (e.g. phonetic) standpoints; the excluded member of the opposition /t/ : /d/ emerges in *Bunde* /'bundə/. If one of these conditions is not fulfilled the neutralization is considered less typical (marginal). In Greek, for example, the opposition /m/ : /n/ is suspended in word-final position, but this gives rise to no morph-variants. If several of these conditions remain un-fulfilled Bazell does not (apparently) recognize neutralization. In English neither /r/ nor /h/ occurs before a consonant whereas /l/ does (*field, help*, etc.). We cannot here, for one thing, operate with neutralization of the opposition /h/ : /l/ since more than one

---

1) As pointed out by Fischer-Jørgensen (1975, p. 374) this is a strangely weak claim; according to Trubetzkoy, for example, only bilateral oppositions may be neutralized (cf. 2.2). It seems likely that what Bazell has in fact wished to say is 'only a single feature *not* shared by the including and the included member' (Hans Basbøll, personal communication); note in this connection that for Bazell neutralization does not cover the suspension of nonminimal oppositions (cf. below).

of the conditions are unfulfilled. Nor should we speak of neutralization of /r/ : /l/, for although these two phonemes share a feature
the remaining three conditions are unfulfilled. This should be described as defective distribution.

In his 1956 article Bazell discusses some of the traditional objections to the concept of neutralization: it is tainted by mentalism;
it is based on a confusion of levels; it violates the principle that the
same phonetic segment should be given the same phonemic interpretation whereever it occurs; it is more simply dealt with as defective distribution; and the application of it is arbitrary. All these objections, Bazell concludes, are invalid. Bazell's rejection of the classical American objection ("once a phoneme, always a phoneme") is
particularly convincing. In Danish the opposition between aspirated
and unaspirated stop consonants is neutralized in utterance-final
position through the occurrence of both types of phones in a
relation of free variation (cf. chapter 1). If the same sound is always
analysed phonemically in the same way, we have to set up two
different phonological forms for every Danish word terminating
in a stop consonant (see, however, chapter 1, note 3). This is quite
unacceptable, and Bazell points out that to "separate this case from
the otherwise clearly analogous case of the neutralisation of the
opposition voiced/unvoiced in German final position is a highly
artificial solution" (1956, p. 27). Not only in the case of oscillation
between features, but also where an intermediate phone occurs in
the position of neutralization is the American method unsatisfactory
since it is often difficult to tell which of two forms is present. "It
is the purpose of the theory of neutralisation to get rid of such
pseudo-problems" (1956, p. 27).

It is impossible, then, to maintain the position that 'neutralization' is nothing but a case of defective distribution. On the other
hand, the concept of defective distribution is obviously necessary
as well, but Bazell defines it in a curiously restricted way (1956, p.
27):

> It would seem preferable to confine the term *defective
> distribution* to cases in which a gap in distribution does not
> function as a regulative principle of speech. For instance
> in English *au* does not occur before labial consonants; but
> this fact, which is valid for the normal vocabulary, does not
> prévent the ready adoption of such forms as *Lebensraum*,
> without modification of the diphthong in this respect,
> whenever occasion presents itself.

148

Notice, however, that in English the only consonant permitted initially in words before another consonant is /s/ and that this does function as a regulative principle of speech. It is inconceivable that Bazell would regard this distributional restriction as an instance of neutralization, for he states expressly that neutralization should be defined in terms of a single feature (1956, p. 28). That it should indeed be interpreted as defective distribution appears from his discussion of the non-occurrence of English /h/ and /r/ before a consonant (1953, p. 21). This gap, which could hardly be considered anything but a regulative principle, is described as *non-trivial* defective distribution. Bazell's conception of defective distribution is thus broader than would appear from the above quotation.

According to Bazell neutralization does not cover the suspension of non-minimal oppositions, i.e. cases where several features lose their relevance. "With such extensions as this, neutralisation would soon become practically synonymous with redundancy" (1956, p. 27). On the other hand he recognizes neutralization in those cases where one feature loses its relevance when accompanied by certain properties *within the same segment:* "the neutralisation (in most European languages) of the opposition oral/nasal whenever the feature "consonantal" is not simultaneously present, is logically analogous to the neutralisation of the opposition voiceless/voiced in final position" (1956, p. 26). The similarity between Bazell's two examples may be brought out by means of contemporary generative rule conventions, the only difference between the following two neutralization rules being the sequential versus non-sequential nature of their environment specifications:

$$[\pm \text{voiced}] \quad \rightarrow \quad [0 \text{ voiced}] \Big/ \underline{\qquad} \#$$

$$[\pm \text{nasal}] \quad \rightarrow \quad [0 \text{ nasal}] \Big/ [\underline{\quad V \quad}]$$

In his 1956 article Bazell points out that grammatical considerations are relevant to the concept of neutralization. If, for example, the interpretation of a given absence of opposition as neutralization complicates morphological description, it may be advisable to reject this interpretation. A case in point is the Greek example mentioned above. Since the absence of opposition between /m/ and /n/ in word-final position gives rise to no morph-variants — there being no morphemes with final -*m* which also appear in word-final position — it may be preferable to regard the nasal consonant in final position as having the same feature composition as in other positions. If, on the other hand, the interpretation of a given absence of contrast as neutralization simplifies morphological description, this is considered an argument in favour of recognizing neutralization.

According to Bazell neutralization is a necessary concept which, however, is still too vague. It should possibly be split up into several concepts, or at any rate defined more precisely. For example, one should perhaps not recognize neutralization if its localization is ambiguous, as in the case of the initial clusters [sl-] and [ʃr-] in English (which, due to the absence of *[ʃl-] and *[sr-], might be interpreted as either /<s/ʃ>l-, <s/ʃ>r-/ or /s<l/r>-, ʃ<l/r>-/). Bazell, however, does not offer any real solution to this problem of delimitation. In particular it remains unclear where the borderline between atypical neutralization and defective distribution should be drawn.

9.2. W. Haas

Haas has dealt with the concept of neutralization in a long article dating from 1957 ('The identification and description of phonetic elements'). He finds himself most in sympathy with linguists of the Prague school and like them regards contrast as a fundamental concept. Whenever in certain environments a contrast is lacking Haas recognizes 'neutralization' (but this broad concept of neutralization is subsequently subdivided, cf. below). Thus not only is an opposition like voiced : voiceless considered neutralized finally in German, but also a multidimensional opposition such as velar : alveolar (or labial : alveolar, cf. 2.2, 2.4 and chapter 5) before /l/ in English and German, cf. English *glue, blue* but not **dlue* and German *klagen, plagen* but not **tlagen*. Haas's concept of neutralization is thus wider (in one sense at least) than Trubetzkoy's, and on the basis of his article it seems clear that he would also, for instance, recognize neutralization between /s/ and any other consonant initially before stops in English.

However, Haas differs from Trubetzkoy in another and even more fundamental way. The fact that an *element's contrastive force* is neutralized is not — according to Haas — sufficient reason for regarding the *element itself* as neutralized. Neutralization of a feature's contrastive force, but not of the feature itself, may be illustrated with the following example (which is mine, not Haas's): in Danish the contrastive force of the feature 'unaspirated' is lost after initial

/s/ (e.g. in *spinde* ['sbenə] 'spin'), but this does not necessarily imply that the feature itself is neutralized; 'unaspirated' may still be assigned to the category of distinctive features which it resembles. Haas considers as too dogmatic Trubetzkoy's idea that in such cases we would disregard the feature itself (e.g. disregard 'unaspirated' in *spinde*):

> Having *selected* a phonetic element by reference to its contrastive force in certain positions, we may recognize it even where there is nothing to contrast it with. After all, having picked out nails as something distinct from screws, we may recognize them also in the absence of screws; no need to regard them as representatives of some 'archi-instrument' consisting of what is common to screw-nail and driving-nail. This is not to deny that it *may* be very useful at times to have a notion at our disposal which is neutral to the difference (Haas 1957, p. 137).[2]

If we choose to operate with neutralization of the feature itself, then this feature (e.g. voiceless) is *not* assigned to the category of distinctive features which it resembles, but the category itself (e.g. voiced/voiceless) is considered absent in the position of neutralization.

In other words, when a feature loses its contrastive force — i.e. when there is neutralization in the broad sense — there are, according to Haas, two possibilities of interpretation: (i) the feature itself remains unneutralized, i.e. there is *defective distribution* of the opposite feature (for instance, of 'aspirated' after /s/ in Danish); (ii) the feature itself is neutralized (see below for examples). In the following discussion I shall refer to neutralization of a feature's contrastive force as *neutralization 1* and to neutralization of the feature itself as *neutralization 2* (this terminology is mine, not Haas's). It should be pointed out that 'neutralization 2' constitutes a subclass of 'neutralization 1'.

In order to decide whether in a given case there is neutralization 2 or not Haas resorts to criteria of convenience. Elements in position of neutralization 1 may be 'freakish', and in such instances one may wish to recognize neutralization 2. If the phonetic element occurring in this position sounds like a compromise between two elements

---

2) It appears that Haas occupies a position between de Groot, who regards phonemes as elements with an *identifying* function, and other Prague phonologists, who regard them as elements with a *distinctive* function.

151

contrasting elsewhere (intermediary realization), if it sounds like one of the two elements but is freely exchangeable with the other (oscillating realization), or if it alternates morphologically with another element, it is 'freakish'. In these cases we are faced with 're-calcitrant' features, which may therefore be regarded as neutralized themselves. As an example of the third type of freakishness Haas mentions 'voicelessness' finally in German *Tag* [tɑ:k], which alternates with the 'voice' of *Tage* ['tɑ:gə]. The first two types of freakishness may be illustrated with the following examples: (i) in English the phonetic element occurring after /s/ in a word like *spill* is intermediary between the [p] of *pill* and the [b] of *bill*; (ii) in Danish, [p] and [b] are freely exchangeable in utterance-final position, e.g. *top* 'top'. In German *Tag*, English *spill* and Danish *top*, consequently, we may recognize neutralization 2 and analyse the words as /tɑ:<k/g>/, /s<p/b>ıl/ and /tɔ<p/b>/. Since the archiphoneme in *Tag* is naturally incapable of contrasting with either of its factors, /k/ and /g/, we may interpret /tɑ:<k/g>/ as phonemically equivalent to /tɑ:g/, and in this way no complications arise in the description of German morphology.

What enables Haas to choose freely between neutralization 2 and the remaining cases of neutralization 1 (i.e. defective distribution of the opposite feature) is his recognition not only of *absolute features* but also of *relative features*. A feature may be relative in either of two ways: (i) it may be defined "as a *relative grade* under a certain category, different gradation-scales and feature-ranges being determined by different environments" (p. 144); (ii) it may be defined "as belonging to a *relative category*, the choice of category being determined by the environment" (p. 144). As an example of the second type of relativity Haas mentions English [h], which may be interpreted as (glottal) 'fricative' in initial position (*hat* [hæt]) but not in post-consonantal position (*pat* [phæt]), where it should be regarded as non-distinctive aspiration. As for the first type of relativity, Haas points out that although some features are most naturally regarded as absolute, i.e. can be defined exclusively by reference to extra-lingual measure, other features are relative. A case in point is degree of opening in Danish vowels. After /r/ the same number of grades of opening is found as in other environments, but a feature like 'half-close' is phonetically dissimilar in *rende* 'run, trickle' and *vende* 'turn'. Conversely, a vowel of the [æ]-type represents the feature 'half-close' in *rende* and the feature 'open' in *vande* 'water' (vb):

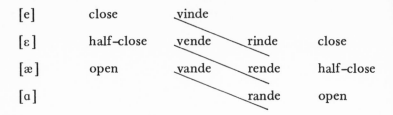

[e]	close	vinde		
[ɛ]	half–close	vende	rinde	close
[æ]	open	vande	rende	half–close
[ɑ]			rande	open

By recognizing relative features Haas is able to operate with neutralization 2 whenever he wishes. When neutralization 2 is called for (i.e. when we are faced with 'freakishness'), the feature involved may be regarded as relative in either of the two ways mentioned above. Thus the recognition of *relative categories* enables us to consider the category of 'voice' absent in final position in German, just as the category of 'glottal friction' is absent in post–consonantal position in English. Similarly, the categories of 'aspiration' and 'voice' may be considered relative in respectively Danish and English, i.e. they may be regarded as absent finally and after /s/ respectively (Danish *top*, English *spill*). Secondly, the recognition of *relative grades* enables Haas to operate with neutralization of multidimensional oppositions (cf. next paragraph).

Haas's modifications of the Praguian conception of neutralization imply "(i) greater freedom of choice in phonological description, and (ii) an extension of the notion of neutralisation ... to cases where only some of a feature's contrasts are neutralised" (p. 148). In German *Tag*, for instance, the phonologist is free to interpret 'voiceless' as an absolute feature and operate with defective distribution of 'voiced' in final position *or* to interpret it as a relative feature of reduced contrastive force. He may, in other words, choose freely between /tɑːk/ and /tɑː<k/g>/, and Haas considers this freedom of choice a great advantage. As regards the second implication, it is pointed out that many cases of 'genuine' neutralization of multidimensional contrasts, such as that between velar and alveolar (or between labial and alveolar) before /l/ in English and German, may now be recognized. In this case Trubetzkoy was forced to operate with defective distribution since the feature involved, 'velarity', although unopposed to 'alveolarity', contrasts with 'labiality' (cf. English *glow*, *blow*, **dlow*). Haas, on the other hand, may operate with neutralization in such instances of partial loss of contrastive force. If the articulatory positions of English and German stops are defined relatively, i.e. as mere grades (front, mid, back), we may say that contrasting grades are reduced by one (to front, back) initially before /l/; in other words, a given point of articulation may be regarded as a relative grade under the category of articulatory place and its feature range may be considered determined by the environment. Now in Northern English there is free variation between [gl] and [dl] (*glow*) and between [kl] and [tl] (*clock*). By defining articulatory positions relatively Haas may interpret these data in either of two ways: (i) [gl, dl] and [kl, tl] may be analysed as /gl/ and /kl/, i.e. it may be assumed that an *unambiguous* feature of extended range ('back') occurs in both [gl, dl] and [kl, tl]; (ii) they may be analysed as /$<$g/d$>$l/ and /$<$k/t$>$l/, i.e. it is assumed that an *ambiguous* feature of extended range ('back') occurs in the initial segment of these clusters. Such an ambiguous interpretation of the feature of extended range may be called for if there are morphological freak-occurrences, e.g. if only [d] and [t] should turn out to occur in derivations like *aglow* and *o'clock*.[3]

If neutralization 2 is recognized, the segment occurring in the position of neutralization represents either an *archiphoneme* or a *sum-phoneme*. Both are ambiguous, but whereas an archiphoneme comprises only the properties shared by two phonemes *a* and *b*, i.e. is a unit of *defective definition*, a sum-phoneme comprises in addition to what is common to *a* and *b* the disjunction of the features in which they differ, i.e. it is a unit of *alternative definition*. As an example of a sum-phoneme the initial segment of Northern English *glow* [gləu, dləu] may be mentioned (provided that this word is analysed not as /gləu/ but as /$<$g/d$>$ləu/). According to Haas the difference between these two types of ambiguity — 'neither-nor' and 'either-or' — is sufficiently important to warrant different terms, and when it is necessary to refer to both types of ambiguity simultaneously the word *homophoneme* may be used.[4]

---

3) "A partial loss of contrastive force, like any total loss, may open a door to phonological or morphological freak occurrences" (p. 150).
4) As pointed out to me by Hans Basbøll it seems doubtful whether there can be any real difference between 'archiphoneme' and 'sum phoneme' if distinctive features are recognized (as they are by Haas). If Northern English *glove*, for example, is interpreted as /$<$g/d$>$lʌv/, the initial segment will be composed phonologically of 'stop closure', 'voicing' and 'backness', and it is hard to see how it is possible to operate with a unit of alternative definition here. I do not believe that there is any basis for distinguishing between 'neither-nor' and 'either-or' homophonemes but that any type of neutralization may be expressed by the figure ⓐⓑ , in which the hatched area represents the archiphoneme, i.e. the features shared by the phonemes *a* and *b*.

On some points the revisions of the Praguian concept of neutralization proposed by Haas are of a largely terminological nature. He has extended the concept of neutralization to all cases of sequentially determined lack of contrast, but his notion of 'neutralization 1 unaccompanied by neutralization 2', i.e. neutralization of a feature's contrastive force but not of the feature itself, actually corresponds to the notion of defective distribution in Prague phonology. The only difference seems to be that Haas here uses the term 'neutralization' and that he devotes special attention to the fact that a reduction of the number of contrasts takes place. Furthermore, his narrow concept of neutralization (neutralization 2) corresponds closely to the Praguian notion of neutralization. It is thus especially by his approach to suspension of multidimensional oppositions that Haas may be said to have made an original contribution to the discussion of neutralization.

As already mentioned, any feature may be regarded as relative, and in this way Haas can introduce neutralization 2 whenever it is *expedient*: "In trying to decide between the two ways of dealing with neutralisation ... we shall choose whichever interpretation seems to afford the more adequate account of the elements that occur in the positions of neutralisation" (p.154). It has been said by Householder about fundamental linguistic attitudes in various parts of the world that the European asks: "is it true?", the American: "is it consistent?", and the Englishman: "will it help?" Although it would certainly be unreasonable to place Haas in the same category as Daniel Jones, one senses in his article a pragmatic attitude towards neutralization. The clarification of the concept called for by Bazell can hardly be brought about as long as the basis for choosing between neutralization and defective distribution is 'descriptive convenience'. Haas operates with a very broad notion of neutralization which is then subdivided, but his criterion for recognizing neutralization 2 in a given form is theoretically unsatisfactory. Nevertheless, his paper contributes on several points to the understanding of phonological neutralization.

9.3. A. Avram

In his lucid 1960 article on neutralization and phonological alternations *Andrei Avram* examines the problem of how to interpret the sounds appearing in positions of neutralization. As his starting point he selects an example illustrating the suspension of the voicing opposition in Rumanian before consonants belonging to the voice correlation (/p/ : /b/, /t/ : /d/, etc.). The question that he attempts to answer is the following: which phonological units should the [s] and [z] of respectively *despărţi* and *dezbrăca* be assumed to represent? Comparing these words, in which the voicing of the sibilant is determined by that of the following consonant, with the word *dezarma*, in which the voicing of [z] is not contextually determined, Avram points out that essentially the possible interpretations amount to three. These will each be treated in turn.

1)   [s]   in *despărţi* realizes /s/;

        [z]   in *dezbrăca* realizes /z/;

        [z]   in *dezarma* realizes /z/.

This interpretation represents the phonetically based either–or approach mentioned in chapter 1 of the present book. According to Avram it implies that we attribute a distinctive value to the voiceless character of the sibilant in *despărţi* and to the voiced character of the sibilant in *dezbrăca*. However, such an interpretation is highly problematic, for the voicelessness of [s] in the former word and the voicing of [z] in the latter being contextually determined they cannot perform the function of differentiating meanings (unlike the distinctive voicelessness of [s] in words *sare, rasă, ros* and the distinctive voicing of [z] in words like *zare, rază, roz* which are not imposed by the context). In fact, the phonetically based either–or analysis of [s] and [z] in *despărţi, dezbrăca* entails a denial of the voicing neutralization before /p/ and /b/. Avram also argues that if we were to apply consistently the principle that the same phonetic segment (e.g. [z]) has to be interpreted identically in different contexts (e.g. *dezarma, dezbrăca*), we would then have to do the same with features and regard, for example, nasalization of vowels in Rumanian (which is brought about by an adjacent nasal) as a distinctive feature because nasalization is distinctive in other segments. In his opinion such an interpretation (based on the "once a phoneme, always a phoneme" principle) would be unacceptable.

2)   [s]   in *despărţi* realizes /z/;

        [z]   in *dezbrăca* realizes /z/;

        [z]   in *dezarma* realizes /z/.

This is the morphologically based either-or analysis (cf. chapter 1): the problem of how to interpret the sibilants in *despărţi* and *dezbrăca* is overcome by resorting to the criterion of 'morphological analogy'; i.e. it is assumed that the prefix *des-/dez-* has the same phonological form, /dez/, whereever it occurs. Since the morphological criterion cannot, however, be applied in all cases this interpretation is also rejected by Avram. In a Rumanian morpheme like *dosp-*, for instance, where the sibilant appears in a single (neutralizing) position and is always realized as [s], the principle of morphological analogy is of no avail (the same applies to the final segment of a German word like *und*, cf. chapter 1). Now if [s] is here assumed to be a manifestation of /s/ (the simplest solution), we are interpreting the same sound in two different ways *in the same position*. Avram considers such an approach unacceptable. "The phonological contents of the fricative in *despărţi* cannot differ from the phonological contents of the fricative in *dospi* only for the simple reason that, in Rumanian, the prefix *des-/dez-* is also attached to words with a vocalic initial; should there be no words of the *dezarma* type, would the phonological contents of the dental fricative in *despărţi* change?" (Avram 1960, p. 276).

3)   [s]   in *despărţi* realizes /<s/z>/;

      [z]   in *dezbrăca* realizes /<s/z>/;

      [z]   in *dezarma* realizes /z/.

This is the both-an analysis discussed in chapter 1 and the one which Avram prefers. If the analyst attaches due attention to the fact that the distinctive features of a phoneme are, by definition, independent of the context he can establish the phonological nature of the sounds occurring in the positions of neutralization without resorting to morphology. In the first place it should be borne in mind that there is nothing paradoxical in assuming that the same phonetic segment, e.g. [z] in *dezarma* and *dezbrăca*, may realize two different phonological units. Depending on what language we are analysing, on what phase in the evolution of a given language we are analysing, or on what context we are faced with within one phonological system, the same phonetic reality may perform different functions. Secondly, it should be pointed out that just as the contextually determined lip rounding of the final [ɔ] in Rumanian *roua* does not prevent us from interpreting this vowel as a representative of the same phonological unit as the unrounded [a] in *casa*, the contextually determined voicelessness of [s] in *despărţi* should not prevent us from interpreting this sibilant as a representative of the same phonological unit as the [z] in *dezbrăca*. In either case the distinction between the two sounds is entirely determined by the context, and the only significant difference between the two examples is that [ɔ] and [a] never oppose each other in Rumanian, i.e. they are variants of a phoneme, whereas [s] and [z] in some positions do (*sare* ≠ *zare*, *rasă* ≠ *rază*, *ros* ≠ *roz*, etc.), i.e. they are variants of an archiphoneme. The archiphoneme, which could also be referred to by other names (hyperphoneme, mixed phoneme, etc.), is regarded by Avram as a higher phonological unit than the phoneme, a unit to whose phonological contents belong all the features which two (or more?) phonemes have in common but not the feature by which they differ. Neutralization is described as "the cancelling, in certain contexts, of an opposition utilized somewhere else" (p. 277). Although it is not stated explicitly in his article it seems clear that Avram regards neutralization and the archiphoneme as concepts which cannot be dissociated.

The three different interpretations of the above Rumanian examples obviously have consequences for the description of the alternation which occurs in the prefix *des-/dez-*. If a phonetically based either-or analysis is preferred it is an alternation between the phonemes /s/ (*despărţi*) and /z/ (*dezarma, dezbrăca*) which takes place; if a morphologically based either-or analysis is preferred the alternation disappears; and if a both-and analysis is preferred it is an alternation between the phoneme /z/ (*dezarma*) and the archiphoneme /<s/z>/ (*despărţi, dezbrăca*) which takes place. In the last case we are faced with an alternation which, in Avram's terminology, is phonological without being phonematical.

As Avram himself points out, his interpretation of the sounds appearing in the positions of neutralization is not new, and his approach to the problem of identifying contrastive units in one position with units uncovered in other positions is clearly influenced by Martinet (to whose 1936 article he refers). However, there can be little doubt that Avram has adduced some weighty arguments in favour of recognizing the concepts of neutralization and the archiphoneme.

Chapter 10
A THEORY OF NEUTRALIZATION

10.1. Problems Connected with the Either-or Analyses

Let us now return to some of the questions raised in chapter 1. Although in the discussion of various phonological theories (chapters 2-9), I have attempted to take up a neutral attitude, it will probably not have escaped the reader's attention that of the different approaches to the problem of multiple complementarity mentioned in chapter 1, I regard the both-and analysis as the most adequate. In this chapter I shall present some arguments against the either-or analyses, attempt to argue in favour of an analysis which permits both-and identifications, and discuss a number of problems that have to be gone into if the concepts of neutralization and the archiphoneme are recognized.

The *phonetically based either-or analysis*, according to which neutralization is nothing but a case of defective distribution, is attended with a number of problems (some of which have already been mentioned):

(i) It sometimes leads to arbitrary decisions, namely in the case of intermediary and oscillating manifestation (cf. chapter 1).

(ii) It covers up genuine indeterminacies in phonological patterns. It is difficult to deny, for example, that Twaddell is somehow right when he expresses the view that to interpret *spill* as either /spɪl/ or /sbɪl/ would be to conceal rather than reveal the phonological facts (Twaddell 1957 (1935), p. 67). It also implies that a distinctive value is attributed to features which are in fact redundant, cf. Avram (1960) and Derwing (1973, p. 185), who points out that an interpretation of English *stop* as /stɒp/ incorrectly implies that a contrast between /t/ and /d/ is operative in this environment. In short, it does not fully respect the principle of contrast.

(iii) It is performed exclusively according to an extralinguistic criterion, namely that of phonetic similarity. Now I do not share Hjelmslev's extreme view that "No extra-lingual criteria can be relevant, i.e. neither physical nor physiological or psychological criteria" (Hjelmslev 1936, p. 49).[1] When considering different structural solutions it is in my opinion legitimate to take into consideration the empirical correlates of the abstract units which are postulated. But in that case, it seems, one should consider not only physical and physiological correlates but also psychological correlates. If this is done it will sometimes turn out to be the case that the data do not point in the direction of an either-or analysis, but that there are units which are psychologically indeterminate (cf. 2.2, 2.4, 2.9 and chapter 5).

(iv) It necessitates a different treatment of phonological phenomena which are clearly analogous. As pointed out by Bazell (cf. 9.1), the 'once a phoneme, always a phoneme' principle forces the analyst to set up two different forms for every Danish word ending in a stop consonant. In this way the absence in word-final position of the opposition aspirate/non-aspirate in Danish is separated from the analogous absence in final position of the opposition voiced/voiceless in languages such as German, Russian and Czech.

(v) It sometimes creates phonological sub-systems which are extremely asymmetrical. By way of illustration we may mention Saigon Vietnamese. According to Thompson (1959, p. 458) the consonant inventory of this language consists of 24 phonemes which may be arranged in the following 6-by-4 system:

	labial	apical non-retroflex	apical re-troflex	frontal	dorsal	glottal
fortis stop	p	t	ṭ	c	k	ʔ
fortis continuant	f	s	ṣ	j	x	–
lenis	w	t'	r	l	g	h
nasal	m	n		ɲ	ŋ	–

All of these consonants are found in syllable-initial position, but in syllable-final position the only contrastive consonants which occur are [p t k ʔ j w g h m n ŋ]. Now if these are identified with the

1) In Fischer-Jørgensen 1949 it is demonstrated that in his actual practice Hjelmslev himself takes phonetic substance into consideration and that it is impossible to perform an adequate phonological analysis which disregards substance completely.

contrastive consonants occurring in initial position according to a phonetically based either-or principle the following highly asymmetrical system of final consonants will be obtained (cf. Jørgen Rischel MS):

p	t	-	-	k	ʔ
-	-	-	j	-	-
w	-	-	-	g	h
m	n	-	ŋ	-	

According to Rischel such a statement in terms of defective distribution clearly fails to indicate the really characteristic feature of final consonants in Saigon Vietnamese. In his opinion the final system should instead be analysed as the following 4-by-3 pattern, in which the feature system has been considerably reduced:

p	t	k	ʔ
w	j	g	h
m	n	ŋ	-

Such a feature restatement is unproblematic if separate phoneme inventories are set up in different positions (Firth, Twaddell), but if initial and final consonants are to be identified with each other it creates problems which seem insoluble by means of an either-or approach.

The *morphologically based either-or analysis* is also beset with a number of difficulties which cannot be ignored. Most of these have been mentioned in the preceding chapters but are here repeated for the reader's convenience:

(i) It may reasonably be claimed, as done by Martinet (1973 (1965), p. 94), that this method sacrifices the results of the phonological analysis in order to simplify the presentation of morphemes. This objection has also been raised by Avram (1960), who argues that it is highly problematic to interpret the same sound in two different ways in the same position: for example, to interpret [s] in Rumanian *despărți* and *dospi* as /z/ and /s/ respectively.

(ii) As a consequence of subordinating phonology to grammar the principle of contrast cannot be fully respected. Although there will be no contrasts which are ignored in the type of phonological representation used by adherents of the morphologically based either-or method, there will be many cases in which a contrast is postulated in a given environment which is never realized here, cf. German /bund##/ and /bunt##/ (where ## symbolizes 'word boundary'). If it is problematic to analyse English *stop* as /stɒp/, due to the fact that there is no opposition between /t/ and /d/ after initial /s/, it also seems problematic to analyse uninflected *Bund* and *bunt* in German as respectively /bund/ and /bunt/, for in word-final position voiced and voiceless obstruents are never opposed to each other in this language. According to Martinet, a phonological analysis consists in accounting for what phonic features the native speaker-hearer is capable of producing, distinguishing and combining to form the words of the language (cf. 2.4). Such an approach to phonology, which to me seems very reasonable, obviously rules out the interpretation of a German word like *Bund* as /bund/ and of a Russian word like *rybka* as /ribkǎ/, for a German is incapable of pronouncing word-final voiced consonants and a Muscovite is unable to pronounce sequences of obstruents which are not voiced or voiceless throughout.

(iii) The morphologically based either-or method leaves a residue of cases in which the operation of identification cannot be performed, namely those in which a morpheme is realized in one way only. Thus the problem of equating the final segment of German *und* with initial /t/ rather than initial /d/ or *vice versa* cannot be solved by this method, and the same goes for the analysis of the postinitial segment of an English word like *still*.

10.2. A Proposed Method of Identification

I shall now propose a method of identification which in certain well-defined situations permits both-and analysis, but which otherwise consists in performing phonetically based either-or identifications or sometimes in refraining from performing the operation of identification. Assuming that a proper segmentation has taken place, the inventory of contrastive segments (micro-phonemes) is established in each position by means of the commutation test. I shall not here discuss the important problem of what exactly is to be understood by position, but only state that if we define it in terms of constituent parts of the syllable the number of different "places" need not be overwhelmingly large. As pointed out by Richel (MS) it will usually be unnecessary to distinguish, for example, between CV and CVC, or between V, CV and CCV, and the positional frame can thus be simplified considerably. In each position the contrastive segments are broken down into constituent features (micro-features) by studying the possible commutations. Comparing a French word like *boue* with words like *mou, pou, vous, doux* and *goût* we can decompose its initial segment into the five micro-features 'non-nasal', 'voiced', 'noncontinuant', 'noncoronal' and 'anterior' (cf. Jakobson 1949, p. 207). The contrastive segments established in a given position are now identified — as far as possible, but by no means exclusively — with contrastive segments established in other positions on the basis of micro-features, i.e. according to the principle proposed by Martinet (1946, p. 43f).

Now it will be recalled that Martinet has defined neutralization as the loss of the relevance of a feature in certain positions (1946, p. 48), that Jakobson and Lotz regard neutralization as the inability of two opposite features to alternate in well-defined situations (1949 (Jakobson 1962, p. 427)), and that Bazell states that neutralization should be defined in terms of a single feature (1956, p. 28). In accordance with this view, and looking at the phonological contrasts of a language from the position of maximum contrast, I shall provisionally define neutralization as *contextually determined loss of one distinctive dimension*. It follows from the definition that any neutralization rule will conform to the pattern $[\pm f] \rightarrow \emptyset / x\_y$. Furthermore I shall lay down the condition that such a loss of a distinctive dimension must be 'clean' in the sense that it must not always be accompanied by simultaneous loss of another distinctive dimension (or of other distinctive dimensions). In other words, there must be at least some cases where the loss is unaccompanied by loss of other dimensions. Consequently $[\pm \text{voiced}] \rightarrow \emptyset /\_\#\#$ in German is a genuine neutralization rule. On the other hand we cannot formulate a neutralization rule such as $[\pm \text{voiced}] \rightarrow \emptyset$ in consonants initially before two consonants in English (recall that only [s] can begin a triple consonant cluster in this language), for such a rule will always be accompanied by $[\pm \text{continuant}] \rightarrow \emptyset, [\pm \text{nasal}] \rightarrow \emptyset, [\pm \text{anterior}] \rightarrow \emptyset$, etc.

If as a result of a neutralization rule a segment in weak position lacks a (dichotomous) feature, and if it is furthermore the case that the micro-features of such a contrastive segment are contained in two or more contrastive segments occurring in strong position, I shall identify it with two such segments, which are allowed to differ only in carrying opposite feature specifications for this feature, if such an identification is not phonetically unrealistic.[2] If there

are more pairs than one in strong position with which the weak segment could be equated without violating the principle of phonetic
realism, I shall equate it with that pair which it resembles most
phonetically (or, more precisely, which it resembles most in terms
of phonetic features). In other words, the operation of identification
— with two strong micro-phonemes — is performed on the basis of
(a) micro-features and (b) structurally redundant phonetic features.
Otherwise I shall equate a micro-phoneme in weak position with one
strong micro-phoneme if (a) its micro-features are contained in this
strong micro-phoneme and (b) on the basis of shared phonetic
features.

In order to illustrate this approach let us first consider the final
segment of an English word like *twelfths* [twelfθs]. Since syllable-
final clusters of four consonants in English can only end in [t] or
[s], the micro-features of this segment may be assumed to be [+
consonantal, + continuant] (note that [-lfθt] may be assumed to be
a possible final cluster in English). Now we can formulate a rule
(whose domain is the syllable, and which applies to English as well
as to several other languages) that the dimension of voice is lost in
the non-initial segment(s) of obstruent clusters (in e.g. English
spear the loss of the distinctive dimension of voice in the post-initial segment is unaccompanied by loss of other distinctive dimensions, cf. *steer, sphere, smear,* etc.). Since the micro-features of the
final segment of *twelfths* are contained in several strong micro-
phonemes, I shall among these have to equate this segment with
strong /s/ and /z/, for a) these micro-phonemes differ only in being
respectively [- voiced] and [+ voiced], b) they contain the micro-
features [+ consonantal, + continuant], and c) this identification is
phonetically more realistic than equating it with /f/ and /v/, or with
/θ / and /ð/, etc.; i.e. all the redundant features of this [s] except
[- voiced] are contained in both these segments. Consider secondly an
English word like *steer.* Since the neutralization rule just mentioned
applies in this case as well, we shall equate the post-initial segment
with both /t/ and /d/ occurring in strong position, for a) these segments are respectively [- voiced] and [+ voiced], b) the micro-
features of [(s) t] (= [+ consonantal, + coronal, - nasal, - continuant],
cf. *spear, sneer, sphere, sly*) are contained in them, and c) this identification is phonetically more realistic (in terms of features) than

---

2) If multivalued features are recognized, a segment in weak position may be
equated with more than two segments in strong position.

equating it with /tʃ/ and /dʒ/. On the other hand we shall identify the [s] of *steer* with only one micro-phoneme occurring in strong position, for in this case no neutralization rule in the above sense can be formulated. This micro-phoneme will be /s/ since the micro-feature characterizing [s(t)-], namely [+ consonantal], is contained in it and since this identification is phonetically realistic (identity of redundant features).

It will be noticed that according to our method of identification we attribute to the [s] in *twelfths* the micro-features contained in the /s/ and /z/ occurring in strong position (apart from [+ consonantal, + continuant], which it contains from the outset). Similarly, we attribute to the [s] of *steer* the micro-features contained in strong /s/ (apart from [+ consonantal]), and we attribute to the [t] of this word a number of micro-features contained in strong /t/ and /d/. (I assume that different members of one phoneme must be structurally identical, i.e. must contain the same relevant distinctive features.) Now in 10.1 I questioned the legitimacy of attributing a distinctive value to features which are in fact redundant, an approach which characterizes the phonetically based either-or method as well as the morphologically based either-or method. It now appears that according to the method advocated here such an attribution of distinctive values to redundant features also takes place. In other words, in our analysis the principle of contrast is not fully respected either (although it is respected to a greater extent than in the pure either-or analyses). Let us therefore consider the alternatives, which, as far as I can see, amount to two. Either we must refrain from performing the operation of identification (Firth, Twaddell), which for reasons given in chapter 1 I am disinclined to do, or identification must be based exclusively on micro-features. The latter alternative — although very satisfactory from a structural point of view — will in many languages result in an enormous amount of archiphonemes and be psychologically decidedly counter-intuitive (it would also imply that the concept of neutralization is swallowed up by that of sequence redundancy). In English *steer*, for example, the initial segment would be an archiconsonant, and in *twelfths* the final segment would be a consonantal archicontinuant. I prefer therefore to hug the phonetic ground, although not to the extent of fully adopting the phonetically based either-or analysis. In agreement with most European linguists I consider paradigmatic contrast a fundamental principle, but on the other hand I do not adhere to a phonological analysis which completely disregards physiological–physical or psychological evidence (cf. 10.1). I believe that the method of identification proposed here, in which the concept of neutralization makes allowance for the principle of contrast, is consistent with such a general attitude, and that psycholinguistic evidence, particularly, may be adduced in support of the concept of neutralization (cf. 2.2, 2.4, 2.9, chapter 5 and 10.10 below).

10.3. *Neutralization, Segment Redundancy, and Defective Distribution*

By defining neutralization as *contextually* determined loss of one distinctive dimension — and I am using the word 'context' in the normal sense of what comes before or after something, i.e. what occurs in a certain position — we keep it apart from the type of redundancy which in generative phonology is termed *segment redundancy*, i.e. from the situation where the value of one or more features may be predicted from that of another (or those of others) within the same segment and is therefore redundant. As an example of segment redundancy we can mention Polabian /j/, in which the values of voicing and palatalization are predictable, and thus redundant, on the basis of other feature values within the same phoneme (cf. 2.2). It will be recalled that Trubetzkoy stressed the psychological difference between segment redundancy and contextually determined invalidation of a phonological opposition.

In 10.2 the initial micro–phoneme of English *steer* was equated with the micro–phoneme /s/ occurring in strong position, and in this way the micro–features contained in that strong segment were attributed to it. By interpreting the first segment of *steer* in this way we assume that all English consonant phonemes except /s/ are absent in this position, i.e. we operate with *defective distribution*. Since, as a result of the identification, we propose that the first phoneme of *steer* contains the same micro–features as strong /s/, we cannot here speak of contextually determined absence of a number of distinctive dimensions. What we shall have to say instead is that in this case no loss of feature relevance takes place and that all English consonant phonemes except /s/ are rendered defective by a following postinitial /t/. More generally, we shall say that we are faced with defective distribution whenever a phoneme cannot occur in a clearly defined context (i.e. when its non–occurrence is not to be explained as an 'accidental gap'). In Saigon Vietnamese, for example, the phonemes /f/, /s/, /ṣ/, /x/, /t'/, /r/ and /l/ may be regarded as defectively distributed, for they do not occur in syllable-final position (cf. 10.8). If we consider an English word like *twelfths*, we notice that there may be both neutralization and defective distribution in one and the same position. After three consonants the distinctive dimension of voice is lost syllable-finally in English, and according to the criteria of contained micro-features and phonetic similarity we must interpret the final segment of this word as <s/z>. However, by attributing all the micro-features of strong /s/ and /z/ except [+ consonantal, + continuant] to the final segment of *twelfths* we reach the conclusion that all English consonants which are not characterized by the feature specification [+ coronal, + anterior, + continuant, + strident] are defectively distributed inasmuch as they do not occur syllable-finally after three consonants.[3]

It appears, then, that according to our definition of neutralization and our method of identification, neutralization is kept clearly apart from both segment redundancy and defective distribution, for in the former case the loss of feature relevance it not contextually determined and in the latter case no (contextually determined) loss of feature relevance is assumed to take place.[4]   In adopting this point of view we carry on the tradition. That neutralization was intended by the originators of this concept to be kept apart from defective distribution is obvious, cf. Trubetzkoy's and Martinet's discussion of the absence of the clusters /tl-/ and /dl-/ in English and German as well as their insistence on the fact that only phonemes which form bilateral oppositions, or which stand in exclusive relation, may be neutralized (2.2, 2.4). Recall also that according to Vion only phonemes which are adjacent in the system, i.e. which form minimal oppositions, may be neutralized (2.9) and that Roman Jakobson distinguishes between neutralization and defective distribution (chapter 5). In short, there is general agreement among pho-

---

3) Or, assuming that <t/d> is also possible in the context /lfθ_$/, we reach the conclusion that all English consonants which are neither characterized by the feature specification [+ coronal, + anterior, + continuant, - nasal] nor by the feature specification [+ coronal, + anterior, - continuant, - nasal] are defectively distributed inasmuch as they do not occur syllable-finally after three consonants.

4) The principle according to which I operate with neutralization or with non-neutralization (defective distribution, segment redundancy) may be regarded as a sort of 'rule of the game', rather than something which is empirically given. It seems, however, that there is good agreement between the results obtained in this way and the empirical data (cf. 10.9).

nologists who operate with the concept of neutralization that it applies to minimal oppositions only and that there must therefore be a concept of defective distribution as well.

Let us return briefly to the Russian examples [s't'in'a] 'wall' and ['aist] 'stork' discussed in chapter 5. Since palatalization is sequentially predictable before dentals, and voicing in obstruents is sequentially predictable before obstruents in Russian, it would seem that we are not here faced with a case of contextually determined loss of *one* distinctive dimension in the sibilants occurring in these words, and that our definition of neutralization does therefore not cover cases of this type. As pointed out in chapter 5, however, each of these neutralization rules can be formulated independently, cf. examples like *snop, sled* [snop, s'l'et] (2.2) and *laska* [laskə] 'caress' (n), *ot goroda* [ad ...] (2.4). In [s't'in'a] and ['aist] these two rules happen to coincide. We shall therefore in both these words operate with two neutralizations and accordingly interpret the sibilants as the archiphoneme $<$s/z/s'/z'$>$.

In 10.2 it was pointed out that a possible, and structurally very satisfactory, alternative approach to the problem of identification would be to base identification exclusively on micro–features. If such an approach were adopted, would it still be possible to distinguish between neutralization and defective distribution? In terms of features a strategy that might be considered would be to operate with neutralization whenever we are faced with contextually determined absence of one distinctive dimension and with defective distribution (of features) when we are faced with contextually determined absence of more distinctive dimensions than one. In other words, one might operate with two types of sequence redundancy, and one might argue in favour of such a subcategorization by claiming that only in the case of neutralization does one find phonological segments which are psychologically indeterminate. In English *steer*, for example, the absence in the initial segment of all micro–features except [+ consonantal] could be considered a case of defective distribution, whereas the absence of the dimension of voice in the postinitial segment could be regarded as an instance of neutralization. Since a method of identification based exclusively on micro–features is not the one I propose, I shall not discuss this possibility any further, but leave it to those phonologists who believe that this approach is more adequate and who are at the same time of the opinion that a distinction between neutralization and defective distribution ought to be retained.

168

10.4. Neutralization and Alternation

In 2.4. it was mentioned that Martinet warned the linguist against the danger of confusing neutralization with morphologically conditioned phoneme alternation. We must now ask whether the definition of neutralization as contextually determined loss of one distinctive dimension ensures a clear–cut distinction between this concept and alternation. For reasons which will be explained in the following such a clear–cut distinction is only obtained if by 'contextually determined' we understand 'determined by phonetic/phonological context'. If 'contextually determined' might also refer to grammatical or lexical properties, it would no longer be possible to separate neutralization from alternation. Since I regard such a separation as necessary, it must therefore be stated explicitly that in order for neutralization to be recognized the context specification of a rule eliminating a distinctive dimension must be phonetic/phonological.

In his article on morphonology (1965, p. 20f) Martinet discusses the pluralization of an Italian word like *amico* [amíko] 'friend' as *amici* [amíči]. Could it be argued here that in the same way that the opposition /t/ : /d/ in Russian is neutralized before obstruents, cf. *pod komom* 'under the lump', *pod gorodom* 'under the town', the opposition between /k/ and /č/ in Italian is neutralized before /i/ (and /e/)? Martinet answers this question in the negative, for there are hundreds of Italian words which show that /k/ may also occur before a front vowel, e.g. the plural form *stomachi* [stómaki] of *stomaco* [stómako]. In Russian, on the other hand, the opposition between /t/ and /d/ is always neutralized before an obstruent. Therefore the Italian example is a case of alternation, not of neutralization, and should accordingly be dealt with in the description of morphology. Now the replacement in Italian of /k/ by /č/ before front vowels is paralleled by a replacement of /g/ by /ǧ/, cf. an example like *astrologo* [astrólogo] 'astrologer' — *astrologi* [astróloǧi]. Since /k, g/ may be assumed to differ from /č, ǧ/ in Italian with respect to the feature 'back' — cf. Martinet 1965, where it is stated that the differentiating feature is here "la profondeur de l'articulation buccale" (p. 21), and Basbøll 1974, where it is said that the "č est en fait un /k/ palatal, comme ǧ est un /g/ palatal (l'affrication étant redondante, dépendant de la place d'articulation)" (p. 32n) — one might within the framework of the present theory of neutralization consider setting up a more general 'neutralization rule' eliminating the backness dimension in consonants before front vowels. (Such a rule would not have to be restricted to stops, for the only Italian consonants which are [+ back] are /k/ and /g/.) We would, however, have to include the nonphonological context specification that it applies to words like *amici, astrologi, dice* 'says' but not to words like *stomachi, luoghi* [lwɔ́gi] (plural of *luogo* [lwɔ́go] 'place'), *amiche* [amíke] (plural of *amica* [amíka] 'female friend'). Consequently, a rule of this type cannot be accepted as a neutralization rule.

Yet another problem remains to be considered, namely whether it is legitimate to operate with *grammatical boundaries* as context specifications in neutralization rules (cf. a rule like [± voiced] → Ø / _## in languages such as German and Russian). In other words, would it be acceptable by 'contextually determined' to understand 'determined either by phonetic/phonological context or by grammatical boundaries' (morpheme, word, etc.)? Such an inclusion in phonological analysis of grammatical boundaries would in no way represent a departure from traditional phonological methods. In Fischer-Jørgensen 1975, for example, the following is said about the inclusion in generative phonological rules of grammatical conditions (p. 204):

> Naturally not all rules are dependent on syntactic structure, but some are. For example, certain rules are dependent on grammatical boundaries. In this particular case, there is no major difference between generative phonology and other phonological theories. It has always been customary to assume that there are special phoneme combinations, neutralizations, etc. which appear at word boundaries, and that assimilation rules apply within certain syntactic groups.

Nevertheless it is problematic to operate with grammatical boundaries in the context specifications of neutralization rules, as will appear from the following example. If, in English, [n] or [l] is followed within the same syllable by a sibilant, then this sibilant will always be voiced if there is an intervening morpheme boundary, as in *sins* [sɪnz], *ells* [elz]. On the other hand there is no such restriction with respect to voicing if the sibilant and [n] or [l] are not separated by a morpheme boundary, for /s/ and /z/ contrast in e.g. *nonce : bronze* and *else : Selz(nick)*. (The absence within non–proper morphemes of syllable–final /lz/ is clearly an accidental gap, i.e. new words like *belze, gulze* could readily be introduced.) Now in order to account for the predictability of sibilant voicing in words of the type *sins*, *ells* one might consider setting up a neutralization rule, the domain of which is the syllable, that eliminates voicing in sibilants preceded by [n, l] if and only if there is an intervening morpheme boundary. According to this rule the final segment of *sins* and *ells* would be the neutralization product <s/z>, and in order to keep these words apart from *since* /sɪns/ and *else* /els/ one would arrive at the phonological representations /sɪn#<s/z>/, /el#<s/z>/. Such an analysis, which at the phonological level distinguishes between *sins, ells* and *since, else* by means of a morpheme boundary, I would not be prepared to accept.

The above example has been discussed by Martinet (1965, p. 22), who points out that one cannot in this case argue from the presence of a morpheme boundary in *sins, ells*, etc., for this boundary does not correspond to a potential pause, and therefore it must not be involved at the phonological level. Suppose, therefore, that we choose to accept as legitimate context specifications only such boundaries as can be defined in phonetic/phonological terms. Such an approach would obviously permit us to operate with syllable boundaries as well as with utterance boundaries (cf. Harris's definition of an utterance as "any stretch of talk, by one person, before or after which there is silence on the part of that person"). It would also allow us to use word boundaries as context specification for neutralization rules, for boundaries of this type correspond to potential pauses (and there will often here be junctural cues). On the other hand, boundaries which are purely grammatical, i.e. which have no possibility of phonetic manifestation, may not be used as context specifications for neutralization rules.

In conclusion, then, it may be said that by the expression 'contextually determined' in the proposed definition of neutralization I understand 'determined by purely phonetic/phonological context'. Given this reading, neutralization is kept clearly apart from alternation, which I propose should be dealt with at a higher level of linguistic description.

10.5. *The Concept of the Archiphoneme*

In the first chapter of this book I quoted Šaumjan and Kortlandt as having said — to my mind correctly — that by recognizing the concept of neutralization the analyst is forced into recognizing a new type of phonological unit as well, i.e. the archiphoneme. In Chapter 2 I argued that there is solidarity between the concepts of neutralization and the archiphoneme (2.6, 2.7, 2.8). Whenever there is neutralization there will also be an archiphoneme and *vice versa*. In a phonological description of German, for example, in which the concept of neutralization is recognized, the phonological units which occur finally in words like *rieb, riet, Sieg* can be neither /p t k/ nor /b d g/, for both of these series are characterized by the distinctive dimension of voice, a dimension which is absent in word-final position. Instead the final segments must be interpreted as the archiphonemes ⟨p/b⟩, ⟨t/d⟩, ⟨k/g⟩, i.e. as respectively labial, dental and velar stop phonemes which contain neither the feature [-voiced] nor the feature [+ voiced].

An archiphoneme may be provisionally defined as a *contrastive segment in weak position whose distinctive features correspond to the intersection of two contrastive segments in strong position which differ in respect of one feature only*. In English *twelfths* [twelfθs], for example, where the two last segments lack the distinctive dimension of voice, we attribute according to our method of identification the micro-features shared by strong /s/ and /z/ to the final segment, apart from [+ consonantal, + continuant] which it contains already, i.e. we interpret it as ⟨s/z⟩. As a result of this feature attribution the final segment of *twelfths* is turned into the intersection of strong /s/ and /z/, two phonemes which differ only in being oppositely specified for the feature 'voiced'. In Mulder 1968 (p. 98) the conception of the archiphoneme as the intersection of two classes is illustrated by means of a so-called Venn-diagram.[5] Following Mulder, and retaining *twelfths* as our example, we may set up the following diagram:

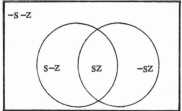

---

5) In Mulder's book on *Sets and Relations in Phonology* the concepts of neutralization and the archiphoneme occupy an important position. Since I am not conversant with set-theory, relation-theory and other systems of mathematical logic, I have chosen to exclude an account of Mulder's views from this book. It should be stated here, however, that his approach is based on neo-Prague principles as these are set forth by Martinet, cf., for example, his definition of the archiphoneme as "a phoneme in a subsystem which, when projected into the over-all system, is represented there by two or more phonemes" (Mulder 1968, p. 114).

The left-hand circle represents the class /s/, the right-hand circle the class /z/, and the square the set of all English phonemes. The product of s and $-z$ is everything that is /s/ but not /z/, i.e. the feature [- voiced], and the product of $-s$ and z is everything that is /z/ and not /s/, i.e. [+ voiced]. The product of $-s$ and $-z$ is everything that is neither /s/ nor /z/. Finally, the product, or intersection, of s and z is everything that /s/ and /z/ have in common, i.e. the features [- vocalic, + consonantal, + strident, + continuant, + coronal, + anterior]. It is perhaps not superfluous to stress the fact that $\langle s/z \rangle$ is not the sum, but the product of /s/ and /z/, cf. Hockett, who refers to the archiphoneme by means of the formula 'both and neither' (1955, p. 165).

It appears from the diagram that in terms of distinctive features an archiphoneme is included in a phoneme, and this explains why some phonologists (e.g. Vachek, cf. 2.6) consider it a subphonemic unit. In the sense, however, that the archiphoneme is a unit in weak position which 'covers' two strong phonemes, the Russian term 'hyperphoneme' does not seem unreasonable, cf. also Martinet's definition of it as an "unité phonologique simple susceptible, en certaines positions, de se dissocier en deux ou plusieurs éléments phonologiquement distincts" (1936, p. 54).

In the above provisional definition I characterized the archiphoneme as an intersection of *two* contrastive segments occurring in strong position. However, in certain well-defined situations, namely those where two neutralization rules affect a given segment simultaneously, the distinctive features of an archiphoneme may correspond with four contrastive segments in strong position which differ with respect to two features. In the case of Russian [s't'in'a] and ['aist], for example, we may set up a Venn-diagram in which there are four circles, representing the classes /s/, /s'/, /z/ and /z'/, which intersect. In such a diagram the product of s, z, s' and z' is everything that /s/, /z/, /s'/ and /z'/ have in common, i.e. [- vocalic, + consonantal, - compact, - grave, - nasal, + continuant] (cf. Cherry, Halle and Jakobson 1953). In other words, the intersection of the four circles indicates the Russian archiphoneme $\langle s/z/s'/z' \rangle$. We therefore have to amend our definition of the archiphoneme by adding that if two neutralization rules affect a segment simultaneously, the resulting archiphoneme must be characterized as a contrastive segment in weak position whose distinctive features correspond with the intersection of four (or possibly three) contrastive segments in strong position which differ in terms of two features. A case of three coinciding neutralizations is found in Igbo (cf. the discussion in 10.8 of vowel harmony in this language). The resulting archiphoneme must here be characterized as a contrastive segment in weak position whose distinctive features correspond with the intersection of eight contrastive segments in strong position which differ in terms of three features.

Throughout this book I have symbolized archiphonemes by means of digraphs, not capital letters. One reason for adopting this method of transcription is that a capital letter notation necessitates an arbitrary choice between two (or more) symbols. Should German *und*, for example, be transcribed as /unT/ or as /unD/? Furthermore, when such decisions must be made, nonphonological considerations may all too easily be brought into play. In Lyons 1968, for example, it is stated that a word–final dental stop in German may within the framework of Prague school phonology be symbolized as a /T/ (p. 116). In the very next sentence, however, Lyons transcribes the German word *Tod* as /toD/, and it lies near at hand to assume that his reason for selecting the letter D in this case is the occurrence of the phoneme /d/ in alternants like *Todes, Tode*. If such a morphologically based choice between two capital letters is accepted, it seems impossible to avoid blurring the distinction between archiphonemes and morphophonemes. Another reason for preferring two–letter representations is that this method of transcription shows explicitly that a contrastive segment in weak position is analysed as the equivalent of two (or more) contrastive segments occurring in strong position. For example, the choice of <t/d> as the symbol of the final segment of German *und* shows with greater clarity than the symbol /T/ that this segment is regarded as the intersection of the /t/ and /d/ occurring in words like *Tusche* and *Dusche*. A third reason for avoiding capital letter representations is that such a method of transcription over–emphasizes the idea that in addition to an inventory of 'regular' phonemes, a language contains a number of special phonemes. As pointed out in Chapter 1, it is possible to regard any neutralization product as referable to two or more regular phonemes; in this sense it may be argued that archiphonemes do not form so detached a part of the inventory as the use of capital letters implies.

A representation of archiphonemes by means of digraphs rather than capital letters has also been proposed by André Martinet. In a discussion following a lecture on the archiphoneme representative (Akamatsu 1975) he argues that in a German example like *Berg* —

Berge the transcription /ber<k/g>, bergə/ is preferable to /berK, bergə/, since the latter invariably suggests the existence of a morphological alternation.. According to Martinet there is in this case no alternation, and therefore /ber<k/g>, bergə/ must be preferred, for inasmuch as the elements b e r and g are found in both forms, this notation suggests similarity rather than disparity. Martinet proposes therefore the following, with which I am in full agreement: "Je suggère donc qu'on écarte délibérement la notation au moyen de capitales et qu'on la remplace par une notation où figurent les phonèmes neutralisés, notation plus compliquée certes mais moins susceptible de bloquer la compréhension des phénomènes" (p. 101).

10.6. *Neutralization and Different Feature Systems*

If neutralization is defined as contextually determined loss of one distinctive dimension, i.e. of one *feature* dimension, the number and nature of the neutralizations which are put forward in the description of a language will obviously depend on the feature system which is adopted. In particular, neutralization will be affected by whether the feature system is purely binary (Roman Jakobson, Chomsky and Halle) or whether multivalued features are recognized as well (Ladefoged). Suppose, for example, that a language contains the nasal consonants [m], [n], [ɲ] and [ŋ], that these are distinctively opposed to each other — and thus constitute different phonemes — before vowels but not before consonants, where only [m] occurs before labials, only [n] before dentals, only [ɲ] before palatals, and only [ŋ] before velars. If we have at our disposal a multivalued feature of 'articulatory place', we can account for the absence of contrast between labial, dental, palatal and velar nasals before consonants by means of the following neutralization rule:

$$[\text{articulatory place}] \to \emptyset \; / \; [^{+ \text{nasal}}\underline{\hspace{1em}}] \; C$$

According to our criterion of contained micro–features any preconsonantal nasal can now be identified with strong /m/, /n/, /ɲ/ and /ŋ/, which differ only in respect of 'articulatory place', i.e. it can be interpreted as the archiphoneme <m/n/ɲ/ŋ>. It will be noticed that in this rule the loss of the distinctive dimension of 'place' is not determined exclusively by context, for in addition to specifying that 'articulatory place' is absent before consonants, the rule specifies that this is only the case within the category of nasals

(I shall assume that the articulatory place of obstruents in this language is not automatically determined before obstruents and that e.g. [pt] and [kt] occur and contrast). If the right-hand side of a neutralization rule is permitted to take this form — and I do not think that we can exclude neutralization rules which apply to a subclass of the contrastive segments which occur in a given position — we must amend our provisional definition of neutralization to "loss of a distinctive dimension which wholly or in part is contextually determined." Loss of a distinctive dimension which is "in part contextually determined" is thus exemplified with the above rule, for here the elimination of 'articulatory place' is dependent on a certain context, namely 'subsequent consonant', *and* on the presence of a simultaneous feature value, namely [+ nasal]. Now in the purely binary feature systems the above nasals would be distinguished from each other in the following way:

	Chomsky and Halle					Roman Jakobson			
	m	n	ɲ	ŋ		m	n	ɲ	ŋ
anterior	+	+	-	-	compact	-	-	+	+
coronal	-	+	-	-	grave	+	-	-	+
back	-	-	-	+					

Since the nasals are kept apart by more features than one we cannot formulate a neutralization rule which would account for the situation before consonants. Thus a tentative rule like [± compact] → Ø/ [+ nasal] C would have to be rejected since it must be accompanied by [± grave] → Ø/ [+ nasal] C, and *vice versa*. Since no neutralization rule in our sense can be formulated, each of the preconsonantal nasals must be identified with one strong micro-phoneme according to the criteria of contained micro-features and phonetic similarity, i.e. [m(C)], [n(C)], [ɲ(C)] and [ŋ(C)] must be equated with respectively /m/, /n/, /ɲ/ and /ŋ/. This implies that the data under discussion are interpreted (unreasonably, in my opinion) as instances of defective distribution: /n/, /ɲ/ and /ŋ/ are considered to be absent before labial consonants, /m/, /ɲ/ and /ŋ/ before dental consonants, /m/, /n/ and /ŋ/ before palatal consonants, and /m/, /n/ and /ɲ/ before velar consonants.

Now it seems that a fairly good case can be made out for a feature system which recognizes multivalued features in addition to binary ones. For example, it is not possible to account for the difference in tongue height between the Danish vowels [i], [e], [ɛ] and [a], which occur in words like *mile* 'dune', *mele* 'sprinkle with flour', *mæle* 'speech, voice', *male* 'paint', by means of the Jakobsonean features 'compact' and 'diffuse' or Chomsky and Halle's features 'high' and 'low'. In order to overcome problems of this type, Wang (1967, 1968) has proposed to operate with the dimensions 'high' and 'mid':

	i	e	ɛ	a
high	+	+	–	–
mid	–	+	+	–

It is doubtful, however, whether such an analysis can be considered truly binary, for 'mid' would seem to imply the existence not only of 'high' but also of 'low' (unless the names 'high' and 'mid' are considered completely arbitrary). Halle's proposal (1973, p. 930) that [i] and [e] should be regarded as tense and [ɛ] and [a] as lax is not very convincing either (cf. Fischer-Jørgensen 1975, p. 386). It therefore seems that the extent to which one should dichotomize has its limits and that as far as vowel height is concerned Ladefoged's system is perhaps superior to either of the purely binary systems.[6] Now if it can be argued that one ought to operate with a multivalued feature of 'height' and that the principle of two-valued thinking therefore cannot be regarded as an absolute one in phonology, the road is open for recognizing other multivalued dimensions as well.[7] For example, the arguments which have been adduced in favour of recognizing a multivalued dimension of 'articulatory place' are fairly good, provided that 'gravity' is also included in the feature system. Since it seems plausible, furthermore, that pre-consonantal nasals in languages of the type discussed above are psychologically indeterminate in respect of place, I would feel

6) In Davidsen-Nielsen and Ørum 1978 it is argued that as compared with Chomsky and Halle's system Ladefoged's system constitutes an improvement in another respect as well, namely by its reintroduction of the feature 'gravity'.

7) In Basbøll and Kristensen 1975 a multivalued feature [dist] is set up which denotes distance from the most constricted pharyngeal vowel. Thus, in Danish, [ɑ] is [1 dist], [æ] is [2 dist], [ɛ] is [3 dist], [e] is [4 dist] and [i] is [5 dist]. This feature is similar to Ladefoged's multivalued height-feature, although it should be borne in mind that [height] — unlike [dist] — is a "vertical" dimension and that these two features are naturally "inversely proportional".

inclined to recognize a multivalued feature of articulatory place and, consequently, to recognize neutralization rules such as [articulatory place] → Ø/ [+ nasal] C (cf. also Basbøll (1974a), who sets up a rule of basically this type in Spanish). Rules of this type may be assumed to exist in languages such as Spanish, Italian and, although in a more restricted form, English.[8] In English the articulatory place of a post-vocalic nasal is automatically determined before syllable-final labial and velar consonants, cf. examples like *dump, nymph, junk*. Before other syllable-final consonants, however, the choice of nasal is not limited to one which is homorganic with the following segment, cf. examples like *dreamed* ([driːmd] or [dremt]), *dreams, winged* and contrasts such as *rimmed, wind, ringed*. (Within morphemes, on the other hand, the articulatory place of a pre-final nasal is, with a few isolated exceptions, predictable before all consonants, cp. *dump, nymph, junk* with examples like *hunt, hand, plunge, stench, dense.)*

Let us consider, finally, how the problem of identification presented by certain French vowels occurring in weak position may be tackled if we operate with (a) the dichotomous features 'high' and 'low' and (b) one multivalued feature of 'height'. Let us assume — although this is an oversimplification — that the following may be said about the distribution and contrastive force of [e] and [ɛ] and of [o] and [ɔ] in French: 1) [e] and [ɛ] are distinguished in word-final position (*les : laids*), but otherwise only the latter vowel occurs in closed syllables and only the former in open syllables, as exemplified by respectively *perdre* ['pɛrdr] and *descendre* [de'sɑ̃ːdr] (cf. 2.2). 2) [o] and [ɔ] contrast in word-final closed syllables (except those which end in /r/), as in *saule : sol*, but otherwise only the former of these vowels occurs in open syllables and only the latter in non-final closed syllables and before homosyllabic /r/, as in respectively *chapeau* [ʃa'po], *beauté* [bo'te] and *poster* [pɔs'te], *port* [pɔr] (cf. 2.8, 2.9, 2.10). Restricting ourselves to the type of French in which there is only one /a/-phoneme, I shall assume that this vowel is [+ back] and that it is distinguished from /ɔ/ by being [- round]. Such an interpretation will permit us to recognize only three distinctive degrees of vowel height. Within the framework of

---

8) In English this implies that the dimension of articulatory place is neutralized before consonants characterized by certain *coefficients* of the place-feature. I do not think that contextual conditions of this type should be ruled out. On the other hand it is obvious that 'neutralization' of some but not all coefficients of a multivalued feature is impossible.

Chomsky and Halle's binary feature system the French vowels may be arranged in the following matrix:

	i	e	ɛ	y	ø	œ	u	o	ɔ	a
high	+	-	-	+	-	-	+	-	-	-
low	-	-	+	-	-	+	-	-	+	+
back	-	-	-	-	-	-	+	+	+	+
round	-	-	-	+	+	+	+	+	+	-

We can now formulate a neutralization rule which eliminates the distinctive dimension [± low] and which applies to the unrounded front vowels when they do not occur in word-final position and to the back vowels when they occur in open syllables, in non-final closed syllables, and before homosyllabic /r/. According to our method of identification the [ɛ] of *perdre*, etc. as well as the [e] of *descendre*, etc. must now be identified with both /e/ and /ɛ/ since the micro-features of these vowels ([- high, - back, - round]) are contained in both these strong vowels and since /e/ and /ɛ/ differ only with respect to the feature 'low'. Similarly, the [o] of *chapeau*, *mollusque*, etc. as well as the [ɔ] of *poster, port*, etc. must be identified with both /o/ and /ɔ/ since their micro-features ([- high, + back + round]) are contained in both these strong segments and since /o/ and /ɔ/ differ only with respect to the feature 'low'. I shall not here discuss an alternative neutralization rule which might be considered, namely one which eliminates the distinctive dimension [± high] instead of [± low], but only point out that such a rule would lead to a different set of identifications.

In a type of description where a multivalued feature of 'height' is recognized, but which otherwise operates with the dichotomous features 'backness' and 'rounding' (cf. Ladefoged 1971), the French vowels can be arranged in the following matrix:

	i	e	ɛ	y	ø	œ	u	o	ɔ	a
height	high	mid	low	high	mid	low	high	mid	low	low
back	-	-	-	-	-	-	+	+	+	+
round	-	-	-	+	+	+	+	+	+	-

Now in the first place it is obvious that we cannot eliminate the dimension of height in weak positions, cf. contrasts such as *bile* :

belle, dimanche : *démanche* and *pou* : *pot, poulie* : *poli, pour* : *port*.
On the other hand it is possible to eliminate within this dimension
one of the three values, say, 'mid'. In weak positions the dimension
of height would then have two values only — high and low — and on
account of oppositions like the ones just mentioned we would have
to regard weak [e], [ε], [o] and [ɔ] as 'low'. According to our
method of identification we must then equate weak [e] and [ε] with
/ε/ since this is the only strong micro-vowel which contains the
micro-features [low, - back, - round], and similarly we must equate
weak [o] and [ɔ] with /ɔ/, which is the only strong vowel which contains the micro-features [low, + back, + round]. Furthermore, we
would have to identify the weak [i] of *bile, dimanche,* etc. — which
contains the micro-features [high, - back, - round] — with strong
/i/, and we would have to identify the weak [u] of *pou, pouli, pour,*
etc. — which contains the micro-features [high, + back, + round] —
with strong /u/. It thus appears that a rule which eliminates the value
'mid' in weak position would lead us to operate with defective
distribution: the phoneme /e/ must be considered absent in all
positions except word-finally, and the phoneme /o/ must be considered absent in open syllables, in non-final closed syllables and
before homosyllabic /r/. In other words, the rule [mid] → Ø in weak
positions is not a neutralization rule but a rule of defective distribution.

We see, then, that the choice of feature system determines the
neutralizations which may be assumed to exist in a language. If
multivalued features are recognized, certain data must be interpreted
as neutralization, but if the feature system we operate with is exclusively binary, these data have to be analysed in terms of defective
distribution instead (cf. the above discussion of preconsonantal
nasals). Conversely, other data can only be interpreted as instances
of neutralization if multivalued features are not recognized (cf. the
above discussion of French vowels). It is beyond the scope of this
book to present arguments which would enable the analyst to come
down generally in favour of one of these two types of feature
systems.

10.7. *Further Restrictions on the Concept of Neutralization?*

As pointed out in chapter 2 phonologists have attempted to restrict
the concept of neutralization by permitting it to apply to certain
oppositions only. Thus Trubetzkoy lays down the condition that

bilateral but not multilateral oppositions may be neutralized, and Martinet requires that the members of a neutralizable opposition should stand in exclusive relation. Vion takes a more catholic view and only requires that neutralized phonemes should be adjacent in the phonological system, i.e. they should form a minimal opposition (2.9, 2.11). According to these proposals, and within the framework of distinctive features proposed by Chomsky and Halle, an opposition like /r/ : /l/ in English is potentially neutralizable, for the totality of features shared by the members of this opposition — [+ sonorant, + consonantal, -nasal, etc.] — does not recur in other English phonemes (Trubetzkoy); /r/ and /l/ are alone in sharing the sum total of their distinctive features except for one (Martinet); and differing only in being oppositely specified for the feature 'anterior' they form a minimal opposition (Vion). In British English, therefore, where [r] occurs only in syllable onsets, the following neutralization rule (in which $ symbolizes 'syllable boundary') might be set up:[9]

$$[\pm \text{anterior}] \rightarrow \emptyset \; \bigg/ \; \begin{bmatrix} + \text{sonorant} \\ + \text{consonantal} \\ - \text{nasal} \\ \hline \end{bmatrix} \; C_0 \,\$$$

As a result of such a rule words like *ball* and *old* are interpreted phonologically as /bɔ:<l/r>, əʊ<l/r>d/. Since such an analysis is decidedly counter-intuitive it seems necessary to consider whether (and how) the concept of neutralization should be restricted in other ways.

---

9) I shall assume that Chomsky and Halle's analysis of [r] and [l] applies not only to American but also to British English, for although the former sound is not as retracted in British as in American English it still differs from the latter in being articulated farther back in the mouth (post-alveolarly). Within the framework of Roman Jakobson's distinctive features the rule accounting for the absence of /r/ in syllable codas could be formulated like this:

$$[\pm \text{compact}] \rightarrow \emptyset \bigg/ \begin{bmatrix} + \text{vocalic} \\ + \text{consonantal} \\ \hline \end{bmatrix} \; C_0 \,\$$$

If a multivalued feature of articulatory place is accepted, one could also formulate a rule which eliminates this feature in liquids occurring in syllable codas.

In order to avoid postulating neutralization of /r/ and /l/ in syllable codas in English and, more generally, in order not to waive the claim that neutralization is a 'psychologically real' concept, let us first consider the possibility of restricting it to proportional oppositions. In German, for example, it does not seem implausible that the final segment of a word like *und* is perceived by the speaker-hearer as a voicing–irrelevant dental stop because the opposition /t/ : /d/ is absent in final position *and* because there are other parallel oppositions which are also absent in this position; in other words, /t/ : /d/ is a proportional opposition and the other German oppositions belonging to this proportion are also absent in final position. In the case of British English /r/ : /l/, on the other hand, the reason why the feeling of the final segment of e.g. *ball* as an anteriority-irrelevant liquid does not arise might be that it is not supported elsewhere in the phonological system, i.e. we are here faced with an isolated phenomenon.

On closer inspection, however, such a condition can hardly be maintained. Suppose that a language contains the stop phonemes /p t k b d g m n ŋ/ and that the oral stops contrast both initially and finally in syllables, whereas /m/, /n/ and /ŋ/ do not contrast in the latter of these positions where only [ŋ] occurs. In such a language /m/ : /n/, /n/ : /ŋ/ and /ŋ/ : /m/ are obviously proportional oppositions since they are parallelled by respectively /p/ : /t/, /b/ : /d/, by /t/ : /k/, /d/ : /g/ and by /k/ : /p/, /g/ : /b/. However, the absence of /m/ : /n/ : /ŋ/ syllable-finally is not supported by any absence in this environment by /p/ : /t/ : /k/ or /b/ : /d/ : /g/. Therefore a condition according to which neutralization is restricted to those cases where a proportional opposition is absent and is accompanied by absence of other oppositions belonging to the same proportion is not satisfied. Note that even if a multivalued feature of articulatory place is recognized one obviously cannot in addition to a proportion like /m/ : /n/ = /p/ : /t/ = /b/ : /d/ operate with a proportion like /m/ : /n/ = /n/ : /ŋ/ = /ŋ/ : /m/. Since for reasons given in 10.5 I think that we should be prepared to recognize neutralization in a case like the one under discussion it seems necessary to reject a condition according to which only proportional oppositions are neutralizable.

It will be noted that we are caught on the horns of a dilemma only if /r/ : /l/ in English is considered a minimal opposition. In fact it is by no means obvious that this opposition should be regarded as minimal. To be sure there are data which point toward a very close relationship between /r/ and /l/. One example is provided by dissimilation products such as *pilgrim, turtle, marble* (cf. Lat. *peregrīnus*, Lat. *turtur*, French *marbre*), but most dissimilations of this type have taken place outside English. In fact, there is only scanty dissimilatory evidence in English which points towards a particularly close relationship between /r/ and /l/. Note also that /r/ is dissimilated into /j/, not /l/, in American English in a word like *February* ['fɛbjʊˌɛrɪ]. (The occurrence of [j] in this word is commonly assumed to be due to both dissimilation and analogy with *January*.) Consequently, /r/ : /l/ should perhaps not be regarded as a minimal opposition in English, and this might be the reason why the interpretation <r/l> in the above example is psychologically unconvincing. That English /r/ : /l/ is a non-minimal opposition is the opinion held by Ladefoged (1975, p. 268), according to whom these segments differ in respect of two features, namely 'lateral' and 'rhotacized'. It seems, then, that there is no strong reason to place any condition on our concept of neutralization, which involves minimal oppositions only, but that the definition of it as contextually determined loss of one distinctive dimension can probably be retained.

Finally, a brief remark about the phonological interpretation of English words like *shred* [ʃred] and *sled* [sled]. In this case I shall choose not to operate with neutralization. In the first place, and as pointed out in 9.1, it seems impossible to localize 'neutralization' in either the first or second segments of these words, i.e. they could be interpreted as either /<s/ʃ>red, <s/ʃ>led/ or as /ʃ<r/l>ed, s<r/l>ed/. This problem of localization does not disappear if /ʃl-/ is regarded as a possible cluster in English (compare a brand name like *Schlitz* [ʃlɪts] with a word like *slits* [slɪts]), for in that case the words could be analysed as /<s/ʃ>red, sled/ or as /ʃred, s<r/l>ed/. Secondly, it is doubtful whether either of the oppositions /s/ : /ʃ/ and /r/ : /l/ should be regarded as minimal. According to Chomsky and Halle, for example, /s/ and /ʃ/ differ in two features: 'anterior' and 'high' (1968, p. 177).

10.8. *Some Sample Neutralization Rules*

In the preceding chapters a large number of neutralizations from a wide variety of languages have been discussed. In this section we shall give a survey of these and a few other neutralizations, classify them according to the feature which is eliminated, and formulate some representative rules.

Tenuis : Media

In Russian the opposition between voiced and corresponding voiceless consonants is suspended in word-final position and before obstruents. Since one feature only is eliminated, and since the loss of this feature is contextually determined, the following neutralization rule can be formulated:[10]

$$[\pm \text{voiced}] \rightarrow \emptyset \left/ \left\{ \begin{array}{l} \_\_ \ \#\# \\ \_\_ \ [-\text{sonorant}] \end{array} \right\} \right.$$

As examples [xlep] 'bread' and [rɪpka] 'little fish' may be mentioned (cf. [xleba] gen.sing. and [rɪba] 'fish'). Voicing neutralizations are found in many other languages. In Czech it takes place in the same environments as in Russian, cf. *let* [let] 'flight', *led* [let] 'ice' and *svatba* ['svadba] 'wedding' (2.3, 2.7). In languages such as German and Dutch the dimension of voicing is eliminated in word-final position, cf. German examples like *rieb, riet, Sieg* and Dutch examples such as *heb, veld, lig* (2.8). In Rumanian it is eliminated before obstruents, cf. e.g. *despărţi, dezbrăca* (9.3), and in Polabian the same took place before all obstruents except /v/ and /j/ (2.2). In English the feature 'voiced' is neutralized in the non-initial segment(s) of homosyllabic obstruent clusters, cf. examples like *act, begged*; an argument for locating this neutralization in the non-initial segment(s) has been given by Mulder (1968, p. 199). In some American dialects the opposition between /t/ and /d/ is neutralized when preceded by a stressed vowel and followed by a weak vowel or syllabic consonant, as in *latter, ladder, metal, medal, bitten, bidden*. In Danish, finally, an analogous suspension of opposition can be demonstrated (cf. chapter 1, chapter 4, 9.1). Here the distinctive dimension of aspiration is lost word-finally, word-medially before schwa-like vowels, and in the non-initial segment(s) of obstruent clusters, cf. examples like *lap* 'patch' = *lab* 'paw', *lække* 'leak' = *lægge* 'lay', *spille* 'play', and *akt* 'act'.

---

10) Being concerned with principles rather than with details I have disregarded an exception to this rule, namely that the opposition of voice remains constant before /v/.

Palatalization

In Russian the distinctive dimension of palatalization is lost before palatalized and plain dentals, for in these two positions only palatalized and plain consonants respectively occur. In Jakobsonean features this suspension of opposition can be expressed by means of the following neutralization rule:

$$[\pm \text{sharp}] \rightarrow \emptyset \left/ \underline{\quad} \begin{bmatrix} + \text{consonantal} \\ - \text{compact} \\ - \text{grave} \end{bmatrix} \right.$$

As examples [s't'in'a, s'l'et] and [stol, slon, snop] can be mentioned (2.2). It should be added that the distinctive dimension of palatalization is eliminated in other contexts as well in Russian, cf. examples like [s'v''eckə] 'candle' and [d''ef'k'i, d''efk'i] 'girls', where the oppositions /s/ : /s'/ and /f/ : /f'/ are neutralized before respectively /v'/ and /k'/ (2.6, chapter 5), and [v'ilas'ip''et] 'bicycle', where the oppositions /p/ : /p'/ and /l/ : l'/ are neutralized before respectively /e/ and unstressed [a] (chapter 5). Recall also that in Polabian the dimension of palatalization was lost before all consonants, in final position, and before all vowels except [o α u ǎ ə̌]; in a word like [püp] 'priest', consequently, the opposition /p/ : /p'/ was neutralized initially as well as finally.

Articulatory Place

In Japanese (the Tokyo dialect), where /m/, /n/ and /ŋ/ contrast initially in syllables, the relevance of articulatory place is lost in syllable-final nasals: before labial consonants only [m] occurs, before dental consonants only [n], before velar consonants only [ŋ], and before vowels, glides and utterance-finally only nasalization of the preceding vowel, or a nasalized velar fricative, occurs (Niels Ege, personal communication). According to Hattori (1957, p. 41-42) speakers of Japanese do not identify a syllable-final nasal with any of the three syllable-initial ones. Now if a multivalued feature of articulatory place is recognized one can formulate the following Japanese neutralization rule:

$$[\text{articulatory place}] \rightarrow \emptyset \left/ \begin{bmatrix} + \text{nasal} \\ \underline{\quad} \end{bmatrix} \$ \right.$$

Neutralization rules which in certain contexts eliminate the dimension of place in nasals may be set up for a large number of languages, thus, for example, Marathi (3.2), Spanish, Italian and English (10.5). Recall in this connection that in the Old Indic Devanagari alphabet the symbol 'anusvara' is used for a nasal whose point of articulation is mechanically regulated by that of a following sound (2.2.).

Vowel Height
If vowel height is dealt with in terms of binary features, a neutralization rule can be established in some types of French which in certain contexts eliminates the feature 'low' (cf. 10.5). Assuming that the distribution of [e] and [ɛ] and of [o] and [ɔ] is the one given in 10.5 we can set up the following informal rule (in this rule I have disregarded [ø] : [œ], but the distribution of these two vowels roughly parallels that of [o] and [ɔ]):

$$
[\pm \text{low}] \rightarrow \emptyset \left/ \left\{ \begin{array}{l} \left[\begin{array}{l} + \text{syllabic} \\ - \text{back} \\ - \text{round} \\ \hline \end{array}\right] \quad \begin{array}{l} \text{in closed syllables and non-} \\ \text{final open syllables} \end{array} \\[2em] \left[\begin{array}{l} + \text{syllabic} \\ + \text{back} \\ + \text{round} \\ \hline \end{array}\right] \quad \begin{array}{l} \text{in open syllables, non-final} \\ \text{closed syllables and before} \\ \text{homosyllabic /r/} \end{array} \end{array} \right. \right.
$$

Possibly the suspension of the Russian oppositions /i/ : /e/ and /o/ : /a/ in unstressed position after nonpalatalized and nonpalatal consonants may be regarded as another example of neutralization of the feature 'low'.

10.9. *Some Difficult Cases*

Before trying out the above theory of neutralization on some cases from various languages where the identification of micro-phonemes in one position with micro-phonemes in others is connected with considerable difficulties, let us first recapitulate how the notion of neutralization and the archiphoneme have been conceived in this chapter.

By *neutralization* I understand a loss of one distinctive dimension which, wholly or in part, is contextually determined, and I have laid down the condition that such a loss must not always be accompanied by loss of another distinctive dimension (or of other distinctive dimensions), i.e. it should be separately observable in some position. Double neutralization occurs if two neutralizations, each of which can be observed in isolation, intersect in a given position (cf. the intersection of the voicing neutralization and palatalization neutralization in the sibilant of a Russian word like ['aist]). Triple neutralization, quadruple neutralization, etc. are also theoretically possible.

By *archiphoneme* I understand a contrastive segment in weak position whose distinctive features correspond to the intersection of two contrastive segments in strong position which differ in terms of one feature only. In the case of double neutralization the archiphoneme is a contrastive segment in weak position whose distinctive features correspond to the intersection of four (or possibly three) contrastive segments in strong position which differ in terms of two features (some might wish to call such a weak segment an archi-archiphoneme). In the case of triple neutralization the archiphoneme represents the intersection of eight (or possibly fewer) strong contrastive segments which differ in terms of three features. If multivalued features are recognized in addition to binary ones, the distinctive features of one archiphoneme may also correspond to the intersection of three or more contrastive segments in strong position which differ in terms of one feature only, cf. e.g. syllable-final nasals in Japanese. Recall, finally, that the operation of identification is performed on the basis of micro-features and structurally redundant phonetic features.

French Vowels

In 10.5 and 10.7 it was pointed out that if the dichotomous features 'high' and 'low' are recognized a French neutralization rule can be formulated which eliminates the distinctive dimension [± low] in vowels in certain environments. According to this rule words like *bile, belle, dimanche, démanche,* and *pou, pot, poulie, poli, pour, port* are interpreted as /bil, b<e/ε>l, dimãʃ, d<e/ε>mãʃ/ and /pu, p<o/ɔ>, puli, p<o/ɔ>li, pur, p<o/ɔ>r/. Suppose, however, that instead of eliminating [± low] we choose to eliminate the distinctive dimension [± high]. Due to contrasts like *dimanche : démanche* and *pou : pot, poulie : poli* the weak [e] and [o] of the last members of these pairs now contain the micro-feature [+ low] in the same way as [ε] and [ɔ] (cf. *bile : belle* and *pour : port*). Now according to such a rule and our proposed method of identification the [i] of *bile, dimanche* must now be identified with both /i/ and /e/, for the micro-features of this vowel — [- low, - back, - round]

— are contained in both these strong segments and /i/ and /e/ differ only with respect to the feature 'high'. Similarly the [u] of *pou, poulie, pour* must be identified with both /u/ and /o/ since its micro-features − [− low, + back, + round] − are contained in both these strong vowels and since /u/ and /o/ differ only with respect to the feature 'high'. On the other hand both [e] and [ɛ], which are characterized by the micro-features [+ low, − back, − round], must be identified with strong /ɛ/, and both [o] and [ɔ], which are characterized by the micro-features [+ low, + back, + round], must be identified with strong /ɔ/. In other words, by eliminating [± high] rather than [± low] we arrive at the phonological forms /b<i/e>l, bɛl, d<i/e>mãʃ, dɛmãʃ/ and /p<u/o>, pɔ, p<u/o>li, pɔli, p<u/o>r, pɔr/.

Now it will be recalled that one of the reasons adduced by Buyssens (2.8) for rejecting the concept of the archiphoneme is that it leads to arbitrary decisions and that the example he used was French *pour* and *port*, which might be interpreted either as /pur, p<o/ɔ>r/ or as /p<u/o>r, pɔr/. As pointed out in 2.10 it is not at all easy from a strictly functional point of view to come down in favour of a rule which eliminates [± low] rather than [± high] or *vice versa* (note that the criterion of partial complementarity is not quite satisfactory). On the other hand it is obvious that a rule which eliminates [± high] leads to phonological forms which are phonetically less realistic than the forms resulting from the alternative rule, cf. the analysis of [demã:ʃ], [po] and [poli] as /dɛmãʃ, pɔ, pɔli/. Furthermore, there can be little doubt that if there are any vowels in French which are psychologically indeterminate to the native speaker it is not the [i] and [u] of words like *bile, dimanche* and *pou, poulie, pour* but rather the vowels occurring in words like *belle, démanche, pot, poli, port* (cf. also Vion's criterion of indecision discussed in 2.9). It seems clear, therefore, that if the empirical correlates − physical as well as psychological − of the postulated phonological units are taken into consideration a neutralization rule which eliminates the distinctive dimension [± low] is preferable to a rule which eliminates [± high], and in this sense it may be claimed that an archiphonemic interpretation of the French vowels under discussion does not lead to arbitrary decisions.

A neutralization rule which in certain environments eliminates the feature 'low' in French is also suggested in Basbøll 1974 b. Basbøll first describes the vowel system of conservative standard French and in so doing sets up the following stressed oral vowel phonemes:

/i e: ɛ y ø: œ u o: ɔ ɑ: a/. In his distinctive feature matrix of these vowels he operates with the features 'high', 'back', 'round' and 'tense', the last of which serves to differentiate between /e: ø: o: ɑ:/ and /ɛ œ ɔ a/. The difference between these two sets of vowels is one of combined quality and quantity, and the use of the feature 'tense' to account for it is well-motivated since /e: ø: o: ɑ:/ are always long when length is realizable; since they have greater constriction (whether palatal, velar, or pharyngeal) than the corresponding lax vowels; and since longer duration may be assumed to accompany the more extreme articulation of these vowels. Basbøll points out that all the vowel pairs which are distinguished by means of the feature 'tense' tend to be neutralized in unstressed position, i.e. a neutralization rule may be set up which in this environment eliminates the distinctive dimension of tenseness in non-high oral vowels. Basbøll next turns to more recent standard French, where the quantity of oral vowels has become predictable from other phonetic surface traits without regard to quality, i.e. the interrelationship between quality and quantity which was the main reason for postulating the tenseness feature no longer exists. Since the vowels of *Beaune* : *bonne, les* : *laids,* etc. are now distinguished solely by means of quality it seems necessary to replace the feature 'tense' by another vowel height feature in addition to 'high', namely 'low'. The oral vowels of recent standard French are thus kept apart by means of the features 'high', 'low', 'back' and 'round' (cf. the matrix in 10.5), the two *a*-phonemes have coalesced into one (which is predictable according to Basbøll's analysis), and the feature 'low' serves to differentiate between /e ø o/ and /ɛ œ ɔ/. In other words, within the descriptive framework proposed by Basbøll a rule which in certain environments neutralizes the opposition between these two sets of vowels is assumed to be one which eliminates the feature 'low'.

Vowel Harmony in Turkish
In Turkish there are in word stems eight vowel phonemes which are distinguished in the following way (cf. Lyons 1968, p. 128):

	i	ï	ü	u	e	a	ö	o
High	+	+	+	+	−	−	−	−
Back	−	+	−	+	−	+	−	+
Round	−	−	+	+	−	−	+	+

In word suffixes the quality of a vowel is very largely determined by the preceding base vowel. The general principles are the following (cf. Lyons 1962 and Waterson 1956):

1) The feature 'back' takes the same value in suffix vowels as in the base vowel, cf. examples like [evim, gözüm, gözler] and [kïzïm, kolum, kollar].

2) If the base vowel is [- round], suffix vowels are [- round] as well, cf. [evim, kïzïm, evler, kïzlar].

3) If the base vowel is [+ round] and the first (or only) suffix vowel is [+ high], then this suffix vowel is [+ round] as well, and the next suffix vowel, if [+ high], is also [+ round], and so on. Examples: [gözüm, gülüm, gözümüz].

4) If the base vowel is [+ round] and a suffix vowel is [- high], then this suffix vowel is [- round], and the following suffix vowels (if any) are also [- round]. Examples: [gözler, kollar, güller, önünden, gözleriniz, kollarïmïzdan].

As a result of these dependencies the only contrastive feature in Turkish suffix vowels is 'high', cf. examples like [evim, evler], where the suffix vowel is independently [+ high] in the former word and independently [- high] in the latter. On the other hand, the features 'back' and 'round' are completely predictable in suffixes, and an idea which immediately suggests itself is therefore to set up only two suffix vowels, one of which is characterized by the features [+ syllabic, - consonantal, + high] and the other of which by the features [+ syllabic, - consonantal, - high].

It seems clear that of the above four rules the first three are of a purely assimilatory nature since in these cases the suffix vowel takes the same value for backness and rounding as the base vowel. In 4, however, the nonhigh suffix vowel is 'non-harmonic' since the value it takes for the feature 'round' is the opposite of that of the base vowel; here vowel harmony is restricted to retention of the feature value [- round] in any following suffix vowels. Now it seems unreasonable phonologically to let the feature value [+ round] in the base vowel be responsible for the value [- round] in a nonhigh suffix vowel, and it is therefore natural to exclude the first part of 4 from the domain of vowel harmony (in the true sense of this word) and to deal with it otherwise. If one attempts to account for 'genuine' vowel-harmony by means of the concept of neutralization, the following informal rules may be set up:

$[\pm \text{back}] \rightarrow \emptyset$ in suffix vowels (or, in the context VC_0—)

$[\pm \text{round}] \rightarrow \emptyset$ in high suffix vowels (or, in the context $[_{+ \text{high}}^{V}] C_0$—)

As a result of these rules and our proposed method of identification the high suffix vowels in words like [gözüm, evim, kolum, kollarïmïzdan] are identified — due to the absence in these vowels of the dimensions of backness and rounding — with the strong vowels /i/, /ï/, /ü/ and /u/, i.e. they are interpreted as the archiphoneme $<$i/ï/ü/u$>$. Furthermore, the low suffix vowels of words like [gözler, evler, kollarïmïzdan] are identified — due to the absence in these segments of the dimension of backness — with the strong vowels /e/ and /a/, i.e. they are analysed as the archiphoneme $<$e/a$>$.

(An alternative analysis of the Turkish data has been suggested by Hans Basbøll (personal communication): all Turkish suffix vowels may phonologically be considered [- round] (and [0 back]), and their phonetic manifestation may be accounted for by means of rules of the following type:

$$1) \quad V \rightarrow [\alpha \text{ back}] \Big/ \begin{bmatrix} V \\ \alpha \text{ back} \end{bmatrix} C_0 \underline{\hspace{1.5cm}}$$

$$2) \quad \begin{bmatrix} V \\ + \text{high} \end{bmatrix} \rightarrow [+ \text{round}] \Big/ \begin{bmatrix} V \\ + \text{round} \end{bmatrix} C_0 \underline{\hspace{1.5cm}}$$

Within such a model of description Turkish words such as [önünden], [kïzïm] and [gözümüz] would be dealt with like this:

	ön$<$i/ï$>$nd$<$e/a$>$n	kïz$<$i/ï$>$m	göz$<$i/ï$>$m$<$i/ï$>$z
Rule 1	↓	↓	↓
	öninden	kïzïm	gözimiz
Rule 2	↓	↓	↓
	önünden	kïzïm	gözümüz

Basbøll also points out that if high suffix vowels are considered [0 round], as I suggest, the following manifestation rule may be set up:

$$\begin{bmatrix} V \\ <+ \text{high}> \end{bmatrix} \longrightarrow \begin{bmatrix} \alpha \text{ back} \\ <\beta \text{ round}> \end{bmatrix} \Big/ \begin{bmatrix} V \\ \alpha \text{ back} \\ \beta \text{ round} \end{bmatrix} C_0 \underline{\hspace{1.5cm}}$$

Such a rule would change e.g. /ön<i/ï/ü/u>nd<e/a>n/ and /kïz<i/ï/ü/u>m/ directly into [önünden] and [kïzïm].

It will be noticed that as a result of the above neutralization rules — [± back] → Ø in suffix vowels and [± round] → Ø in high suffix vowels — and our proposed method of identification we operate with *defective distribution* of the vowel phonemes /o/ and /ö/ in suffixes; for since the feature 'round' remains unneutralized in low suffix vowels, the suffix vowels of words like [evler] and [kollar] contain in addition to [- high] the feature value [- round]. In other words, according to the analysis proposed here there are only two suffix vowels in Turkish, one of which is characterized by the features [+ syllabic, - consonantal, + high] and the other of which contains the features [+ syllabic, - consonantal, - high, - round].

In chapter 5, in 10.3, and at the beginning of this section, it was pointed out that in order for neutralization to be recognized in a given form it should be possible to formulate a rule which eliminates one distinctive dimension only. In the case of Russian examples like [s't'in'a] and ['aist] where more distinctive dimensions than one are involved, namely palatalization and voicing, it was argued that it is legitimate to speak of neutralization because each of these contextually determined losses of feature relevance can be observed and formulated separately (cf. examples like [snop] and [laskə]). Now although the situation is less clear-cut in Turkish it can be argued also in this case that it is possible to formulate two separate neutralization rules and that the loss of backness can be observed in isolation in examples like /evl<e/a>r/ and /koll<e/a>r/. On the other hand neutralization of the feature 'round', being always accompanied by backness neutralization, can never be observed separately, i.e. a relation of inclusive distribution exists between the environments specified in the two rules. Since it is possible, however, to separate one of the two rules from the other and observe it in isolation I am inclined to believe that neutralization should be recognized also in cases like vowel-harmony in Turkish.

As regards the manifestation of Turkish archiphonemes like <i/ï/ü/u> and <e/a>, rules may be set up which are of a simple assimilatory nature, since the former archiphoneme is realized as [i], [ï], [ü], [u] after base vowels which are respectively [- back, - round], [+ back, - round], [- back, + round], [+ back, + round] and <e/a> is manifested as [e], [a] after base vowels which are respectively [- back], [+ back]. In the case where vowel-harmony in respect of rounding is determined by a low suffix vowel the manifestation rule is also straightforward. In /gözl<e/a>r<i/ï/ü/u>n<i/ï/ü/u>z/, for example, the last two archiphonemes are realized as high vowels which are [- back] on account of the base vowel and [- round] on account of the first suffix vowel.

Since the values of the feature 'back' and 'round' are in fact predictable in any Turkish suffix vowel it could be argued from a strictly functional point of view that the only neutralization rules which could receive consideration are [± back] → Ø in suffix vowels and [± round] → Ø in suffix vowels. Being contextually identical these two rules could not according to our theory be recognized as neutralization rules. We would therefore have to conclude that neither the backness–dimension nor the rounding–dimension is lost in suffixes, but that suffix vowels contain the same number of features as base vowels in Turkish (in basically the same way that the [s] of English *sty* is assumed to contain the same features as that of *sigh*). Instead of operating with two suffix vowels we would then have to operate with six, namely /i/, /ï/, /ü/, /u/, /e/ and /a/. Such a solution, which has been proposed by Voegelin and Ellinghausen (1943), is not very attractive.

If identification is based exclusively on micro–features (cf. 10.2) any low suffix vowel would be identified with /e/, /ö/, /o/ and /a/ (in the same way that any high suffix vowel would be identified with /i/, /ï/, /ü/ and /u/). From a purely functional point of view this would be the appropriate thing to do, but it would not permit us to account naturally for the fact that suffix vowels following a low suffix vowel are unrounded; for example, the lack of rounding in the last two vowels of a word like [gözleriniz] cannot be explained if the first suffix vowel is interpreted as <e/ö/a/o>. Such an interpretation would necessitate a completely ad hoc rule converting <e/ö/o/a> to <e/a>, and not until this rule had applied could the rounding rule be used. As compared with a strictly functional analysis the <e/a> interpretation of a low suffix vowel has the advantage that it provides a natural explanation of the unrounded character of following suffix vowels, for in addition to the feature [- high] this archiphoneme contains the feature [- round]. The solution proposed here, according to which vowel–harmony is dealt with in terms of neutralization and according to which low suffix vowels are phonologically [- round], constitutes a compromise between the prosodic and the phonemic approaches to the data under discussion in the sense that only two suffix vowels are assumed, viz. <i/ï/ü/u> and <e/a>, and that the phonemes /o/ and /ö/ are considered absent in suffixes and thus defectively distributed. As compared with the prosodic analysis of vowel harmony in Turkish it has the advantage not only of predicting that suffix vowels are un-rounded after a low suffix vowel but of providing an assimilatory explanation of this fact as well, cp. the prosodic representation of a word like [gözleriniz] as /FRgazlariniz/ (in which /F/ symbolizes 'front', /R/ symbolizes 'rounding', and /a/ and /i/ symbolize respectively 'high vowel' and 'low vowel') with the archiphonemic representation /gözl<e/a>r<i/ï/ü/u>n<i/ï/ü/u>z/.

Vowel Harmony in Igbo

Vowel harmony in Igbo (a language of which I have no special knowledge) has been discussed in prosodic terms by J. Carnochan in a 1960 paper. At the outset of his paper Carnochan refers to Ida C. Ward, who has come to the conclusion that there are eight vowel phonemes in Igbo, namely /i e ɛ a u ɵ o ɔ/. These vowels are distin-guished by means of 'height', 'rounding' and 'particular degree of closeness' (this last dimension may possibly be regarded as a tense-ness–feature), as shown in the following matrix:

	i	e	ɛ	a	u	ɵ	o	ɔ
High	+	+	−	−	+	+	−	−
Raised	+	−	+	−	+	−	+	−
Round	−	−	−	−	+	+	+	+

In descriptions of Igbo it has been pointed out that in words of two or more syllables vowels agree as regards the value taken by the feature 'raised', cf. [izu] 'stealing' and [ezɵ] 'buying'. This means that a neutralization rule could be set up which eliminates the fea-ture 'raised' in all vowels except one in polysyllabic words. According to Carnochan, however, there are many exceptions to this rule, cf. examples like [litara, ebɔci, lɔruru], and he therefore suggests a fresh appraisement of vowel harmony and an investigation of it in various grammatical structures. Illustrating vowel harmony with short verbal pieces (subject-verb constructions) he gives the following examples involving 3rd person singular "tense 2" (roughly = present tense) forms:

[o siɛ]	'he cooks'	[o zuo]	'he steals'
[ɔ sea]	'he says'	[ɔ zeɔ]	'he buys'
[o tɛɛ]	'he rubs'	[o goo]	'he buys'
[ɔ saa]	'he washes'	[ɔ bɔɔ]	'he cuts up'

Here the phonetic shape taken by the pronoun – either [o] or [ɔ] (which differ only with respect to the feature 'raised') – is determined by the vowel of the verb stem. If the stem vowel is [– raised], the pronominal vowel is [– raised] as well, and if the stem vowel is [+ raised], the pronominal vowel is also [+ raised]. Carnochan interprets these data prosodically, but in a type of phonological description in which the concept of neutralization is recognized it seems that a rule can be formulated which eliminates the feature 'raised' in certain pronominal forms followed by a verb. Such a rule is of a fairly general nature, for it also applies to 3rd person singular "tense 1" (roughly = past tense) forms (e.g. [o siri] 'he cooked' vs. [ɔ sere] 'he said'), to 2nd person singular "tense 1" forms (e.g. [i siri] 'you cooked' vs. [e sere] 'you said'), and to the impersonal "tense 1" forms (e.g. [ɛ siri] 'it is cooked' vs. [a sere] 'it is said'). Since there are contrasts like [e sere]:[a sere] and [a sere] : [ɔ sere] the features 'high' and 'round' retain their distinctive value in these pronominal vowels;, i.e. a rule can be formulated which neutralizes one feature only, namely 'raised', and the vowels representing the personal pronouns 'he', 'you' and 'it' may be interpreted as respectively <o/ɔ>, <i/e> and <ɛ/a>.

In the above examples of 3rd person singular "tense 2" forms, the 'raising' of the suffix vowel is correlated with that of the stem vowel in the same way that the 'raising' of the pronominal vowel is, cf. [o siɛ] 'he cooks', where [+ raised] in [ɛ] goes together with [+ raised] in [i], and [ɔ sea] 'he says' where [– raised] in [a] goes together with [– raised] in [e]. In this case, however, the rounding of the suffix vowel is also correlated with that of the stem vowel, cf. [siɛ, sea, tɛɛ, saa], where the final vowel in each word is unrounded, and [zuo, zeɵ, goo, bɔɔ], where it is rounded. Within the framework of a phonological description in which the concept of neutralization is recognized this means 1) that the scope of the raising–neutralization must be extended to cover these suffix vowels as well, and 2) that a neutralization rule which in this environment eliminates the rounding–feature must be set up. Since both rounding and raising are neutralized in these suffix vowels we must according to the proposed method of identification analyse the final segments in words like [siɛ, sea, tɛɛ, saa, zuo, zeɵ, goo, bɔɔ] as a neutralization product of the vowel phonemes /ɛ/, /a/, /o/ and /ɔ/, i.e. as the archiphoneme <ɛ/a/o/ɔ>.

Consider finally the following 2nd person singular "tense 1" constructions:

[i siri]	'you cooked'	[i zuru]	'you stole'
[e sere]	'you said'	[e zɵrɵ]	'you bought'
[i sɛrɛ]	'you quarrelled'	[i zoro]	'you hid'
[e sara]	'you washed'	[e zɔrɔ]	'you got up'

Here the suffix vowels are identical with the stem vowels, i.e. the features 'raised' and 'round', as well as 'high', have lost their distinctive value. Within the framework of our theory this means 1) that the scope of the raising–neutralization and rounding–neutralization must be extended to cover examples like these as well, and 2) that a neutralization rule which in this context eliminates the feature 'high' must be set up. Since all three features — raising, rounding, height — are neutralized here we must according to our method of identification analyse the final segments of words like [siri, sere, sɛrɛ, sara, zuru, zɵrɵ, zoro, zɔrɔ] as neutralization products of all the vowel phonemes found in Igbo. Note that we are in this case faced with three neutralization rules which coincide.

Apart from the fact that three and not two neutralization rules must be set up to account for vowel harmony in Igbo, the situation is much the same as in Turkish and poses the same problem, namely that only one type of neutralization can be observed in isolation. In Turkish the distribution of the backness–neutralization includes that of the rounding–neutralization. In Igbo, within the material put forward by Carnochan, the distribution of the raising–neutralization includes that of the rounding–neutralization, and the distribution of the rounding–neutralization, in turn, includes that of the height-neutralization. Raising–neutralization can be observed in isolation in the initial vowels of examples like [i siri, ɛ siri, o siri], which are analysed as respectively <i/e>, <ɛ/a>, <o/ɔ>, i.e. as vowels which carry distinctive values of the 'height' and 'rounding' features. Rounding–neutralization can be observed unaccompanied by height-neutralization in verb forms like [siɛ, sea, tɛɛ, saa, zuo, zɵɵ, goo, bɔɔ], where the final vowels are interpreted as <ɛ/a/o/ɔ>. Height-neutralization can never be observed unaccompanied by raising-neutralization and rounding–neutralization, cf. examples like [siri, sere, sɛrɛ, sara, zuru, zɵrɵ, zoro, zɔrɔ], where the suffix vowels are interpreted as a neutralization product of /i e ɛ a u ɵ o ɔ/.

If the archiphoneme covering all the vowel phonemes of Igbo is symbolized as /V/ we can set up phonological forms like these:

/<o/ɔ> sa<ɛ/a/o/ɔ>/	[ɔ saa]	'he washes'
/<o/ɔ> si<ɛ/a/o/ɔ>/	[o siɛ]	'he works'

13⁺

/<ɛ/a> sirV/	[ɛ siri]	'it is cooked'
/<ɛ/a>serV/	[a sere]	'it is said'

These representations may be compared with the following prosodic formulas set up by Carnochan:

L [(A)w (CAA)y]	[ɔ saa]	'he washes'
R [(A)w (CIA)y]	[o siɛ]	'he works'
R [(A)y (CIrə)y]	[ɛ siri]	'it is cooked'
L [(A)y (CIrə)y]	[a sere]	'it is said'

In these formulas /A/, /I/, /C/ and /ə/ symbolize respectively 'low vowel', 'high vowel', 'consonant', 'syllabic' and are regarded as phonematic units. On the other hand /L/, /R/, /w/ and /y/ symbolize respectively 'lowered', 'raised', 'rounded', 'unrounded' and are regarded as prosodic elements whose domain is the whole construction in the case of /L/ and /R/ and one or two syllables in the case of /w/ and /y/.

In Firthian studies it has often been pointed out that a prosodic approach is particularly well suited to dealing with vowel harmony and that a phonemic approach to such vowel dependencies is inadequate. In Turkish and Igbo, however, it seems that a statement in terms of neutralization (in which syntagmatic relations will also be emphasized) is a possible and adequate alternative. In this connection one final remark may be added. In a description of vowel harmony in Lhasa–Tibetan, which is of the type in which degrees of closure are interrelated, R.K. Sprigg (1961) draws attention to the advantages of a prosodic analysis over other types of phonological analysis as regards the description of interrelated vocalic features of successive syllables. However, Sprigg compares a prosodic statement of vowel harmony with a phonemic statement, not with a phonological statement in which the concept of neutralization is recognized. Since this case involves one distinctive dimension only, namely 'closeness', and since a given example of 'closure piece' must be either open or close, it would not seem impossible to formulate an adequate rule which in certain environments (e.g. in one of two successive syllables in certain grammatical structures) eliminates a vowel height feature, e.g. 'low'.

The Consonants of Saigon Vietnamese

In Saigon Vietnamese, a language of which I have no special knowledge (apart from having read Thomson 1959 and Rischel MS), the following system of consonant phonemes, all of which occur initially in syllables, is set up by Thompson (cf. 10.1):[11]

	labial	apical non-retroflex	apical re-troflex	frontal	dorsal	glottal
fortis stop	p	t	ṭ	c	k	ʔ
fortis continuant	f	s	ṣ	j	x	–
lenis	w	tˤ	r	l	g	h
nasal	m	n		ɲ	ŋ	–

A comparison of the system of final consonants with that of initial ones reveals that in addition to the dimensions established in weak position, the dimensions of retroflexion (i.e. [± distributed]) and backness are needed in strong position, cf. e.g. /s-/ : /ṣ-/ and /ɲ-/ : /ŋ-/.[12] It would therefore be natural to formulate the following rules (in which $ symbolizes syllable boundary):

$$[\pm \text{distributed}] \rightarrow \emptyset \ / \ \underline{\quad} \$$$

$$[\pm \text{back}] \rightarrow \emptyset \ / \ [+ \text{consonantal}] \ \$$$

Now it will be recalled that in 10.2 I laid down the condition that in order for neutralization to be recognized, a loss of distinctive dimension must be 'clean' in the sense that it must not always be accompanied by simultaneous loss of another distinctive dimension. This condition is violated here, for whenever [± distributed] is eliminated

---

11) Thompson's classification of [j] (which he describes as a relatively high front semivowel) as a fortis consonant does not seem unproblematic, and his category of lenis consonants looks like a somewhat mixed bag.

12) As opposed to /k/ and /ŋ/, which are termed mediovelar, and /t/, /ṭ/ and /n/, which are termed apical, /c/ and /ɲ/ are (according to Thompson) frontals, i.e. they are "characterized by the acoustic effect of the front of the tongue touching ... the alveolar ridge" (459–460). However, considering the way they are placed in Thompson's overall table I shall assume that they may be regarded as [– anterior], i.e. as being articulated in the same zone as e.g. English /tʃ/ and /dʒ/. If they were regarded as [+ anterior], we would have to keep them apart from respectively /t/, /ṭ/ and /n/ by means of the feature [+ high].

[± back] is eliminated as well, and *vice versa*. The fact that [+ consonantal] must be specified for the elimination of backness but not of retroflexion is due simply to the absence of retroflexion as a relevant dimension in vowels. In other words, neither of these 'neutralization rules' can be observed in isolation, and unless the above condition is weakened they therefore have to be rejected. Note, however, that the two rules are of fundamentally the same nature, for the former eliminates the distinction between advanced and retracted apicals and the latter the distinction between advanced and retracted dorsals (in the broad sense of this term). Since 'distributed' and 'backness' are in complementary distribution, it is possible to set up a more abstract cover feature, e.g. 'advanced', and theorize that it is this dimension which is eliminated (Jørgen Rischel, personal communication):

$$[\pm \text{advanced}] \rightarrow \emptyset / \underline{\quad} \$$$

I therefore tentatively propose that if two (perhaps more) features are in complementary distribution and conspire in such a way that it is possible to set up a more abstract feature which covers both these features, it is legitimate to operate with neutralization. In Saigon Vietnamese I shall therefore assume that there is neutralization of the dimension(s) by which e.g. /s-/ : /ṣ-/ and /ɲ-/ : /ŋ-/ are kept apart.

Let us now attempt to identify syllable-final consonants with syllable-initial consonants in Saigon Vietnamese. First, the microphoneme /t/, which as a result of neutralization lacks the dimension of retroflexion, and the micro-features of which are contained in more strong micro-phonemes than one, must be identified with two strong micro-phonemes. These must differ only in being respectively [+ distributed] and [- distributed], and the identification must not be phonetically unrealistic. Now these strong micro-phonemes must be /t/ and /ṭ/. Even if we assume that the micro-features [+ consonantal, + coronal, + anterior, - nasal] are contained in /tʿ/, and that /tʿ/ and /ṭ/ differ only in carrying opposite feature specifications for the retroflexion feature, an identification of /-t/ with /tʿ-/ and /ṭ-/ can be rejected according to the principle of phonetic similarity. Similarly, a possible identification of /t/ with /s-/ and /ṣ-/ can be ruled out according to the same principle. Secondly, the final microphoneme /k/, which as a result of neutralization lacks the distinctive dimension of backness, and whose micro-features are contained in more segments than one occurring in strong position, must be identified with two strong phonemes which differ only in being respectively [+ back], [- back]. Since the only initial micro-phonemes which contain the micro-features of /-k/, and which differ only in carrying opposite feature specifications for the backness feature are /c-/ and /k-/, we shall identify /-k/ with these strong segments. In this case the criterion of phonetic similarity need not be brought into play (except insofar as features themselves are phonetically based). Thirdly, the final micro-phoneme /ŋ/ can, according to the same principles as those employed in identifying /-k/ with /c-/ and /k-/, be identified with both /ɲ-/ and /ŋ-/. It will be noticed that the identifications which we have made so far have been phonetically realistic.

In the remaining cases we are unable to perform phonetically realistic identifications of a final micro-phoneme with two initial ones which differ exclusively in carrying opposite feature specifications for a neutralized feature, and in which the micro-features of the weak segment are contained. For example, we cannot equate /-p/, which lacks the distinctive dimensions of retroflexion and backness, with /t-/ and /ṭ-/ or /s-/ and /ṣ-/, or with /c-/ and /k-/ or /ɲ-/ and /ŋ-/, for the micro-features of /-p/ are not contained in any of these pairs of strong micro-phonemes. Therefore we shall equate each of the remaining final micro-phonemes with one initial micro-phoneme only, and according to the principles of contained micro-features and phonetic realism we must identify /-p/, /-ʔ/, /-w/, /-j/, /-g/, /-h/, /-m/ and /-n/ with respectively /p-/, /ʔ-/, /w-/, /j-/, /g-/, /h-/, /m-/ and /n-/. In this way all the final micro-phonemes of Saigon Vietnamese have been equated with initial ones like this:

Strong position		Weak position
p	←——————→	p
t, ṭ	←——————→	t
c, k	←——————→	k
ʔ	←——————→	ʔ
w	←——————→	w
j	←——————→	j

(cont.)

200

(cont.)   Strong position   Weak position

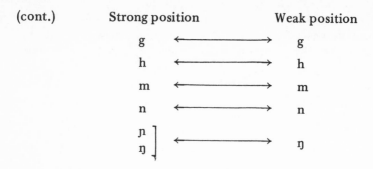

In contradistinction to a statement exclusively in terms of defective distribution such an identification will not, it seems, fail to indicate the really characteristic feature of final non-syllabics in Saigon Vietnamese, i.e. it will not result in an extremely asymmetrical phonological sub-system. In terms of the features which Thompson operates with there will be no more than four distinctive places of articulation finally, and the fortis stops and nasals which occur in this position will be the following:

p $\langle t/\underset{.}{t}\rangle$ $\langle c/k\rangle$ ʔ
m   n $\langle \textbardbl/\eta\rangle$ -

Now there can be little doubt that it is data like the consonants of Saigon Vietnamese which Twaddell and the Firthians would cite in support of their polysystemic theories. It is therefore important to stress the fact that an analysis which permits both-and identifications, and which recognizes neutralization products such as $\langle t/\underset{.}{t}\rangle$, $\langle c/k\rangle$ and $\langle \textbardbl/\eta\rangle$, does not lead to the same amount of asymmetry as a pure either-or analysis in cases of this type.

Korean Consonants
Let us assume, first, that in a given language the only distinctive stop consonants which occur finally in syllables are [p t k] and that the following system of distinctive stop consonants is found initially in syllables:

b   d   g
p   t   k
ph   th   kh

In this language a rule like [± voiced] → Ø / __ $ will always be accompanied by [± aspirated] → Ø /_ $, and *vice versa*. As in the case of Saigon Vietnamese, however, it is possible to set up a cover feature, namely 'voice onset time' (cf. Abramson and Lisker 1967), and assume that it is this dimension which is eliminated in syllable codas. Within the framework of Ladefoged's feature system it is not even necessary to operate with any cover feature, since it can simply be said that the feature 'aspirated', which specifies when voicing starts with respect to the timing of the articulation, and which may specify a three-way opposition, is eliminated finally in syllables (cf. Ladefoged 1975, p. 261). In either analysis it is possible to operate with neutralization and thus to interpret final [p], [t], [k] as the archiphonemes <b/p/ph>, <d/t/th>, <g/k/kh>.

A situation of this type exists in Korean. In this language the only distinctive stop consonants which occur in syllable codas (before orals or utterance-finally) are unaspirated [p t k] (cf. Kim 1970 and Tcheu 1967). Initially in syllables the following system of stop consonants is found:

p	t	c	k
p^h	t^h	c^h	k^h
ph	th	ch	kh

In this case a highly natural solution would be to operate with a multivalued feature of aspiration (voice onset time) which is neutralized in final position. According to our proposed method of identification final [p], [t] and [k] will be analysed as the archiphonemes $<p/p^h/ph>$, $<t/t^h/th>$ and $<k/k^h/kh>$ respectively, for (a) [p], [p^h] and [ph], etc. differ only with respect to aspiration, (b) the micro-features of [-p], [-t], [-k] are contained in respectively [p- p^h- ph-], [t- t^h- th-] and [k- k^h- kh-], and (c) this identification is phonetically more realistic than one involving [c- c^h- ch-].

An alternative analysis of the Korean data has been put forward by Tcheu (1967). Instead of operating with three degrees of aspiration Tcheu sets up a series of lax stops (in my notation [p^h t^h c^h k^h]), a series of tense stops ([p t c k]), and a series of aspirated stops ([ph th ch kh]). As in the above analysis final [p] is equated with initial [p], [p^h], [ph]; and final [k] with initial [k], [k^h], [kh]. On the other hand [t] is equated with all the remaining obstruents in Korean, i.e. with [t], [t^h], [th], [c], [c^h], [ch] and tense and lax [s]. Such an analysis is perfectly legitimate if the operation of identification is based on micro-features, for the micro-features of final [t] are contained in all these initial obstruents, and none of the micro-features by which these eight obstruents are kept apart are contained in final [t]. It should not be overlooked, though, that if identification is based exclusively on micro-features it becomes very difficult to separate neutralization from defective distribution (cf. 10.3), and Tcheu's analysis of final [t] in Korean as a central archi-obstruent /T/ seems to show that he would also interpret e.g. the [s] of an English word like *spin* as an archiconsonant, i.e. as a neutralization product. It is unlikely, furthermore, that an archi-archiphoneme like /T/, which embraces eight initial micro-phonemes, reflects any psychological reality in the minds of Koreans.

Concluding Remarks

It is clear from the discussion of the above difficult cases that our conception of neutralization has to be modified in two respects. On the basis of the data from Turkish and Igbo, first, it appears that the condition according to which neutralization can be recognized only if a contextually determined loss of one distinctive dimension is separately observable has to be weakened. I shall now say that if the context specifications of two potential neutralization rules are not identical, then these rules may be recognized as genuine neutralizations. Although in Turkish, for example, it is never possible to observe loss of the rounding dimension unaccompanied by loss of the backness dimension, I shall recognize both the elimination of rounding and of backness as neutralization rules, for since the former applies in high suffix vowels and the latter in all suffix vowels the context specifications of these two rules are not identical. Secondly, it appears from the discussion of Saigon Vietnamese that neutralization should probably also be recognized in those cases where two (or more) losses of distinctive dimension occur in exactly the same context if it is possible to set up a more abstract feature which covers both these dimensions. The last situation is admittedly problematic and should perhaps be regarded as a borderline case of neutralization.

10.10. Empirical Data

In 10.2 neutralization was defined as contextually determined loss of one distinctive dimension, and in 10.4 the archiphoneme was defined as a contrastive segment in weak position whose distinctive features correspond with the intersection of two strong segments and which is identified with two such segments differing with respect to one feature only. In this section I shall discuss some empirical data which appear to support neutralization and archiphonemes understood in this sense. It should be pointed out that the approach adopted is not 'empirical linguistics' in the sense that it is attempted to discover whether there are sound segments in various languages which are psychologically or neurophysiologically indeterminate and then to set up a theory of neutralization which accounts for precisely such cases. What I shall do instead is to investigate whether the proposed method of identification is reasonable in the light of various extralinguistic data (e.g. orthography, slips of the tongue) as compared with the either–or methods of identification. Such an approach, which would seem to provide a useful check on linguistic hypotheses, is basically similar to the 'two–pronged attack' proposed by Chomsky and Halle. After having attempted to make the strongest legitimate universal claim about the structure of language they seek "to construct an evaluation procedure for selecting one among various grammars permitted by the proposed linguistic theory and compatible with the given data" (1965, p. 107). Compare also Twaddell, who states that it would be nice if a postulated phonological unit should turn out to be an "objectively determinable reality" (1935 (1957, p. 67)).

Orthographical Evidence
In a paper by Blair Rudes (1976) the following is said about the relationship between phonology and orthography (p. 117):

> It appears true that, when a language is first given an alphabetic orthography by speakers of the language, the orthography will, within limits set by the number of symbols available, represent the autonomous phonemes or contrastive units of the language. This transfer from phonemes to graphemes goes quite smoothly until cases of contextual neutralization are encountered. Here, the speaker developing the orthography encounters the same sort of arbitrary decision as is faced by the symbolic phonemicists, and the results are equally non–uniform.

This hypothesis, which seems highly plausible, is confirmed in a number of writing systems. Thus Trubetzkoy (1933a, p. 111) draws attention to a special symbol — the 'anusvara' — which in the Old

Indic Devanagari alphabet is used for a nasal whose point of articulation is mechanically regulated by that of a following sound, and which has therefore no phonological value (cf. 2.2).[13] He also points out that in the Avestan alphabet the dental stop which occurs word–finally and before obstruents, and which in these positions is voicing–irrelevant, is symbolized with a special letter which is identical with neither *t* nor *d*. Thirdly, Trubetzkoy argues that in Old Greek the letters ʃ and ψ were introduced in order to represent an /s/ preceded by a stop consonant which was neutral both with respect to the voicing opposition and with respect to the aspiration opposition. In these three cases we are faced with special letters which are used to symbolize neutralized phonemes, but it is obvious that the concept of neutralization is supported just as well (if not better, cf. chapter 1) if there is vacillation between two letters, consistently kept apart elsewhere, in positions of neutralization. Some cases of this type are discussed in the following.

Old English

In early West–Saxon (c. 900) the system of short monophthong vowel phonemes may be assumed to have been the following (cf. Kuhn 1961, p. 536, table IV; and Sprockel 1965, p. 135 ff):

i	y	u
e		o
æ		ɑ

It appears from this table that the vowels [y], [o] and [ɑ] are interpreted as separate phonemes, not as allophones of /u/ and /æ/. This analysis is based on the following facts: 1) There are minimal pairs, e.g. *cynne* (dat. sg. of *cynn* 'race') ≠ *cunne* (subj. of *cunnan* 'can, know'), which reveal that [y], which arose through *i*–umlaut of /u/, had at this stage become phonologized. 2) Similarly, there are

---

13) According to Thumb (1958, p. 206) the anusvara represents in modern pronunciation a nasalized vowel before sibilants, /h/ and /l/; an [m] in word–final position; and a nasal consonant which is homorganic with the following sound word–medially before consonants (cf. examples like *manāṃsi, devam tatra, sambharanti* where it appears before *s*, word–finally and before *bh*). Prosodically, it is added, the anusvara functions as a consonant. It is assumed that the anusvara was originally a homorganic nasalized vowel which was tagged on to an oral vowel, i.e. words like *aṃsa* and *puṃs* were supposedly pronounced [ããsa, puũs].

minimal pairs which show that [o], which was at an earlier stage a variant of /u/ occurring before an open vowel in the following syllable, had by now become phonologized, cf. *worpen* ≠ *wurpen* (past part. and past subj. pl. of *weorpan* 'throw'). 3) The vowel [ɑ] was no longer in complementary distribution with [æ], and although instances of minimal contrast are hard to find (note, however, *bac* 'bake' (imp. of *bacan*) ≠ *bæc* 'back' and *far* 'go' (imp. of *faran*) ≠ *fær* 'journey'), there are several distributional facts which indicate that it had become phonologized (cf. Chatman 1958, p. 225).

Let us assume that the short monophthongs of Old English are kept apart by means of the following feature specifications:

	i	e	æ	y	u	o	ɑ
High	+	−	−	+	+	−	−
Low		−	+			−	+
Back	−	−	−	−	+	+	+
Round	−		+				

It appears from this table that /o/ and /ɑ/ are considered distinctively opposed to each other in terms of height, i.e. the difference in rounding between these vowels is regarded as redundant (cf. Campbell 1959, where *o* is said to represent a rounded back vowel which is "rather less open than that of NE *not*" (p. 15)). Now before nasal consonants the system of contrastive vowels is reduced, there being only two distinctive degrees of vowel height in this context. Thus the three-way distinctions /i/ : /e/ : /æ/ and /u/ : /o/ : /ɑ/ are found before nonnasals, cf. examples like *flite* (dat. sg. of *flit* 'strife') ≠ *fete* (pres. sg. subj. of *fetan* 'fall') ≠ *fæte* (dat. sg. of *fæt* 'vessel') and *cure* (pret. sg. subj. of *cēosan* 'choose') ≠ *(ge)core* (dat. sg. of *gecor* 'decision') ≠ *care* (dat. sg. of *caru* 'grief'), but before nasals there is never more than a two-way contrast between high and non-high vowels, cf. *bindan* 'bind' (strong verb) ≠ *bendan* 'bend' (weak verb) and *cunne* (subj. of *cunnan* 'know') ≠ *canne* 'cup'. In other words, a system of seven contrastive short vowels has in this environment been reduced to a system of five. Consequently, it is possible to formulate the following neutralization rule:

$$[\pm \text{low}] \rightarrow \emptyset \ / \ \begin{bmatrix} + \text{ syllabic} \\ - \text{ long} \end{bmatrix} \ [+ \text{ nasal}]$$

According to our proposed method of identification the first vowel of *bendan*, whose micro-features are [- high, - back], must be equated with strong /e/ and /æ/, and the first vowel of *canne*, whose micro-features are [- high, + back], must be equated with strong /o/ and /a/. In other words, these vowels are interpreted as the archiphonemes <e/æ> and <o/a>.

In early West-Saxon manuscripts there is vacillation before nasals between the letters *a* and *o* and between the letters *æ* and *e*, cf. examples like *gangen ~ gongan* 'go', *hana ~ hona* 'cock', *nama ~ noma* 'name' and *Dænisc ~ Denisc* 'Danish', *Ængle ~ Engle* 'the English'. In Sprockel 1965 statistics based on the Parker Chronicle are given of this vacillation. It appears from the data that *o* predominates at an early stage, but that *a* becomes the more common letter later on. Of the two letters symbolizing the *i*-umlaut reflex of P.Gmc. /a/ before nasals it is *æ* which predominates in early Old English and *e* which is the more common letter at a later stage. (In early West Saxon texts, however, *e* is by far the more common letter.)

In conclusion it may be said, first, that it is clearly possible to account for the above data by means of the concept of neutralization. Secondly, it can be argued that this analysis finds support in Old English orthography, where two pairs of letters, consistently kept apart in other contexts, vacillate in the position before a nasal consonant. To be sure, the *i*-umlaut reflex of P.Gmc. /a/ in contexts other than that of a following nasal is also written with both *æ* and *e*, but in contradistinction to the position before nasals, where both letters occur in the same stems (e.g. *Ængle ~ Engle*), there is in this case apparently no vacillation in the sense that one and the same morpheme may be spelled sometimes with *æ* and sometimes with *e* (cf. Sprockel 1965, p. 10f). It seems, then, that a fairly strong case can be made for regarding the nonhigh short vowels occurring before nasals in Old English as entities which were psychologically indeterminate and which could therefore be written with the letters *e, o* as well as with the letters *æ, a*.

Irish and Scots Gaelic

In his 1976 article Blair Rudes points out that in Middle and Early Modern Irish the voicing-irrelevant stops which occurred after /s/ were written not with the letters *p, t, c(k)* (as in e.g. English, French, German) but with *b, d, g*. This spelling is retained in Modern Scots Gaelic, cf. examples like *sbeach* 'wasp, bee', *sdair* 'history', and *sgamall* 'cloud'. However, in Modern Irish, after the spelling reform in the 1940's and 1950's, these clusters are written with *sp, st, sc*. Rudes now argues that since the same phonetic/phonological material may be written in two different ways, the choice between *b, d, g* and *p, t, c* depending only on time and place, the stops after /s/ must psychologically be voicing–irrelevant neutralization products:

> This orthographic difference between Scots Gaelic (and Early Modern Irish) and Modern Standard Irish shows clearly the fact that the voiceless lenis stops which follow *s* in Gaelic are felt by the speakers to belong to neither the voiced phoneme nor to the voiceless phoneme, but represent an archiphoneme for which voicing is non-contrastive (p. 118).

It should be added that in Irish the voicing neutralization is not limited to the position after /s/; it also applies to the position after /ʃ/ and /x/. Consequently, voicing–irrelevant stop consonants are found not only in examples like *cuspóir* 'object, target',*stad* 'a stop, halt', *scoil* 'school', but also in e.g. *sgéal* 'story'(which is pronounced with a [ʃ] before the palato–velar stop) and *bochta* 'poverty, want' (which is pronounced with [x]). Furthermore, the elimination of the feature 'voiced' after /s, ʃ, x/ applies both to the palatalized and to the non-palatalized series of stop phonemes. In *sgéal*, for example, it is the opposition /k'/ : /g'/ which is neutralized, whereas in *scoil* it is the opposition /k/ : /g/. Now according to Quiggin (1906, p. 141) Modern Irish orthography hesitates between the letters *p, t, c* and *b, d, g* in the position after /s, ʃ, x/. This statement obviously applies to the situation before the spelling reform. However, even recent Irish orthography cannot be completely uniform in this respect, for in a description of the Irish of Erris dating from 1968 it is pointed out by Mac an Fhailigh that there is vacillation between *p, t, c* and *b, d, g* after /s, ʃ, x/ (p. 25). The vacillation between two sets of letters, consistently kept apart elsewhere, in positions where the voicing opposition is not found, indicates that the stop consonants are here psychologically indeterminate entities, and it may thus be regarded as empirical evidence which supports the concept of neutralization.[14]

14) The following has been pointed out to me by R.B. Walsh (personal communication): in Old and Middle Irish *sp, st, sc* is standard usage, but in 'Classical Irish' (c. 1200 to 1600) *sg* is regularly used instead of *sc;* *sb, sd* are not infrequently used instead of *sp, st;* and *chd* occasionally replaces
(cont.)

208

Slips of the Tongue
Speech error evidence has been used to shed light on various linguistic phenomena (cf. e.g. Fromkin 1973). Errors of this type may also be studied with special reference to the concept of neutralization. In particular, it is interesting to investigate the situation where, by a slip of the tongue, a segment is shifted from weak position to strong position. If such a shifted segment appears in the position of relevance sometimes as one and sometimes as the other member of the opposition involved, this would seem to support an analysis of that segment as a neutralization product.

A speech error investigation of the stop consonants after /s/ in English, German and Danish has been carried out with this object in mind (cf. Davidsen-Nielsen 1975, to which the reader is referred for details). Informants were asked to record nonsense words such as (English) *gaspate* [gə'speɪtʰ], *kaspate* [kʰə'speɪtʰ], *skamate* [skə'meɪtʰ] one by one in rapid succession, and in this way a corpus of 142 slips of the tongue was obtained. In this corpus — and I shall here restrict myself to a discussion of the English data — there were three basic types of errors: transposition (e.g. *kaspate* → *paskate*), *s*-movement (e.g. *kaspate* → *skapate*) and *s*-loss (e.g. *gaspate* → *gabate*). It appeared that both [p t k] and [b d g] emerge, cf. examples like *spakate* → *skapate, paskate*, or *pakate*, where it is [p] which is produced, and *spagate* → *skabate, baskate*, or *bagate*, where it is [b] which is produced. To me the most natural interpretation of the data is the following: the stops after /s/ are encoded as voicing-irrelevant neutralization products. When by a slip of the tongue they are moved to strong position they are realized as [p t k] if the interfering segment, i.e. the segment which is interchanged with the archisegment or which attracts the [s], is voiceless, and as [b d g] if the interfering segment is voiced. In the case of *s*-loss there is no such pattern of distribution, but both voiced and voiceless stops occur, cf. e.g. *gaspate* → *gapate* or *gabate*. In other words, the stops after /s/ are considered ambiguous with respect to voicing, and

(cont.)

cht. Learned editors of Bardic poetry tend to normalize to *sg* but to *sp, st, cht.* Walsh also points out that Rudes' term 'Modern Standard Irish' is misleading, there being no such thing as a standard of spoken Modern Irish. The only 'standard' which exists is the written one devised by the civil service in the 1940's and 1950's for use in official documents and in school textbooks.

when through a speech error they are moved to strong position they are disambiguated as either /p t k/ or /b d g/. With a few isolated exceptions such an interpretation accounts both for the data contained in the investigation and for the data of the same type derived from other sources (i.e. for natural slips of the tongue in addition to provoked laboratory slips).

Obviously it is not enough to put forward a theory which accounts adequately for the recorded instances of slips affecting stops after /s/. It is also necessary to consider alternative analyses and to investigate whether they might possess the same explanatory power. If it is assumed that these stops are encoded as [- voiced], it is possible, first, to explain many instances of *transposition* by assuming that it is features rather than whole segments which are affected. In *spakate* → *skapate* and *spagate* → *skabate*, for example, it may be argued that it is the values of the feature 'articulatory place' which are switched and that the voicing feature remains unaffected. If a nasal is involved, however, such an interpretation is not without difficulties. In an example like *spell mother* → *smell buther* (Fromkin 1971, p. 35) one would have to say that a transposition of the values of the nasality feature takes place and that this is accompanied by a change of [- voiced] to (redundant) [+ voiced] in the postinitial segment (note that there are no voiceless nasals in English). In an example like *skamate* → *smaga(te)* it would be necessary to assume that a transposition takes place both as regards articulatory place and nasality and that here again a change of [- voiced] to [+ voiced] occurs in the segment after /s/. (In this case it seems much simpler to argue that <k/g> and /m/ are transposed and that the neutralization product is here disambiguated as /g/.) As regards *s-movement*, cf. examples like *spakate* → *paskate* and *spagate* → *baskate*, one would have to argue that in addition to an s-shift a transposition of the values of the voicing feature takes place whenever [b d g] emerge. It is difficult to see why such a concomitant feature shift must take place and why e.g. *spagate* → *paskate* is not found.[15] In an example like *skamate* → *gasmate* one would have to

---

15) In Danish an example is found of an /s/ being attached to a following /g/, namely in the common swear-word *sgu*, which arose through contraction of *så Gud* 'so God', and which is pronounced exactly like *sku* 'should'. Note also an English example like *let's go* pronounced [sgəu]. With such examples in mind it is difficult to see why the /s/ of *spagate* cannot be attached to the /g/ without affecting the voicing of the postinitial stop segment, i.e. why it does not change into *paskate*.

say that in addition to *s*-movement a transposition of the value of the feature 'voiced' takes place in principle but that it cannot be effected fully, due to the fact that [- voiced] in the nasal is impossible. Such an analysis seems quite cumbersome. In the case of *s-loss*, finally, an interpretation of the post–initial segment as [- voiced] provides no explanation of examples like *gaspate* → *gabate* and *spagate* → *bagate*. It should be added, though, that there are very few examples of this type.

If all the speech errors affecting the stop consonants after initial /s/ are taken into account a good case can be made for an analysis of these consonants as voicing–irrelevant neutralization products, for it seems relatively clear that such an analysis has greater overall explanatory power than an interpretation of the stops after /s/ as [- voiced] (or [+ fortis]). An interpretation of these stop consonants as [+ voiced] (or [- fortis]) runs into the same basic difficulties as the [- voiced] analysis, cf. Davidsen-Nielsen 1975, p. 21.

In Danish, where /p t k/ and /b d g/ are distinguished solely by aspiration, and where the stop consonants after initial /s/ are unaspirated, the post–initial stops have traditionally been interpreted as /b d g/. However, since the Danish speech error material is of the same type as in English, such an analysis is open to discussion. Thus it is difficult to account for examples like *spakat* → *pas(kat)* and *spakat* → *pakat* if the stops after /s/ are analysed phonologically as [+ voiced] (or as [- aspirated]). There are also other data which do not point in the direction of an /sb sd sg/ analysis in Danish. In 1975 I examined and recorded the speech of a three–year–old Danish boy who was unable to pronounce initial *s*-clusters (and most other clusters as well). Instead of simply deleting the /s/, which is commonly done by Danish children of the same age, he moved it to the end of the syllable. For example, he pronounced *smør* [smœ‌ɳ] 'butter' and *snegl* [snai̯ʔl] 'snail' as [mœɳs] and [nai̯ʔs]. In the case of *sp, st, sk* the stop consonants which thereby emerged were /p t k/, cf. examples like *spand* [spanʔ] 'bucket' → [pʰanʔs] and *ske* [skeʔ] 'spoon' → [kʰeʔs]. According to the boy's father — a university lecturer in German familiar with linguistics and phonetics — this *s*-shift was at a certain stage a completely general rule, but at the time when I recorded the boy's speech this rule had begun to disintegrate. For one thing he would in some cases delete the /s/ instead. The stop consonants which then emerged were usually /p t k/, cf. *stol* [stoʔl] 'chair' → [tʰoʔl] and *sten* [steʔn] 'stone' → [tʰeʔn], but this was not without exception, cf. *skorsten* ['skɒ:‚steʔn] 'chimney' → ['gɒːʃeʔn]. Moreover, he frequently pronounced *sk* as a [ʃ], e.g. *skib* [skiʔp] → [ʃiʔp], and in a few cases he pronounced *st* as a [ʃ], e.g. in *i stykker* [i 'støgɒ] 'broken' → [i 'ʃøgɒ]. Now although it is naturally possible that data obtained from other Danish children may more easily be explained in terms of an /sb sd sg/ analysis it seems clear that in this particular case the material does not point toward an interpretation of the post-initial stop consonants as phonologically voiced (or unaspirated).

In languages where the articulatory place of a preconsonantal nasal is determined automatically by that of the following sound segment it would naturally be interesting to see what happens if such a nasal is affected by a slip of the tongue. If through a slip it is moved from the position of reduced contrast to strong position and here surfaces not in the shape of a single invariable nasal but sometimes as a labial, sometimes as a dental, etc., this might perhaps be regarded as evidence for an archiphonemic interpretation. The only speech error material of this type which I am familiar with is the English data established by Victoria Fromkin (1973, p. 250). As mentioned in 10.5 there is in English no general rule according to which the dimension of articulatory place is eliminated in preconsonantal nasals, cf. contrasts like /(r)ɪmd/ ≠ /(w)ɪnd/ ≠ /(r)ɪŋd/. However, the following more restricted rule, whose domain may be assumed to be the syllable, may be set up:

$$[\text{articulatory place}] \rightarrow \emptyset \Big/ \begin{bmatrix} + \text{nasal} \\ \underline{\hspace{1cm}} \end{bmatrix} \begin{bmatrix} + \text{consonantal} \\ - \text{coronal} \end{bmatrix}$$

According to such a rule words like *limp, nymph* and *bank* are interpreted phonologically as /lɪ<m/n/ŋ>p, nɪ<m/n/ŋ>f, bæ<m/n/ŋ>k/ (on account of contrasts like *simmer* ≠ *sinner* ≠ *singer* I shall assume that /ŋ/ has phonemic status in English). Now in Fromkin's material it is only the following slips of the tongue which shed light on the problem under investigation:

a) *the rank* [ræ̃ŋk] *order of the subjects* → *the rand* [ræ̃nd] *orker* . . .

b) *the red tide will stink* [stĩŋk] *up the sea* → *will* [stĩn] *up the* [sijk]

c) *the bank* [bæ̃ŋk] *will pay 5.6%* → . . . *ban* [bæ̃n] *will* [ʃejk] . . .

d) *sink* [sĩŋk] *a ship* → [sĩmp] *a* [ʃɪk]

These speech errors, in which the preconsonantal nasal involved is in each case an [ŋ], do not, in the first place, seem to be compatible

14⁺

with an analysis of the nasal as /ŋ/, for if a velar nasal had been encoded, slips like [bæŋk … pej] → [bæŋ … pejk], [stɪ̃ŋk … sij] → [stɪ̃ŋ … sijk] and [ræ̃ŋk ɔ:də] → [ræ̃ŋd ɔ:kə] were to be expected (note the existence of monosyllabic words like *hanged, fanged,* which demonstrate the permissibility of the cluster [ŋd]). Nor do they point towards an analysis of the nasal as /m/, for if a labial had been encoded one would have expected slips like [bæ̃m … pejk], [stɪ̃m … sijk] and [ræ̃md ɔ:kə] (cf. *damned, crammed,* etc.). On the other hand the data appear to be compatible both with an analysis of the nasal as <m/n/ŋ> and with an analysis of it as /n/. If it is an archinasal which is encoded it is highly natural for it to surface as [n] before an alveolar consonant in [ræ̃nd ɔ:kə]; and in examples c) and b), where the nasal is moved to word-final position and is followed by a (semi)-vowel, it also seems natural enough for it to emerge as an [n]. In [sɪ̃ŋk ə ʃɪp] → [sɪ̃mp ə ʃɪk], where the nasal is not disambiguated but remains in weak position, it is obviously perfectly natural for an archinasal to be realized as an [m] before the labial consonant. If it is assumed, secondly, that the nasal which is encoded in these examples is /n/, there are no problems at all with a), b) and c), and in d) it is possible to argue that /n/ is realized as an [m] before a homosyllabic labial consonant. Obviously a much larger corpus of slips is needed before any conclusion can be reached, but with this reservation in mind it may be said that the above speech errors point towards an analysis of nasals occurring before velar consonants in English as realizations of either /n/ or <m/n/ŋ>.

In Danish, where [m], [n] and [ŋ] are distinctively opposed to each other before consonants which are [+ coronal], cf. examples like *vams* 'doublet' *dans* 'dance', *gængs* 'current' (adj.), it is possible to set up basically the same rule as in English, i.e. a rule which eliminates the dimension of articulatory place before noncoronal obstruents. According to this rule the nasals occurring in words like *dump* 'dull' and *hank* 'handle' are interpreted as manifestations of an archinasal. However, it has been pointed out by Hans Basbøll (1973) that there are certain facts relating to the formation of compounds which support an /n/-analysis rather than an <m/n/ŋ>-analysis in this language. In compounds, [ŋ#C] and [m#C] are obligatorily opposed to each other in Danish, cf. examples like *sangbog* 'songbook' and *sambo* 'room-mate', which are always pronounced with [ŋ] and [m] respectively. On the other hand there is no obligatory contrast in compounds between [n#C] and [m#C] or between [n#C] and [ŋ#C]. Thus a word like *Rhinpost* 'Rhine post' may be pronounced not only with an [n] but also with an [m], and in the latter case it becomes phonetically identical with *rimpost* 'rhyme post'. Similarly, a compound like *tinkrus* 'pewter tankard' may be pronounced not only ['tenˌkʁuʔs] but also ['teŋˌkʁuʔs], thereby coalescing with *tingkrus* 'jug for odds and ends (things)'. There is thus in Danish a productive rule which optionally assimilates the /n/ of simplex words like *Rhin* 'Rhine' and *tin* 'pewter' to a following consonant in the formation of compounds. However, there is no corresponding rule which assimilates the [m] of a word like *tam* 'tame' (cf. *tamgæs* '(tame)geese', which is invariably pronounced ['tamˌgɛs]) or the [ŋ] of a word like *sang* 'song'. If the nasals occurring in compounds like *Rhinpost* and *tinkrus* are interpreted as /n/ (cf. the isolated forms [ʁiˑʔn] and [ten], which are invariably pronounced with [n]), an assimilation rule can be set up according to which /n/ (but not /m/ or /ŋ/) is optionally realized prejuncturally in compounds as an [m] before a labial consonant and as an [ŋ] before a velar consonant. In order to ensure that such an assimilation rule becomes as general as possible it can now be argued that it applies in uncompounded words as well, thus, for example, in *dump* and *hank*, which may accordingly be interpreted as /donp/ and /hank/. It seems, then, that in English and Danish an analysis of nasals occurring before noncoronal consonants as /n/ is a distinct possibility and that in the latter language certain facts relating to the formation of compounds can be dealt with more satisfactorily if this analysis is adopted than if the nasals are interpreted as neutralization products. It should be borne in mind, though, that the situation is less clear-cut in these languages than in e.g. Spanish and Italian, where a rule eliminating the place feature can be formulated in more general terms.

10.11. Surface Contrast and Neutralization in Generative Phonology

In a 1968 article it was pointed out by W. S-Y. Wang that in addition to an implicit awareness of morphophonemic alternations the speaker must have "some general idea of the network of contrasts in his language as it is reflected at the phonemic level of phonological representations" (p. 707n). Wang therefore concludes that there are two levels of phonological representation which are more abstract than the phonetic, namely the phonemic and the morphophonemic. Subsequently it has been demonstrated convincingly by S.A. Schane that a number of historical sound changes can be explained neither in terms of morphophonemes nor in terms of allophones, but only in terms of phonemes. Schane is of the opinion that until generative phonology can capture the notion of surface contrast "it fails to characterize an important aspect of linguistic systems" (1971, p. 504). Unlike Wang, however, he does not conclude that an autonomous phonemic level should be incorporated as an intermediate stage in generative phonology, but instead that a phonemic representation "is to be characterized as a representation of relevant surface contrasts which is deducible from the function of the rules within a generative phonology" (p. 503). Data demonstrating the relevance of surface contrast have also been put forward by Kiparsky (1972), and O'Connor argues that something is lost if a system of surface contrast is glossed over; instead he advocates a combination of the phonemic and the morphophonemic approaches to phonology (1973, p. 213f). Altogether it seems abundantly clear that the notion of surface contrast is an important one and that it therefore deserves a non-marginal position in any phonological theory. Since it is questionable whether the role assigned to it in generative phonology by Schane is prominent enough — note that surface contrast phenomena will here be scattered throughout the phonological component in a large number of rules — it is worth examining whether the proposals made by Wang and O'Connor might be implemented in a satisfactory way. Any thorough and detailed discussion of this problem is clearly beyond the scope of this book, and I shall therefore only give a brief sketch of one way in which it might possibly be tackled.

It will be remembered that Halle rejects a phonemic level because the existence of such a level prevents the formulation of maximally simple and general phonological rules, for example in the description of voicing assimilation in Russian (cf. 7.1). Recall furthermore, however, that if a concept of (surface) neutralization is recognized, the difficulties presented by an autonomous phonemic level to the analyst who wishes to formulate adequate phonological rules are very considerably reduced. It would be particularly interesting, therefore, to examine whether it is feasible to incorporate such a phonemic level in a generative-transformational description. A generative phonology of this type would have a good deal in common with glossematic phonology, where a distinction is made between ideal and actualized notation (cf. chapter 4), and with Prague phonology, where morphonology is also included, although it is usually regarded as an independent discipline intermediate between phonology and morphology. (To Martinet, however, morphonology does not exist, but is plain morphology.)

Since no definite markedness theory has as yet been worked out I shall assume that morphophonemic representations are not of the type where features are given the values 'marked' or 'unmarked'. Let us assume instead that features are normally given the values 'plus' or 'minus', but that in the case of irresoluble neutralizations it is permissible to use blanks. Morphophonemic representations of this type will be fairly similar to the ones proposed by Shibatani and Crothers (cf. 7.6), although they will contain a larger number of blanks. Abuse of blanks may be avoided by observing the well-formedness condition, and redundancies may be expressed by means of morpheme structure rules. These morphophonemic representations are converted to phonemic representations, partly by means of regular phonological rules and partly by means of neutralization rules. In an English word like *electricity* the morphophoneme |k| will, in orthodox generative phonology, be turned into the phoneme /s/ by means of a phonological rule, i.e. the value of features like 'anterior', 'coronal', 'continuant', 'strident' will in this segment be changed from minus to plus before the following high front vowel. In a German word like *Rad*, on the other hand, the morphophoneme |d| will be turned into the archiphoneme $<t/d>$ by means of a neutralization rule, i.e. [+ voiced] → [0 voiced] /__##. The rules connecting morphophonemic and phonemic representations are, in other words, partly feature switching rules, partly feature neutralizing rules. In the case of irresoluble neutralization a blank will be carried over from the morphophonemic to the phonemic representation; for example, the postinitial segment of English *spin* will be characterized as [0 voiced] both on the morphophonemic level and on the phonemic level. As a result, any type of neutralization (resoluble, irresoluble) is expressed on the phonemic level with a blank, and the only function of blanks is to indicate that there is neutralization. Now the level which is reached by subjecting morphophonemic representations of this type to phonological rules and neutralization rules expresses all the surface contrasts of the language. It should not be overlooked, though, that since neither defective distribution nor segment redundancy is expressed by means of blanks, some redundant information will also be contained in phonemic representations of this type. (Recall in this connection that in the phonological forms which arise if the method of identification proposed in

10.2 is used, the principle of contrast is not respected fully either, for in the case of defective distribution, although not in the case of segment redundancy, a distinctive value is here attributed to features which are in fact redundant.) Finally, the conversion of phonemic representations to phonetic representations is effected by means of phonetic manifestation rules. These rules, which account for phonetic details, and which in some cases replace a plus or a minus with a certain degree of a feature along a physically defined scale, take care of the manifestation of phonemes and archiphonemes. In a word like German *Speck* [ʃpek] 'bacon', for example, [0 voiced] is changed to [− voiced] in both stop segments. Note that a model of description like the one which has just been outlined presents no basic difficulties in the description of voicing assimilation in Russian, for this assimilation can be described as a purely phonetic process, cf. /m'o<k/g>bi/ → [m'og bi] and /ž'eč bi/ → [ž'eǯ bi].

Even though the inclusion in generative phonology of a phonemic level in which neutralizations are expressed does not prevent the formulation of adequate phonological rules to the same extent that the inclusion of a post–Bloomfieldian phonemic level does, it seems unlikely that it will be welcomed by many generativists. In generative phonology the principles that different allomorphs should be derived from the same underlying form and that phonological rules should be maximally simple and general are given top priority, and it cannot be denied that even a level of surface contrast like the one discussed here will be an impediment in the formulation of rules. In a German word like *Rad*, for example, [+ voiced] in the stop segment must be changed first to [0 voiced] and subsequently to [− voiced], and in *Rat* [− voiced] must be converted to [0 voiced] and then back again to [− voiced]. Note also that it is not unproblematic to include both morphophonemes and archiphonemes in one relatively integrated phonological component, for as pointed out by Bjarne Hartoft (MS) these two concepts are diametrically opposed to each other in the sense that the former may be said to represent the influence of the paradigm on the syntagma, whereas the latter may be said to represent the influence of the syntagma on the paradigm. In a type of phonological description where a fundamental role is assigned to the morphophoneme, the archiphoneme will not fit in easily. In other words, within the territory delimited by generative boundary posts there is little or no room for concepts like surface contrast and (surface) neutralization. In Kipling's words: "East is east and west is west, and never the twain shall meet." It should be added that there are also other difficulties connected with the introduction of a phonemic level in generative phonology. Thus Schane argues that in Nupe the phonetic rule which palatalizes consonants before front vowels is ordered before the morphophonemic rule which converts all low vowels to /a/ (1971, p. 518).

Since a revised model of generative phonology like the one outlined above is thus unlikely to gain a foothold, I shall briefly discuss an alternative and probably more promising model which has been proposed by Jørgen Rischel in his book on West Greenlandic phonology (1974, p. 316ff). In this language the morphophoneme /t/ is realized with affrication as a [ʄ] before the morphophoneme /i/, and this also happens before the lowered pharyngealized variety of /i/ which occurs before uvulars, but not e.g. before the rather close front variety of /a/ which occurs in certain environments. Consequently, this affrication cannot be explained on the phonetic level. Now in cases of this type, where considerably different realizations of a morphophoneme have the same effect, Rischel postulates the existence of an allophonic association pattern. Those features of allophones united by such a pattern which are irrelevant to certain rules (e.g. those features of /i/ allophones in West Greenlandic which are irrelevant to the affrication of /t/) are called *recessive*. By means of this concept Rischel is capable of establishing a strict bipartition of rules. Phonetic readjustments by means of recessive features, e.g. greater or lesser palatal friction of West Greenlandic /k/ before different realizations of /i/, are termed *phonetic rules*. Rules which disregard recessive features, cf. the affrication in West Greenlandic of /t/ before any realization of /i/, are termed *phonological rules*. Phonetic rules may be regarded as well-formedness conditions which apply anywhere, but they occupy a subordinate position in the sense that phonological rules pay no respect to them.

The transcription which results from the application to underlying forms of phonological rules exclusively is called the *categorial surface representation*. "It is a surface representation in the sense that no rule which is phonological rather than phonetic is necessary to correlate it with a more detailed phonetic representation, and it is categorial in the sense that features varying over a certain range according to phonetic rules, are given fixed values" (p. 363). Now if generative and autonomous statements are capable of converging on the phonetic rule component, and this would not seem to present any grave difficulties, it is possible to establish a version of generative phonology in which there is room for both morphophonemic and traditional phonemic representations, as shown in the following graph (p. 364):

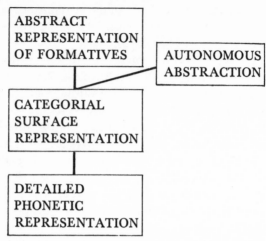

Although the categorial surface representation is relatively closely related to the autonomous phonemic representation, the latter on the whole represents a higher degree of abstraction than the former. It seems clear, therefore, that this type of intermediate representation does not prevent the formulation of adequate phonological rules to the same extent that any type of intermediate phonemic level would. Furthermore, Rischel's model has the advantage of completely separating abstraction based on the principle of morpheme identity from abstration based on the principle of (surface) contrast. Since it is becoming progressively clearer to generative phonologists that the structural generalizations which are captured by a traditional phonemic representation are in no way devoid of interest, and since the categorial output representation can hardly be highly controversial, Rischel's approach to the problem of incorporating a traditional phonemic level (in which resoluble as well as irresoluble neutralizations may be indicated) into generative phonology probably represents the most promising proposal which has as yet been put forward.

10.12. Final Remarks

In those cases where a phonetic feature can be demonstrated to perform a distinctive function in some contexts and to be non-distinctive in others, the phonologist may be said to be faced with a dilemma. How should he deal with the segment in the position where this feature is non-distinctive? Should he equate it with the phonologically and phonetically related segment in strong position which is positively specified for this feature, or should he equate it with the one which is negatively specified for it? In such cases some linguists believe that the consequences connected with either of these identifications are highly undesirable and that a forced choice should therefore be avoided. They claim that these two alternatives do not represent the only possibilities and attempt to escape through the horns of the dilemma by equating the segment in weak position with two phonologically and phonetically related segments in strong position, differing only in being oppositely specified for the feature which is non-distinctive in weak position. It has been one of the purposes of this book to demonstrate that there is nothing outlandish about this approach to the problem of identification; i.e. there is nothing outlandish about the interdependent concepts of neutralization and the archiphoneme. In particular, it is worth pointing out that these concepts were not introduced by weak-hearted phonologists who threw up their hands when faced with difficulties of identification, but by phonologists who after having examined the problem thoroughly came to the conclusion that a both-and identification was the most appropriate approach to it. It would therefore be unjustified to characterize neutralization and the archiphoneme as handy devices for the linguist who cannot make up his mind and does not wish to commit himself. To be sure the both-and analysis is connected with difficulties, but so are all the other analyses which have been put forward, and a number of non-trivial arguments can be adduced in support of the notions of neutralization and the archiphoneme.

It is not only in phonology that the concept of neutralization may be utilized. It has been widely used in the description of morphology, although it has here most often been termed *syncretism*. In a language like Latin regular syncretisms occur in several paradigms, and as far as case is concerned word forms like *aevum* (sg. neut., 'time'), *dominae* (one of the oblique singular forms of *domina*, nom. sg. fem., 'lady') and *dominō* (one of the oblique forms of *dominus*, nom. sg. masc., 'lord') may be analyzed as the syncretisms <nominative/accusative>, <genitive/dative> and <dative/ablative> respectively. The notion of neutralization (syncretism) has also been used in diachronic morphology. By way of illustration it can be mentioned that the distinction in Proto-Indo-European between the case suffixes -ay (dative singular) and -y (locative singular) is syncretized at a later stage, namely in Greek, where the reflexes of these two suffixes are in complementary distribution (cf. Hoenigswald 1960, p. 37). An example of how the concept can be used in syntactic studies has been given by Lyons (1968, p. 253). In Latin, sentences like *Clodia amat Catullum* 'Clodia loves Catullus" and *Clodiam amat Catullus* 'Catullus loves Clodia' are distinguished by the opposition of the nominative and the accusative cases. However, a sentence like *Dico Clodiam amare Catullum*, where a transitive sentence has been embedded in an indirect discourse construction, and where both the subject and the object are in the 'accusative' case, is ambiguous, i.e. it may be translated either as 'I say that Clodia loves Catullus' or as 'I say that Catullus loves Clodia'. The linguist may now account for this ambiguity by arguing that the opposition between underlying *dico* + *Clodia amat Catullum* and *dico* + *Clodiam amat Catullus* is neutralized on the level of syntactic surface structure.[16]

According to Hjelmslev the concept of neutralization (syncretism), which has been put forward in order to account for linguistic data, may with advantage be used to shed light on various non-linguistic phenomena (1943, p. 82). One field in which neutralization seems to be a fruitful notion is that of music. It has been pointed out to me (Christian Kock, personal communication) that an aesthe-

---

16) In Martinet 1968 a distinction is proposed, at the level of linguistic description above phonology, between *syncretism* and real *neutralization*. By syncretism Martinet understands a formal confusion of units which are meant and understood, with the help of context, as distinct. It is exemplified with the French sentence *Je cherche un homme qui travaille*. In conjunction with *travailler* and third person singular there is no formal distinction between the indicative and the subjunctive. However, the speaker knows whether he wishes to say "I seek a man who is working" or "I seek a man who is willing to work", and the listener, if in doubt about the intended meaning, knows at least that the speaker has either the indicative or the subjunctive mood in mind. By real neutralization Martinet understands the impossibility of distinguishing between two sense units in a given context. By way of illustration he mentions *il faut que je fasse* . . . . In this case *que je fasse* has no definite modal value, i.e. what we find here is not a formal confusion but a semantic suspension of the modality opposition. That this is so appears from the fact that *il faut que je fasse* . . . is semantically (although not stylistically) equivalent to *il me faut faire* . . . . Within the framework of the present theory one might say that the dimension of modality is eliminated in the context of *il faut que*.

tically important neutralization is found in the opening of Beethoven's ninth symphony, where for a long while no one plays anything but the tonic and the dominant (D and A). As these two notes are common to the major and minor key, the major–minor opposition is neutralized. Subsequently, this ambiguity is resolved as the key turns out to be D minor. The same suspension is used by Wagner in the beginning of the overture to *Der fliegende Holländer*. Not until the Dutchman's leitmotif has been called twice by the horns does disambiguation take place, once again in favour of the minor key. This neutralization helps create the necessary air of ambivalence around the Dutchman.

As pointed out in Chapter 1, the concepts of neutralization and the archiphoneme are by no means generally accepted. What I have tried to argue in this book is that for the analyst who attaches great importance to paradigmatic contrast, these concepts represent an adequate and highly natural approach to the problem of multiple complementation (in the sense of Hockett 1955, p. 164ff). That a theory of neutralization is in no way unrealistic appears from a number of empirical data. In other words, neutralization and the archiphoneme are more than expedient theoretical constructs. If neutralization is recognized, an important problem which must be solved is that of delimiting it and separating it from the other type of sequence redundancy, namely defective distribution. Although such a delimitation is not without difficulties, I believe it can be done in the way proposed here, i.e. at the level of features.

223

BIBLIOGRAPHY

Chapter 1
INTRODUCTION
p. 13–21

Akamatsu, T. (1975). De la notion de "représentant de l'archiphonème". *Actes du deuxième colloque de linguistique fonctionelle,* Clermont-Ferrand, 93–101.

Hockett, C.F. (1955). *A Manual of Phonology.* Baltimore.

Hooper, J.B. (1974). The archi-segment in natural generative phonology. Reproduced by the Indiana University Linguistics Club. October, 1974. Subsequently published in *Language* 51 (1975), 536–560.

Kortlandt, F.H.H. (1972). *Modelling the Phoneme.* The Hague.

Martinet, A. (1965). De la morphonologie. *La Linguistique,* 1965, 1, 16–30. (An excerpt translated into the English is published in E.C. Fudge, ed. (1973). *Phonology.* Harmondsworth, 91–100.)

Moulton, W.G. (1962). *The Sounds of English and German.* Chicago.

Šaumjan, S.K. (1967). Die Zweistufentheorie der Phonologie im Licht der modernen Wissenschaftslogik. *Phonetica* 16, 121–142.

— (1968). *Problems of Theoretical Phonology.* The Hague. Translation of *Problemy teoretičeskoj fonologii.* Moscow 1962.

Schane, S.A. (1968). On the non-uniqueness of phonological representations. *Language* 44, 709–716.

Trubetzkoy, N.S. (1939). Grundzüge der Phonologie (= *Travaux du Cercle Linguistique de Prague* 7). French translation by J. Cantineau (1949). *Principes de phonologie.* Paris. English translation by C.A.M. Baltaxe (1971). *Principles of Phonology.* Berkeley.

Chapter 2
PRAGUE PHONOLOGY
p. 22–59

Akamatsu, T. (1975). De la notion de "représentant de l'archiphonème". *Actes du deuxième colloque de linguistique fonctionelle,* Clermont-Ferrand, 93–101.

- (1976). Peut-on dissocier "neutralisation" et "archiphonème"? *La Linguistique* 12, 2, 27-32.

Buyssens, E. (1972). Phonème, archiphonème et pertinence. *La Linguistique* 8, 2, 39-58.

- (1974). Contre la notion d'archiphonème. *Proceedings of the Eleventh International Congress of Linguists,* Bologna-Florence, Aug. 28 – Sept. 2, 1972, 765-768.

- (1975). A propos de l'archiphonème. *La Linguistique* 11, 2, 35-38.

- (1977). A propos de l'archiphonème. *La Linguistique* 13, 2, 51-54.

Cantineau, J. (1955). Le classement logique des oppositions. *Word* 11, 1-9.

Cohen, A. (1952, reprinted 1965). *The Phonemes of English.* The Hague.

Fischer-Jørgensen, E. (1975). *Trends in Phonological Theory.* Copenhagen.

Groot, A.W. de (1939). Neutralisation d'oppositions. *Neophilologus* 25, 127-146.

Jakobson, R. (1929). Remarques sur l'évolution phonologique du russe (= *Travaux du Cercle Linguistique de Prague* 2). Reprinted in Jakobson 1962.

- (1962, 2nd ed. 1971). *Selected Writings* I. The Hague.

Ladefoged, P., and D.E. Broadbent (1957). Information conveyed by vowels. *Journal of the Acoustical Society of America* 29, 98-104.

Martinet, A. (1936). Neutralisation et archiphonème. *Travaux du Cercle Linguistique de Prague* 6, 46-57.

- (1946). Où en est la phonologie? *Lingua* 1, 34-58.

- (1949, reprinted 1955). *Phonology as Functional Phonetics.* London. (= Publications of the Philological Society 15).

- (1956). *La description phonologique avec application au parler franco-provençal d'Hauteville (Savoie).* Geneva.

- (1960). *Éléments de linguistique générale.* Paris.

- (1965). De la morphonologie. *La Linguistique,* 1965, 1, 16-30. (An excerpt tranlated into the English is published in E.C. Fudge, ed. (1973). *Phonology.* Harmondsworth, 91-100.)

- (1968). Neutralisation et syncretisme. *La Linguistique,* 1968, 1, 1-20. (An excerpt translated into the English is published in E.C. Fudge, ed. (1973). *Phonology.* Harmondsworth, 74-84.)

Mathesius, V. (1929). La structure phonologique du lexique du tchèque moderne. *Travaux du Cercle Linguistique de Prague* 1, 67-84. Reprinted in J. Vachek, ed. (1964, 3rd ed. 1967). *A Prague School Reader in Linguistics.* Bloomington, 156-176.

Trnka, B. (1939). On the combinatory variants and neutralization of phonemes. *Proceedings of the Third International Congress of Phonetic Sciences* 1938, Ghent, 23-30.

– (1958). On some problems of neutralization. *Omagiu lui Jorgu Iordan.* Bucarest, 1958, 861-866.

– (1966, rev. ed.). *A Phonological Analysis of Present-Day Standard English.* Tokyo.

Trubetzkoy, N.S. (1929). *Polabische Studien* (= Akademie der Wissenschaften in Wien, Sitzungsberichte 211, 4). Vienna.

– (1931). Die phonologische Systeme. *Travaux du Cercle Linguistique de Prague* 4, 96-116.

– (1933a). Charakter und Methode der systematischen phonologischen Darstellung einer gegebenen Sprache. *Archives néerlandaises de phonétique experimentale* 8-9, 109-113.

– (1933b). La phonologie actuelle. *Journal de Psychologie* 30, 227-246.

– (1934). Das morphonologische System der Russischen Sprache (= *Travaux du Cercle Linguistique de Prague* 5_2).

– (1936a). D'une théorie des oppositions phonologiques. *Journal de Psychologie* 33, 5-18.

– (1936b). Die Aufhebung der phonologischen Gegensätze. *Travaux du Cercle Linguistique de Prague* 6, 29-45. Reprinted in J. Vachek, ed. (1964, 3rd. ed. 1967). *A Prague School Reader in Linguistics.* Bloomington, 187-205.

– (1939). Grundzüge der Phonologie (= *Travaux du Cercle Linguistique de Prague* 7). French translation by J. Cantineau (1949). *Principes de phonologie.* Paris. English translation by C.A.M. Baltaxe (1971). *Principles of Phonology.* Berkeley.

Vachek, J. (1966). *The Linguistic School of Prague.* Bloomington.

Vion, R. (1974). Les notions de neutralisation et d'archiphonème en phonologie. *La Linguistique* 10, 1, 33-52.

Projet de terminologie phonologique standardisée (1931). *Travaux du Cercle Linguistique de Prague* 4, 309-323.

Chapter 3
BRITISH AND AMERICAN PHONOLOGICAL THEORIES
p. 60-72

Bloch, B. (1941). Phonemic overlapping. *American Speech* 16, 278-284. Also published in M. Joos, ed. (1957). *Readings in Linguistics* I. Chicago, 93-96.

Bloomfield, L. (1933). *Language*. New York.

Chomsky, N. (1964). Current issues in linguistic theory. In J.A. Fodor and J.J. Katz, eds. *The Structure of Language*. Englewood Cliffs, N.J., 50-118. Also published separately in the Hague under the same title.

Derwing, B.L. (1973). *Transformational Grammar as a Theory of Language Acquisition*. Cambridge.

Firth, J.A. (1935a). The use and distribution of certain English sounds. *English Studies* 17, 8-18. Reprinted in Firth 1957, 34-46.

— (1935b). Phonological features of some Indian languages. *Proceedings of the Second International Congress of Phonetic Sciences,* 1935, Cambridge, 176-182. Reprinted in Firth 1957, 47-53.

— (1936). Alphabets and phonology in India and Burma. *Bulletin of the School of Oriental Studies* 8 (2 and 3). Reprinted in Firth 1957, 54-75.

— (1948). Sounds and prosodies. *Transactions of the Philological Society,* Oxford, 127-152. Reprinted in Firth 1957, 121-138, and in Palmer 1970, 1-26.

— (1950). Personality and language in society. *Sociological Review* 42 (2). Reprinted in Firth 1957, 177-189.

— (1957). *Papers in Linguistics*. London.

Fischer-Jørgensen, E. (1975). *Trends in Phonological Theory*. Copenhagen.

Halle, M. (1959). *The Sound Pattern of Russian*. The Hague.

Hockett, C.F. (1955). *A Manual of Phonology*. Baltimore.

— (1958). *A Course in Modern Linguistics*. New York.

Jones, D. (1962, 2nd. ed.). *The Phoneme: its Nature and Use*. Cambridge.

Lockwood, D.G. (1972). Neutralization, biuniqueness, and stratificational phonology. In V.B. Makkai, ed. *Phonological Theory, Evolution and Current Practice*. New York, 656-669.

Palmer, F.R., ed. (1970). *Prosodic Analysis*. London.

Pike, K.L. (1947). *Phonemics*. Ann Arbor.

Robins, R.H. (1957). Aspects of prosodic analysis. *Proceedings of the University of Durham Philosophical Society* I, Series B, No. 1, 1-12. Reprinted in Palmer 1970, 188-200.

— (1964). *General Linguistics — an Introductory Survey*. London.

Trager, G.L., and H.L. Smith (1951). *An Outline of English Structure (Studies in Linguistics,* Occasional Papers No. 3). Norman, Oklahoma. Reprinted: *American Council of Learned Societies* (1957). Washington, D.C.

Twaddell, W.F. (1935). On defining the phoneme. *Language Monograph* 16. Reprinted in M. Joos, ed. (1957). *Readings in Linguistics* I. Chicago, 55-80.

Chapter 4
GLOSSEMATICS
p. 73-84

Basbøll, H. (1971, 1973). A commentary on Hjelmslev's analysis of the Danish expression system. *Acta Linguistica Hafniensia* 13 (173-211) and 14 (1-24).

Fischer-Jørgensen, E. (1973). Supplementary note to Hans Basbøll's commentary on Hjelmslev's analysis of the Danish expression system. *Acta Linguistica Hafniensia* 14, 143-152.

Hjelmslev, L. (1935). *La catégorie des cas.* Première partie. Aarhus.

– (1939). Note sur les oppositions supprimables. *Travaux du Cercle Linguistique de Prague* 8, 51-57.

– (1943). *Omkring Sprogteoriens Grundlæggelse.* Copenhagen. English translation by Francis J. Whitfield (1953, revised ed. 1961). *Prolegomena to a Theory of Language.* Madison.

– (1951). Grundtræk af det danske udtrykssystem med særligt henblik på stødet. *Selskab for nordisk filologis årsberetning for 1948-49-50.* English translation by Francis J. Whitfield (1973). Outline of the Danish expression system with special reference to the *stød. Essais Linguistique* II (= *Travaux du Cercle Linguistique de Copenhague* XIV), 247-266.

– (1954). La stratification du langage. *Word* 10, 169-188.

– (1970). Le système d'expression du français moderne (summary by Eli Fischer-Jørgensen). *Bulletin du Cercle linguistique de Copenhague* 1941-1965, 217-224.

Martinet, A. (1968). Neutralisation et syncrétisme. *La Linguistique* 1, 1-20.

Schane, S.A. (1968). *French Phonology and Morphology.* Cambridge, Mass.

Siertsema, B. (1965, 2nd ed.). *A Study of Glossematics.* The Hague.

Togeby, K. (1951). *Structure immanente de la langue française* (= *Travaux du Cercle linguistique de Copenhague* VI). Copenhagen.

Uldall, H.J. (1936). The phonematics of Danish. *Proceedings of the Second International Congress of Phonetic Sciences* 1935, 54-57.

– (1957). *Outline of Glossematics* (= *Travaux du Cercle linguistique de Copenhague* X). Copenhagen.

228

Chapter 5
ROMAN JAKOBSON'S THEORY OF DISTINCTIVE FEATURES
p. 85-94

Bazell, C.E. (1956). Three conceptions of phonological neutralisation. In Halle et al. (eds.). *For Roman Jakobson, Essays on the Occasion of his Sixtieth Birthday*. The Hague, 25-30.

Chomsky, N., and M. Halle (1968). *The Sound Pattern of English*. New York.

Davidsen-Nielsen, N. (1975). A phonological analysis of English *sp, st, sk* with special reference to speech error evidence. *Journal of the IPA* 5, 3-25.

Fischer-Jørgensen, E. (1975). *Trends in Phonological Theory*. Copenhagen.

Fromkin, V.A., ed. (1973). *Speech Errors as Linguistic Evidence*. The Hague.

Jakobson, R. (1959). A new outline of Russian phonology. *International Journal of Slavic Linguistics and Poetics* I/II. Reprinted in Jakobson 1962, 533-537.

― (1962, 2nd ed. 1971). *Selected Writings* I. The Hague.

Jakobson, R., and J. Lotz (1949). Notes on the French phonemic pattern. *Word* 5, 151-158. Reprinted in Jakobson 1962, 426-434.

Jakobson, R., G. Fant, and M. Halle (1952). *Preliminaries to Speech Analysis*. Cambridge, Massachusetts.

Jakobson, R., and M. Halle (1956). *Fundamentals of Language*. The Hague.

Ladefoged, P. (1971). *Preliminaries to Linguistic Phonetics*. Chicago.

Martinet, A. (1946). Où en est la phonologie? *Lingua* 1, 34-58.

Schane, S.A. (1968). On the non-uniqueness of phonological representations. *Language* 44, 709-716.

Trubetzkoy, N.S. (1929). *Polabische Studien* (= Akademie der Wissenschaften in Wien, Sitzungsberichte, 211, 4). Vienna.

Chapter 6
PHONOLOGICAL THEORY IN THE SOVIET UNION
p. 95-106

Avanesov, R.I. (1955). Kratčajšaja zvukovaja edinica v sostave slova i morfemy. *Voprosy grammatičeskogo stroja,* 113-139. Moscow.

― (1956). O trex tipax naučno-lingvističeskix transskripcij. *Slavia* 25, 3, 347-371.

Fischer-Jørgensen, E. (1975). *Trends in Phonological Theory.* Copenhagen.

Halle, M. (1963). 'Phonemics'; in T.A. Sebeok (ed.). *Current Trends in Linguistics* 1, *Soviet and East European Linguistics.* The Hague, 5-21.

Kortlandt, F.H.H. (1972). *Modelling the Phoneme.* The Hague.

Krámský, J. (1974). *The Phoneme.* Munich.

Martinet, A. (1936). Neutralisation et archiphonème. *Travaux du Cercle Linguistique de Prague* 6, 46-57.

Postowalowa, W.I. (1975). 'Die Phonologie'; in B.A. Serébrennikow. *Allgemeine Sprachwissenschaft* II. Berlin (94-159). Translation of the original Russian version, Moscow 1972.

Reformatskij, A.A. (1957). De la neutralisation des oppositions. In A. Martinet (ed.). La notion de neutralisation dans la morphologie et le lexique (= *Travaux de L'institut de Linguistique* II, Paris, 103-107).

– (1970). *Iz istorii otečestrennoj fonologii.* Moscow.

Šaumjan, S.K. (1967). Die Zweistufentheorie der Phonologie im Licht der modernen Wissenschaftslogik. *Phonetica* 16, 121-142.

– (1968). *Problems of Theoretical Phonology.* The Hague. Translation of *Problemy teoretičeskoj fonologii.* Moscow 1962.

Ščerba, L.V. (1911). Court exposé de la prononciation russe. Supplement to *Le maître phonetique,* Novembre-Décembre 1911.

Zinder, L.R. (1960). *Obščaja fonetika.* Leningrad.

Chapter 7
GENERATIVE PHONOLOGY
p. 107-136

Bolozky, S. (1975). A note on archi-segments. *Glossa* 9, 253-258.

Cairns, C.E. (1969). Markedness, neutralization, and universal redundancy rules. *Language* 45, 863-885.

Chomsky, N., and M. Halle (1968). *The Sound Pattern of English.* New York.

Davidsen-Nielsen, N. (1975). A phonological analysis of English *sp, st, sk* with special reference to speech error evidence. *Journal of the IPA* 5, 3-25.

– (1976). A theory of the exceptions to the Germanic and High German consonant shifts. *Acta Linguistica Hafniensia* 16, 45-56.

Derwing, B.L. (1973). *Transformational Grammar as a Theory of Language Acquisition.* Cambridge.

Fischer-Jørgensen, E. (1975). *Trends in Phonological Theory.* Copenhagen.

Fromkin, V.A. (1971). The non-anomalous nature of anomalous utterances. *Language* 47, 27–52.

Halle, M. (1959). *The Sound Pattern of Russian*. The Hague.

— (1962). Phonology in generative grammar. *Word* 18, 54–72. Reprinted in J.A. Fodor and J.J. Katz, eds. (1964). *The Structure of Language*. Englewood Cliffs, New Jersey, 334–352 and in V.B. Makkai, ed. (1972). *Phonological Theory, Evolution and Current Practice*. New York, 380–392.

Hooper, J.B. (1974). The archi–segment in natural generative phonology. Reproduced by the Indiana University Linguistics Club. October, 1974. Subsequently published in *Language* 51 (1975), 536–560.

Householder, F.W. (1967). Distinctive features and phonetic features. In *To Honor Roman Jakobson*, vol. II. The Hague, 941–944.

Hudson, G. (1974). The role of SPC's in natural generative phonology. *Papers from the Parasession on Natural Phonology*. Chicago Linguistic Society.

Johns, D.A. (1969). Phonemics and generative phonology. *Papers from the Fifth Regional Meeting of the Chicago Linguistics Society*, 374–381. Also published in V.B. Makkai, ed. (1972). *Phonological Theory, Evolution and Current Practice*. New York, 549–553.

Lightner, T.M. (1963). A note on the formulation of phonological rules. *Quarterly Progress Report of the Research Laboratory of Electronics* 68, Massachusetts Institute of Technology, 187–189.

Linell, P. (1974). Problems of Psychological Reality in Generative Phonology (= *Reports from Uppsala University Department of Linguistics* 4).

Matthews, P.H. (1974). *Morphology*. Cambridge.

Postal, P.M. (1968). *Aspects of Phonological Theory*. New York.

Read, C. (1971). Pre–school children's knowledge of English phonology. *Harvard Educational Review* 41, 1–34.

Rischel, J. (1974). *Topics in West Greenlandic Phonology*. Copenhagen.

Rudes, B.A. (1976). Lexical representation and variable rules in natural generative phonology. *Glossa* 10, 111–151.

Schane, S.A. (1968). On the non–uniqueness of phonological representations. *Language* 44, 709–716.

Shibatani, M., and J. Crothers (1972). On the status of blank features in phonology. *Project on Linguistic Analysis Reports*. Second Series, 16, September 1972, 71–78. Also published in *Glossa* 8 (1974), 261–270.

Stampe, D. (1973). *A Dissertation on Natural Phonology*. Doctoral dissertation, University of Chicago.

Stanley, R. (1967). Redundancy rules in phonology. *Language* 43, 393–436.

Trubetzkoy, N.S. (1934). Das morphonologische System der russischen Sprache (= *Travaux du Cercle Linguistique de Prague* 5$_2$).

Chapter 8
STRATIFICATIONAL PHONOLOGY
p. 137-145

Jakobson, R. (1941). *Kindersprache, Aphasie und allmeine Lautgesetze.* Uppsala. Reprinted in R. Jakobson (1962, 2nd ed. 1971). *Selected Writings* I. The Hague, 328-401. English translation (1968). *Child Language, Aphasia and Phonological Universals.* The Hague.

Lamb, S.M. (1964). The sememic approach to structural semantics. *American Anthropologist* 66, part 2, 57-78.

Lockwood, D.G. (1969). Markedness in stratificational phonology. *Language* 45, 300-308. Reprinted in V.B. Makkai, ed. (1972). *Phonological Theory, Evolution and Current Practice.* New York, 649-655.

— (1972a). Neutralization, biuniqueness, and stratificational phonology. In V.B. Makkai, ed. (1972). *Phonological Theory, Evolution and Current Practice.* New York, 656-669.

— (1972b). *Introduction to Stratificational Linguistics.* New York.

Sullivan, W.J. (1974). The archiphoneme in stratificational description. *Proceedings of the Eleventh International Congress of Linguists.* Bologna-Florence, Aug. 28 — Sept. 2, 1972, 287-299.

Trubetzkoy, N.S. (1931). Die phonologische Systeme. *Travaux du Cercle Linguistique de Prague* 4, 96-116.

— (1939). Grundzüge der Phonologie (= *Travaux du Cercle Linguistique de Prague* 7). French translation by J. Cantineau (1949). *Principes de phonologie.* Paris. English translation by C.A.M. Baltaxe (1971). *Principles of Phonology.* Berkeley.

Chapter 9
OTHER CONTRIBUTIONS
p. 146-157

Avram, A. (1960). Neutralization and phonological alternations. *Revue de Linguistique* 5, 273-278.

Bazell, C.E. (1953). *Linguistic Form.* Istanbul.

— (1956). Three conceptions of phonological neutralisation. In M. Halle et al., ed. *For Roman Jakobson. Essays on the Occasion of his Sixtieth Birthday.* The Hague, 25–30.

Fischer–Jørgensen, E. (1975). *Trends in Phonological Theory.* Copenhagen.

Haas, W. (1957). The identification and description of phonetic elements. *Transactions of the Philological Society,* 118–159.

Martinet, A. (1936). Neutralisation et archiphonème. *Travaux du Cercle Linguistique de Prague* 6, 44–57.

Chapter 10
A THEORY OF NEUTRALIZATION
p. 158–221

Abramson, A.S., and L. Lisker (1967). Some effects of context on voice onset time in English. *Language and Speech* 10, 1–28.

Akamatsu, T. (1975). De la notion de "représentant de l'archiphonème". *Actes du deuxième colloque de linguistique fonctionelle,* Clermont–Ferrand, 93–101.

Avram, A. (1960). Neutralization and phonological alternations. *Revue de Linguistique* 5, 273–278.

Basbøll, H. (1974a). The phonological syllable with special reference to Danish. *Annual Report of the Institute of Phonetics* 8, University of Copenhagen, 39–128.

— (1974b). The feature tenseness in the modern French vowel system: a diachronic perspective. *Annual Report of the Institute of Phonetics* 8, University of Copenhagen, 173–200.

— (1974c). Structure consonantique du mot italien. *Revue Romane* 9,1, 27–40.

— (1973). Noter til dansk fonologi. Mimeographed.

Basbøll, H., and K. Kristensen (1975). Further work on computer testing of a generative phonology of Danish. *Annual Report of the Institute of Phonetics* 9, University of Copenhagen, 265–291.

Bazell, C.E. (1956). Three conceptions of phonological neutralisation. In M. Halle et al., ed. *For Roman Jakobson. Essays on the Occasion of his Sixtieth Birthday.* The Hague, 25–30.

Campbell, A. (1959). *Old English Grammar.* Oxford.

Carnochan, J. (1960). Vowel harmony in Igbo. *African Language Studies* I, 155–163. Reprinted in F.R. Palmer, ed. (1970). *Prosodic Analysis.* London, 222–229.

Chatman, S. (1958). The ɑ/æ opposition in Old English. *Word* 14, 224-236.

Cherry, E.C., M. Halle, and R. Jakobson (1953). Toward the logical description of languages in their phonemic aspects. *Language* 29, 34-46.

Chomsky, N., and M. Halle (1965). Some controversial questions in phonological theory. *Journal of Linguistics* 1, 97-138.

Chomsky, N., and M. Halle (1968). *The Sound Pattern of English*. New York.

Davidsen-Nielsen, N. (1975). A phonological analysis of English *sp, st, sk* with special reference to speech error evidence. *Journal of the International Phonetic Association* 5, 3-25.

Davidsen-Nielsen, N., and H. Ørum (1978). The feature 'gravity' in Old English and Danish phonology. To appear in *Acta Linguistica Hafniensia*.

Derwing, B.L. (1973). *Transformational Grammar as a Theory of Language Acquisition*. Cambridge.

Fischer-Jørgensen, E. (1949). Remarques sur les principes de l'analyse phonémique. *Travaux du Cercle Linguistique de Copenhague* 5, 214-234.

— (1975). *Trends in Phonological Theory*. Copenhagen.

Fromkin, V.A. (1971). The non-anomalous nature of anomalous utterances. *Language* 47, 27-52.

— (1973, ed.). *Speech Errors as Linguistic Evidence*. The Hague.

Halle, M. (1973). Review of P. Ladefoged, *Preliminaries to Linguistic Phonetics*. *Language* 49, 926-933.

Hartoft, B. (MS). Kortdiftongerne i VP. Funktion, form og forhistorie. Unpublished M.A. thesis.

Hattori, S. (1957). On neutralization. *Travaux de L'institut de Linguistique* II. Paris, 41-43.

Hjelmslev, L. (1936). On the principles of phonematics. *Proceedings of the Second International Congress of Phonetic Sciences* 1935, 49-54.

— (1943). *Omkring Sprogteoriens Grundlæggelse*. Copenhagen. English translation by Francis J. Whitfield (1953, revised ed. 1961). *Prolegomena to a Theory of Language*. Madison.

Hockett, C.F. (1955). *A Manual of Phonology*. Baltimore.

Hoenigswald, H.M. (1960). *Language Change and Linguistic Reconstruction*. Chicago.

Jakobson, R. (1949). On the identification of phonemic entities. *Travaux du Cercle Linguistique de Copenhague* 5, 205-213. Reprinted in R. Jakobson (1962, 2nd ed. 1971). *Selected Writings* I. The Hague, 418-425.

Jakobson, R., and J. Lotz (1949). Notes on the French phonemic pattern. *Word* 5, 151-158. Reprinted in Jakobson 1962, 426-434.

Kim, C.-W. (1970). A theory of aspiration. *Phonetica* 21, 107-116.

Kiparsky, P. (1972). Explanation in phonology. In S. Peters, ed. *Goals of Linguistic Theory*. Englewood Cliffs, New Jersey, 189-225.

Kuhn, S.M. (1961). On the syllabic phonemes of Old English. *Language* 37, 522-538.

Ladefoged, P. (1971). *Preliminaries to Linguistic Phonetics*. Chicago.

– (1975). *A Course in Phonetics*. New York.

Lyons, J. (1962). Phonemic and non-phonemic phonology. *International Journal of American Linguistics* 28, 127-133. Reprinted in E.C. Fudge, ed. (1973). *Phonology*. Harmondsworth, 190-199.

– (1968). *Introduction to Theoretical Linguistics*. Cambridge.

Mac an Fhailigh, E. (1968). *The Irish of Erris, Co. Mayo*. Dublin.

Martinet, A. (1936). Neutralisation et archiphonème. *Travaux du Cercle Linguistique de Prague* 6, 46-57.

– (1946). Où en est la phonologie? *Lingua* 1, 34-58.

– (1965). De la morphonologie. *La Linguistique*, 1965, 1, 16-30. (An excerpt translated into the English is published in E.C. Fudge, ed. (1973). *Phonology*. Harmondsworth, 91-100.)

– (1968). Neutralisation et syncrétisme. *La Linguistique*, 1968, 1, 1-20. (An excerpt translated into the English is published in E.C. Fudge, ed. (1973). *Phonology*. Harmondsworth, 74-80.)

Mulder, J.W.F. (1968). *Sets and Relations in Phonology*. Oxford.

O'Connor, J.D. (1973). *Phonetics*. Harmondsworth.

Quiggin, E.C. (1906). *A Dialect of Donegal*. Cambridge.

Rischel, J. (MS, 1962). Componential analysis of phonemic patterns.

– (1974). *Topics in West Greenlandic Phonology*. Copenhagen.

Rudes, B.A. (1976). Lexical representation and variable rules in natural generative phonology. *Glossa* 10, 111-151.

Schane, S.A. (1971). The phoneme revisited. *Language* 47, 503-521.

Sprigg, R.K. (1961). Vowel harmony in Lhasa Tibetan: prosodic analysis applied to interrelated vocalic features of successive syllables. *Bulletin of the School of Oriental and African Studies* 24, 116-138. Reprinted in F.R. Palmer, ed. (1970). *Prosodic Analysis*. London, 230-252.

Sprockel, C. (1965). *The Language of the Parker Chronicle*, Vol. I: Phonology and Accidence. The Hague.

Tcheu, S.-K. (1967). La neutralisation et le consonantisme coréen. *La Linguistique*, 1967, 2, 85-97.

Thompson, L. (1959). Saigon phonemics. *Language* 35, 454–476.

Thumb, A. (1958). *Handbuch des Sanskrit* I/1, Lautlehre (3rd ed., revised by R. Hauschild). Heidelberg.

Trubetzkoy, N.S. (1933a). Character und Methode der systematischen phonologischen Darstellung einer gegebenen Sprache. *Archives néerlandaises de phonétique expérimentale* 8–9, 109–113.

Twaddell, W.F. (1935). On defining the phoneme. *Language Monograph* 16. Reprinted in M. Joos, ed. (1957). *Readings in Linguistics* I. Chicago, 55–80.

Voegelin, C.F., and M.E. Ellinghausen (1943). Turkish structure. *Journal of the American Oriental Society* 63, 34–65.

Wang, W.S.-Y. (1967). Phonological features of tones. *International Journal of American Linguistics* 33, 93–105.

— (1968). Vowel features, paired variables and the English vowel shift. *Language* 44, 675–708.

Waterson, N. (1956). Some aspects of the phonology of the nominal forms of the Turkish word. *Bulletin of the School of Oriental and African Studies* 18, 578–591. Reprinted in F.R. Palmer, ed. (1970). *Prosodic Analysis*. London, 174–187.

INDEX OF NAMES
(including phonological schools)

References to bibliographical items are marked with a 'b' after the page number. Example: '227b' means that the name in question is to be found in the bibliography on p. 227.

238

INDEX OF SUBJECTS
For names of authors and schools, see the index of names.

marked, unmarked, markedness 29, 52,
53, 117, 118ff, 121, 122, 125 (note
9), 141, 142, 143, 215
metalinguistics 70
microlinguistics 70
micro-phonemes 61
modifying elements 31
morpheme structure rules (MS rules)
110
morphologically based either-or
analysis 16ff
MS conditions 114
MS rules, see: morpheme structure
rules
multilateral oppositions 27, 34
M/U representation 117

natural generative phonology 126, 134,
136
neutralization
contextually determined ∼ 36
structurally determined ∼ 36
double ∼, triple ∼, quadruple ∼ 185
neutralization rules (N-rules) 118,
119, 136
neutralization variant 44

operator method 103
opposition 22, 27, 28
∼vs. difference 74
orthography 40, 41, 203
overlapping 70, 71, 75, 78

partial complementarity 47, 49
phoneme inventory, establishment of
14ff
phonemic level 107ff, 213ff
phonemoids 102
phonetic realization of archiphonemes
37
phonetic rules (vs. phonological rules)
217
phonetic similarity 16ff
phonetically based either-or analysis
16ff
phonological opposition 22
phonons 138
plerematic plane 74
plus-minus notations 125
polysystemic analysis 15, 20

position 97, 161
strong ∼, weak ∼ 97
positions of relevance 28, 29
positions of suspension 28, 29
pre-taxemes 73
privative oppositions 27, 43
proportional oppositions 27, 180
prosodies 67, 196
psychological
∼evidence 21
∼reality in phonology 30, 31, 58,
60, 61

relative categories 151, 152
relative (vs. absolute) features 151
relative grades 151, 152
relevance, degree of ∼ 50, 51
positions of ∼ 28, 29
representation of archiphonemes,
see: transcription
resoluble neutralizations 134, 135,
215

segment redundancy 25, 165
segment structure rules 114
sequence structure rules 114
slips of the tongue (or speech
errors) 90, 91, 129, 130, 208ff
strong position 97
structurally determined neutralization 36
sum-phoneme 153
surface contrast 107, 135, 213ff
suspendable oppositions 28, 29
suspension, positions of 28, 29
syncretism 76ff, 219, 220
obligatory ∼, optional ∼ 76
resoluble/irresoluble ∼77

taxemes 73
transcription 86ff, 101, 173
true generalization condition 114

universal marking 142
unmarked, see: marked
unpaired phonemes (phonèmes
hors couple) 23

variants, variations 97

weak position 97
well-formedness condition 114